ILMATAR'S INSPIRATIONS

Ilmatar's

Nationalism, Globalization, and the Changing

Inspirations

Soundscapes of Finnish Folk Music

Tina K. Ramnarine

THE UNIVERSITY OF CHICAGO PRESS CHICAGO AND LONDON

Tina K. Ramnarine is lecturer in ethnomusicology and social anthropology at
Queen's University Belfast. She is the author of *Creating Their Own Space: The Development
of an Indian-Caribbean Musical Tradition* and is also a professional classical violinist
with a special interest in folk fiddling traditions.

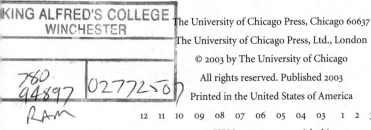
The University of Chicago Press, Chicago 60637
The University of Chicago Press, Ltd., London
© 2003 by The University of Chicago
All rights reserved. Published 2003
Printed in the United States of America

12 11 10 09 08 07 06 05 04 03   1 2 3 4 5

ISBN: 0-226-70402-5 (cloth)
ISBN: 0-226-70403-3 (paper)

Library of Congress Cataloging-in-Publication Data

Ramnarine, Tina K.
Ilmatar's inspirations : nationalism, globalization, and the changing soundscapes
of Finnish folk music / Tina K. Ramnarine.
p. cm. — (Chicago studies in ethnomusicology)
Includes bibliographical references (p.) and index.
ISBN 0-226-70402-5 (cloth : alk. paper) — ISBN 0-226-70403-3 (pbk. : alk. paper)
1. Folk music—Finland—History and criticism.   I. Title.   II. Series.
ML3619.R35   2003
781.62'94541—dc21
2002152512

♾ The paper used in this publication meets the minimum requirements of the
American National Standard for Information Sciences—Permanence of Paper for
Printed Library Materials, ANSI Z39.48-1992.

For Anja, Sophia, and Isabela

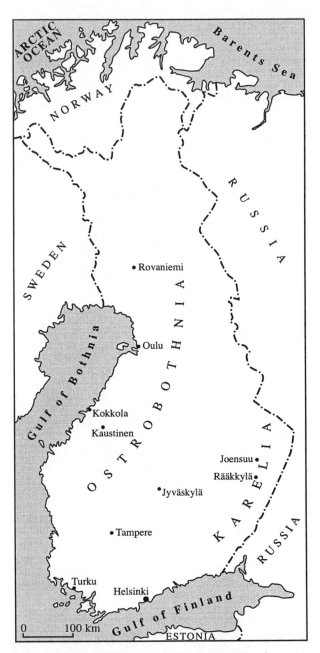

Map of Finland, showing the main places mentioned in the text.

Contents

Preface xi
Acknowledgments xxi

THEORETICAL AND HISTORICAL PERSPECTIVES

1. Introduction: Place, Identity, Representation 3
   "National Art": Folk Music, Art Music 6
   History 8
   Continuity and Change 13
   Identity and Representation 17
   Borrowing from the Traditions of "Others" 22

2. The Folk and the Nation 24
   Interest in Folklore before Lönnrot and the Kalevala 27
   Lönnrot and the Kalevala 30
   The Kalevala, Song Traditions, and the Kantele 38
   Myth, Music, Landscape, Identity 42

ETHNOGRAPHY: THE TRANSMISSION, PERFORMANCE,
AND REPERTOIRE OF NEW FOLK MUSIC

3. The Folk Music Revival in Finland:
   Toward "New Folk Music" 47
   Revival, Transformation, Authenticity 48
   The Kaustinen Festival and Konsta Jylhä 51

The Role of Folklorists in the Finnish Revival Movement 53
*The Role of Jazz and Rock Musicians
in the Revival Movement* 58
Institutionalizing Folk Music during the Revival 63

4. New Folk Music in the Urban Center 67
The Setting: The Sibelius Academy 68
Learning Folk Music at the Sibelius Academy 70
Performing Folk Music in the Urban Center 81

5. Värttinä: Women's Songs from the East 88
An Interview with Sari Kaasinen: Making the Music 89
Gender and Region 93
Reception, Aesthetics, Politics 107

6. New Folk Music in a Rural Context 124
Formal Folk Music Education in the Village of Kaustinen 125
The Kaustinen Festival: "Roots in Finland" 1992 134
From Five Strings to Electric Models 146

7. A Family of Folk Musicians: The Järveläs 150
The Fiddle in Finland: A Historical Perspective 151
Biography, Locality, "Authenticity" 155
Composing New Folk Music: The Ostrobothnian Example 160
Local Musicians, Global Stages 168

FOLK MUSIC, WORLD MUSIC

8. Musical and Social Identities:
Borrowing from the Traditions of "Others" 173
New Folk Music and Karelianism 176
Saami Music in Helsinki 181
Learning from Senegalese Musicians 184
The Finnish Tango 188
Irish Music in Helsinki 190
Appropriation, Originality, Representation 192

9. Global Commodities: The New Folk Music Recording
   in World Music Markets 200
   Sonic Representations: Music in Many Places 204
   Small Record Companies in Finland 205
   The Finnish Performing Music Promotion Center (ESEK) 207
   Music as Product: Questions of Ownership 208

10. Epilogue 212
    Musical Spaces 214
    Writing History 218

Notes 221
Bibliography 237
Discography 251
Index 253

Preface

The last of the summer berries were being sold at the harbor market and sea-gulls hovered expectantly over the fishermen's fresh deliveries when I arrived in Helsinki. On one of those October days in 1991 I took a bus into the city center and walked from the terminus to a gray building in Frederikinkatu (Frederik Street). I was in Finland to find out about contemporary Finnish folk music. I had already been interviewing musicians and music journalists, attending concerts, buying recordings, and meeting other researchers in Finland, but this was my first visit to the Folk Music Department at the Sibelius Academy. Climbing the stairs to the second floor, I walked through corridors saturated with the sounds of musicians practicing—violinists, accordionists, guitarists, *kantele* players, and singers.

Over the last two decades, several "new musics" have been heard in European contexts. Often, these new musics have emerged from and been a part of folk revival movements (as in Scandinavia and Central and Eastern Europe). Socio-political circumstances, government policies, technological developments, education systems and commercial processes have played their roles in shaping musicians' aesthetic and musical perspectives. During the early 1990s, public perceptions of folk music in Finland began to change with the establishment of "new folk music" (a literal translation of the term *uusikansanmusiikki*)[1] on national and international stages. This was an ongoing process of redefining folk music that had received renewed impetus from the activities of folklorists and jazz and rock musicians during the folk revival of the late 1960s and 1970s. The changes in public understandings of folk music have been paralleled by changing paradigms in folk music scholarship. Yet well-rehearsed issues in studies of folk music resurface in examining contemporary expressions. Musical changes and new contexts for folk music have been discussed, for example, in relation to societies undergoing political transition in Central and Eastern Europe

(Slobin 1996). These discussions focus on showing how folk music and people's ideas about it play important roles in political arenas. Analyzing the use of folk music in contemporary contexts as a medium through which different political realities can be expressed and shaped resonates with the study of the construction of folk music as a forum for national self-contemplation in nineteenth-century cultural politics (Boyes 1993; Sykes 1993). But contemporary folk musicians and their audiences often make distinctions between past and present practice. Thus, the Hungarian revival movement is seen as having created "a category of music entirely unlike those previously existing in Hungary" (Frigyesi 1996, 54), and the largest folk-based music market in the former Yugoslavia during the mid-1980s was for "newly composed folk music" (Rasmussen 1996). Newly composed folk music offers a challenge to the model of folk music as preserved repertoire transmitted from generation to generation. So too do the transmission strategies of Finnish new folk music. In Finland, the transmission of folk music in formal contexts such as the Sibelius Academy has been actively encouraged through the involvement of institutes of learning and of the state. Finnish "new folk music" emerged in the late 1980s as a result of institutional initiatives to revive folk culture, as well as of the work undertaken by folklorists and revival musicians. The provision of folk music at the level of higher education has promoted a sense of training for professional careers among musicians, who, through their experimental and commercially oriented recordings and public performances, reach out to world markets and audiences and represent "Finnish" music and cultural identity in a global, as well as national, arena.

This book is an account of Finnish new folk music. Folk music in Finland encompasses a broad range of musical activities and repertoires including arrangements of folk songs for choral and wind ensembles, overlapping folk song and church hymn repertoires (Louhivuori 1992), amateur folk music instrumental groups (Järviluoma 1997, 2000), and folk music practices as a means of reinforcing musical-political ideologies in youth movements such as the League of Finnish Youth and the Finnish Democratic Youth League (Kurkela 1989b). New folk music, however, has become the dominant musical representation of the Finnish folk music scene and a significant marker of Finnish "identity" in both national and global arenas. This book analyzes the multilayered processes—musical, institutional, political, and commercial—that have shaped and are shaped by new folk music activities and notions of national identity. Examples of new folk music groups include Niekku, JPP, Värttinä, Koinurit, Tallari, Salamakannel, Pirnales, and Pinnin Pojat. This is not an exhaustive account of these groups although they do all appear in these pages. In organizing my narrative, I focus on two examples: JPP and Värttinä. Other groups that appear here are revival groups: Nelipolviset, Piirpauke, Karelia, Tuulenkantajat, Pohjantahti, and Primo. The two groups that I have selected for more detailed discussion draw on different musical and regional traditions that have been incorporated into, and that are important in, the new folk music scene. JPP is a *pelimanni* (literally "folk musician") group that plays fiddle dance music from the western regions of Finland (from Ostrobothnia). During the 1960s folk revival movement, this tradition was the dominant representation of folk music. But representations of folk music are subject to change. Värttinä became one of the most successful new folk groups during the 1990s. The repertoire of this group focuses on vocal traditions from the eastern regions of Finland, particularly from Karelia. It therefore invokes Karelianist tropes that had been significant to the construction of a Finnish national identity during initial moves toward national self-determination during the nineteenth century. The contrasting musical styles of these two groups sit comfortably together in the new folk music scene. This is a scene characterized by an embrace of diverse musical and regional traditions to be found within and beyond national borders.

My involvement with this music predated my field research in Finland (1991–92) and began when I undertook a short research project in the late 1980s on the *Kalevala* song tradition. My interest in Finnish musical life deepened when I subsequently took up an appointment as a violinist in a Finnish symphony orchestra. At that time, commercial recordings of Finnish new folk music were only just beginning to be released, and even on a national scale they attracted little attention. I came across them because the recorded canon of new folk music included the *Kalevala* songs that had also played an important role in the folk revival movement of the 1960s and 1970s. The revival movement continues to expand. New forums for conveying an enthusiasm for Finnish folk music and promoting it in a global market include entries on the World Wide Web and performance spaces in a global arena.

By the early 1990s, when I was once again in Finland undertaking field research, Finnish new folk music was becoming increasingly prominent. So too, was "world music." The increase in popularity of both new folk and world music in Finland was not coincidental. Although new folk and world music seem to be separated by their locations in a national and local or in a global arena, they are in fact linked in the music market place and in formal educational contexts like the Sibelius Academy. Finnish new folk music has become part of the "world music" scene. By studying it I was thrown into the dialectics of local-global relations and into rethinking connections between music, place, and identity.[2]

When I first visited the Folk Music Department at the Sibelius Academy I was going to meet an Irish singer, Harry Bent, who was giving Irish folk song lessons to a Finnish kantele student, Arja Kastinen. The teaching room was full of wooden flutes, kanteles of various sizes, and photographs of kantele players. I had arranged to observe the lesson, in which a song recorded by the Irish singer Dolores Keane was rehearsed and both student and teacher compared the placing of ornaments in Irish and Finnish folk song performance, and then to interview Harry. As it turned out, Harry had not been active in "Irish" music before he moved to Finland in the mid-1980s. He had been trained as a classical singer and had joined a jazz band, singing in Dublin on Sunday mornings. At a summer festival gig in Helsinki he had stood in for a singer who could not be at the performance and has stayed with the band, Korkkijalka, playing Irish traditional music, since then. Other members include Jyrki Heiskanen, organizer of the Kaustinen International Festival of Folk Music, who plays the tin whistle, and Kari Reiman, also a fiddler in one of the most well-known Finnish new folk groups, Värttinä (Harry Bent, personal interview, 10 October 1991). That Finnish folk musicians are learning Irish folk song as part of their specialized training in musical performance leads us to question folk music as national expression.

We can also ask, What is Finnish "new folk music"? The term "new folk music" is a chronological marker on one level, for it follows "folk music." Yet the term is ambiguous, for new folk musicians do not always define their area of music making as "new folk." They locate themselves within a more encompassing "folk" category. The editor of *Uusikansanmusiikki* referred to this ambiguity in discussing the title of this music magazine. Before its incarnation as *Uusikansanmusiikki* (*New Folk Music*), the magazine had been entitled *Kansanmusiikki* (*Folk Music*). The new title thus indicated changes to the magazine itself, which had undergone some revamping. It also suggested that the magazine now catered to an audience whose main interest lay in contemporary folk music practice. The editor perceived no need to resolve the ambiguity. Potential readers of new folk music join the readership for folk music (Martti Heikkilä, managing editor, personal communication, July 1992). The term may be ambiguous, but new folk music is distinctive in several ways. It is characterized by processes of institutionalization and by patterns of transmission and performance which challenge received understandings of "folk music." Yet the main institutions involved in the production of new folk music are the Department of Folk (not New Folk) Music at the Sibelius Academy and the Folk Music Institute in the village of Kaustinen.

Confusion also surrounds the term "world music." Frith has succinctly defined world music as the "sounds of countries other than North America and Western Europe," which have begun to be "recorded, packaged and sold as a successful new pop genre" (Frith 1989, 5). This is a center-periphery view of a transnational flow of music in which more powerful nations control the music markets of less powerful ones (Garofalo 1993). With its references to place and to genre, the definition is as problematic as it is illuminating. The identification of world music as sounds beyond North America and Western Europe is a nod in the direction of the "cultural imperialism thesis" (Mitchell 1996, 49), but various musics from these geographic areas are increasingly labeled "world" music. What is considered "world" music in one country may, in another, be regarded as "folk" music. This has happened to Finnish new folk music, which has been marketed outside Finland under the label of "world" music. As for world music as a popular genre, then, new folk musicians conform to pop aesthetics in many ways to make their music relevant to modern audiences, as we shall see. Nevertheless, they are "folk" performers. The two sets of ideologies that explore place and time—global and local, and modern and traditional—and which are "crucial components in the emerging global musical aesthetics" of "world music" (Erlman 1993, 7) apply, therefore, to Finnish new folk music.

I undertook field research in two main places—in Helsinki, an urban center and the capital of Finland, and in Kaustinen, a rural village in the region of Ostrobothnia in northern Finland. These two locales are prominent centers for new folk music. The settings themselves (one urban, the other rural) were important, furthermore, in terms of analyzing continuities and disjunctures between folk and new folk and between new folk and world music. While folk music has been traditionally associated with rural contexts, contemporary practice leads us to revise our ideas about its performance spaces.

Everywhere I went I was asked, "But why do you want to study Finnish new folk music?" Finnish scholarship has focused on folk music of the past: on players, repertoires, collectors, and instruments.[3] Notions of the past and of musical traditions whose histories are tied to a Finnish nationalist history are significant to today's performers, too. Yet when I arrived in Finland in the early

1990s to look at what present-day performers were doing, I was following an intuitive sense that new folk music was a burgeoning trend that in its very contemporaneity necessitated a reconceptualization of folk music (Bohlman 1988).[4] It pointed to some departures in response to what was happening with contemporary musics, which were at that time occupying ethnomusicological attention: local-global questions, micromusics in interaction with supercultural structures (Slobin 1993), and the musical construction of place (Stokes 1994), as well as renewed interest in music histories (Blum, Bohlman, and Neuman 1993). Finnish folk music's continuing representational role as a symbol of the nation offers interesting perspectives on these areas of inquiry. It is a marker of identity in which place, history, and tradition are emphasized. Yet new folk music is also a reminder of change in folk music, and such change offers a challenge to the nationalist ideologies that informed the construction of folk music as a symbol of the nation. There is a tension between nationalist views of folk music as ancient, enduring, and unique and modern-day musical aesthetics which encourage musical changes to the "nation's traditions" as new folk musicians reach out to audiences worldwide. In outlining these areas of exploration at this stage, however, I am suggesting a theoretical positioning only explicitly made in retrospect. As I was in the field, I was simply caught up in the excitement of seeing the development of new folk and world music in Finland. Revising this text a decade after I first began to study this music, I realize that I was fortunate to observe and participate in the Finnish new folk music scene during the period when it was just beginning to attract substantial interest in the international as well as national marketplace. One of the main aims of this book, therefore, is to provide an ethnographic account of Finnish new folk music at this critical moment. Through ethnography, as a narrative form of "obsessional empiricism" (Reily 1998), I chart the practices, discourses, and musical concepts of new folk music practitioners. Through inclusion and analysis of interview materials and observational notes, the ethnography reveals how new folk musicians think and talk about the relationship between past and present folk music practices, about the role of folk music in representations of national identity, and about the interaction of Finnish folk music with "other" musics. It reveals the creative processes involved in new folk music compositions and performances. This ethnographic material also highlights the problematics of representation, identity, and musical spaces, which in turn generates theoretical perspectives on folk music revival processes and musical hybridity in the global era.

This book focuses on processes of transmission and performance and on musicians' ideas about folk music. Given that many new folk musicians are "professional" performers, how do they learn new folk music? What kinds of repertoires do they learn? Why do they study Cuban drumming or Estonian folk singing as part of their training in Finnish folk music? Where do they perform? How do they conceptualize their own musical practices? These are some of the questions addressed through ethnographic description in the following pages. The book is organized into three parts. Part 1 is concerned with the historical background from which new folk music emerges. It is my intention that the historical narrative presented should "yield a plot to fix the relations between phenomena" (Strathern 1988, 6), in particular, between notions of the past, folk music, national identity, and the emergence of a "national art." In the introduction the main themes and theoretical frameworks that have shaped my analysis of new folk music are outlined: history, musical continuity and change, identity and representation, and musical borrowings. Chapter 2 discusses folklore studies, the collection of folk song texts, and the political significance attached to the publication of a national epic, the *Kalevala*. The aim is to show how folk music in Finland became closely identified with the nation and why an understanding of this nationalist history is essential to interpreting contemporary practice and representations of Finnish new folk music.

Part 2 turns to ethnography and focuses on the transmission and performance of new folk music in an urban and in a rural context. The third chapter deals with the folk revival of the late 1960s and the trends in both performance and transmission (in formal educational contexts) that have directly influenced the development of Finnish new folk music. It is based on accounts of the revival that I collected in the field in tracing new folk music history. These accounts demonstrate that the diversity of musical expression found in new folk music since the early 1990s is a continuation of early folk revival approaches. During the 1960s and 1970s, revivalists were interested in pelimanni repertoires—particularly fiddle traditions from Ostrobothnia, in the eastern vocal traditions that had shaped the national epic, and in British and American folk-rock models. Chapter 4 examines the ways in which various folk music traditions are transmitted and performed in the city through ethnographic description of the Department of Folk Music at the Sibelius Academy and of various urban folk performance contexts. While different traditions meet in the urban setting (thus offering possibilities for increased musical exchanges and igniting fears of musical homogenization), regional identities are nevertheless stressed. At a macro level, then, in the urban capital and within the nation-state, music is used to mark identities on micro (regional and village) levels. Discussion of Värttinä in chapter 5 focuses on the importance of this new folk group in regional and national spheres. The sixth chapter turns to different kinds of repertoires and examines the significance of new folk music in the rural setting, Kaustinen, highlighting the global in the local. Notions of continuity and musical authenticity that are facilitated by the rural location are juxtaposed with an exploration of the multiplicity of identities in a small and locally bounded context. A specific ballad performance given by a Finnish-American in collaboration with a Finnish folklorist is considered as an example of the questioning of musical boundaries and identities. Both emerge as fluid. Persistent notions of maintaining a Finnish identity in a Finnish-American milieu, however, lead to a discussion of how symbols of cultural cohesion such as "kantele" and "*Kalevala*" help to create a "Finnish" identity for both Finns and Finnish-Americans (as well as people of Finnish heritage who live in other countries) alike. Chapter 7 introduces a family of musicians from Kaustinen and focuses on pelimanni fiddle repertoires.

Part 3 examines the correlations between "folk" as "local" and "world" as "global" music. In chapter 8 I argue that such a polarization is simplistic, for Finnish new folk musicians are involved in musical dialogues with musicians from across the globe. I am reminded here of Slobin's observation that "we need to think of music as coming from many places and moving among many levels of today's societies" (1993, x). This is true even in the composition of music that represents the nation. In focusing on musical dialogues, exchanges, and collaborations I demonstrate the importance of musical encounters between individual musicians as a determining factor in the making of musical choices. The transnational and intercultural musical activities that occur at the level of individual engagement contribute to the complexity and hybridity of both "folk" and "world" music. They also contribute to the questioning of musical "places" and to the negotiation of the "experience of nationness" (Bhabha 1994). Notions of musical collaboration in the form of "intercultural" musical exchanges between musicians are often marked in performance by the fixing of musical differences between the performers. This point is illustrated through considering the interactions between Finnish new folk musicians and performers associated with other musical styles and repertoires, including tango, Saami *joiku*, and West African *mbalax*. There is a shift, in chapter 9, from examining music as the result of interactions between, and as the expressions of, individuals to a consideration of music as a product and of the new folk music recording as a global commodity, which is a sonic representation of "Finnish" music. Why are representations of Finnish music in the world important? How are power relations affected through achieving international recognition of a nation's "culture"? These questions are addressed by looking at how music is promoted, supported, and disseminated in the construction of identity by state and commercial organizations.

An epilogue serves as conclusion. New folk musicians have contributed important dimensions to questions about "Finnish" musical practice. My focus is on changing perceptions of the folk musician, who is now seen as an individual creative and traveling agent rather than an anonymous part of a fixed collective, and on musical practice in shifting spaces.

Acknowledgments

My thanks go first and foremost to the many people active in diverse capacities in the music field whom I interviewed in exploring the Finnish new folk music world. These were performers, teachers, students, music journalists, and representatives of various state, institutional, commercial, and educational organizations. Visits to the Folk Music Department of the Sibelius Academy and to the Folk Music Institute, where I participated in workshops and performances, and to festivals in Helsinki and in Kaustinen, contributed substantially to my research material. I am indebted to all those who gave their time in exchanging ideas, discussing, and performing music with me. In particular, my thanks are due to Hannu Saha, director of the Folk Music Institute, and to Hannu Tolvanen, administrator of the Department of Folk Music at the Sibelius Academy, who shared his knowledge of the Finnish music world in answering innumerable questions. Special thanks also to Tim Ingold, who first showed an interest in this research project; to Harri Englund, Börje Englund, Rachel Holstead, and Jonathan McIntosh for practical assistance; to Arto Järvelä, Sari Kaasinen, Seppo Paakkunainen, Santtu Karhu, Minna Raskinen, Eric Peltoniemi, Viljo Määttälä, Papp Sarr, Yamar, Sakari Kukko, and Jukka Liedes, who provided lots of information; to Maija Karhinen for her Finnish folk dance classes; to Sami Fagerström for his enthusiasm; to Eero Tarasti, who has encouraged my interest in Finnish music; and to my mother, who first introduced me to Finnish music. Anneli Asplund offered comments on an early draft, and readers for the University of Chicago Press provided comments that were very helpful in the stages of revising the manuscript. I would also like to thank the editorial team at the University of Chicago Press for their encouragement, helpfulness, and attention to detail throughout this project.

The research was made possible by a scholarship from the University of Manchester. Assistance from the Folk Music Institute enabled me to visit the Kaustinen Festival and to participate in the Ala-Könni courses. In addition, individual musicians and representatives of institutes have generously given me books, reports, recordings, and access to library and archive materials.

Theoretical and Historical Perspectives

I have often heard related,
And have heard the song recited,
How the nights closed ever lonely,
And the days were shining lonely,
Only born was Väinämöinen,
And revealed the bard immortal,
Sprung from the divine Creatrix,
Born of Ilmatar, his mother.

Thus was ancient Väinämöinen,
He the ever famous minstrel,
Born of the divine Creatrix,
Born of Ilmatar his mother.

Kalevala, rune 1

[In the rune about Väinämöinen, Ilmatar, daughter of the Air, descends into the sea, which wakes life within her. For seven centuries no child is yet born. She cries to Ukko, ruler of heaven, "free the damsel from her burden." Then a beauteous teal, seeking a resting place, alights on her knee and establishes her nest there. As Ilmatar's knee jerks from the heat of the brooding teal, the eggs roll into the water. From its fragments, the earth, arch of heaven, sun, moon, stars, and clouds are fashioned. Väinämöinen rests still in his mother's body until, falling headlong into the water, he sojourns up to eight years on the surface of the ocean, near a barren, treeless country.]

Introduction

PLACE, IDENTITY, REPRESENTATION

Music unites. Music divides. Every song is a "folk" song, for as Big Bill Broonzy allegedly claimed, "I never heard a horse sing 'em!" Broonzy's statement is cited by Nettl (1983, 303) and by Ling (1997, 1) to draw attention to the difficulties in defining folk music and in delineating musical boundaries. Brăiloiu notes a further difficulty in the notion of "folk music" or "folk song." If every song is indeed a folk song, who are the "folk" who perform these songs and to whom they can be attributed (Brăiloiu 1984)?

Contemporary representations of a musical tradition as being both "folk" and "Finnish" reveal the extent to which a musical practice continues to be intertwined with ongoing ideological orientations and historical processes. Finnish folk music was constructed as a site of cultural contemplation during the nineteenth century, when the move toward national self-determination gathered momentum. As in many parts of Europe, the "folk" were regarded as the preservers of an ancient cultural heritage and as the bearers of performance traditions attesting to the distinct character of the emergent Finnish nation. The folk and the traditions to which they adhered were conceived of as being as timeless as was the (dormant) nation itself. Images of continuity, of a distinct people who were submerged under imperial rule but who had managed to retain their culture, framed nationalist perceptions. Thus, nineteenth-century Finnish nationalists looked to a mythical past and they found the evidence for such a past in the texts of folk songs. While it seemed that folk songs had once been prevalent, nineteenth-century scholars involved in the nationalist enterprise had to engage in processes of collecting cultural treasures, which they believed had been stored in the collective memory of the folk, and of reassembling the remnants of these almost-forgotten traditions.

Finnish folklorists were guided by the views of the German philosopher Johann Gottfried von Herder (1744–1803), for whom the "folk" were peasants and bearers of past traditions. Much of the folk music research undertaken by pioneers in the field throughout Europe, such as the Hungarian composers and scholars Béla Bartók (1881–1945) and Zoltán Kodály (1882–1967), the Romanian ethnomusicologist Constantin Brăiloiu (1893–1958), the English folk collector Cecil Sharp (1859–1924), and the Finnish musicologist Armas Otto Väisänen (1890–1969), followed Herder's conceptualizations of the "folk." As recently as 1955, the International Folk Music Council defined folk music as the orally transmitted traditions of rural communities that have remained impervious to influences from other genres such as popular and art music (JIFMC 1955, 23). Even Ling uses the terms "folk music" and "folk songs" to refer to "rural music taught, without being written down, by one generation to the next," despite his observations that "it is difficult if not impossible to isolate folk music as a genre" and that "different kinds of music interweave and overlap" (1997, 1). In drawing a distinction between rural folk music and urban folk music (which he labels "popular music" or "city music folklore"), Ling reproduces Bartók's views on the differences between folk music in rural and in urban centers.

Bartók's assertion that music differs according to the location of musical practices in rural or urban centers stemmed from a fear for the continuity of folk traditions. The integrity of folk music, supposed to have been preserved and transmitted intact over the preceding millennia and acting as a mediator between past and present, now seemed threatened by rapid change. Processes of urbanization, modernization, and musical exchange challenged the quality of "timelessness" which nationalists and scholars alike attributed to folk music. In attempting to identify the antiquity and birthplaces of particular pieces, Bartók and Kodály adopted Ilmari Krohn's (1867–1960) system of song classification (used by Krohn, a Finnish musicologist, in the collection *Suomen Kansan Sävelmiä* [*Finnish Folk Compositions*], published in five volumes from 1896 to 1945). It is a classification system that groups songs together according to structural similarities. Bartók later grouped the folk repertoire into three classes referring to the relation between the past and the present: "old-style melodies," "new-style melodies," and "mixed genera"—songs which do not belong to the other two. The categorization "mixed genera" was one in which the authenticity of the nation's folk traditions seemed to be compromised. Yet "mixed genera" seem to have been pervasive. Bartók grappled with classification issues in the early 1930s. In his essay *What Is Folk Music?* (Bartók 1976), he drew attention to the confusion concerning concepts of folk music, which he attributed to the widespread misconception that a country's folk music is homogeneous. The musical material he collected was diverse, "completely without uniformity" (Bartók 1976, 5). In continued attempts to define folk music, he turned to categorizing it broadly into two kinds, one being "popular art music," otherwise described as "urban folk music," and the other being "rural folk music" or "peasant music." [1]

Bartók later asserted the value of "peasant" folk music above the urban type (in a climate in which "pastiche" folk music was more well known and used by art composers for its "exotic" qualities), describing "peasant folk music," nearly a decade later, as "pure folk music." He perceived rural folk music as having its origins in the more distant past. At a lecture given in 1940 in the United States, his definition of this music had become rather elaborate: "Pure folk music is the spontaneous expression of the musical feelings of a community, a community which is more or less isolated from the higher and artificial civilization, especially from the civilization of the towns. Therefore, pure folk music is to be found chiefly in districts where people are more or less illiterate, where it supplies their bodily and mental needs by traditional means often many hundreds, even thousands of years old, almost without any foreign influence. It is a fact that under such conditions the expression of music is almost without exception connected with traditional customs and ceremonies as, for instance, crop gathering, and so on. This music, therefore, is a social act and not an individual one" (Bartók 1976, 173). For Ling, as for Bartók, the place of folk music is still in the rural context. Its location emerges as an important marker of musical authenticity. The connection between folk music and place nevertheless extends beyond the rural context. Folk music is habitually described in terms of its location in a national arena: hence, "Finnish folk music," "Bulgarian folk music," "English folk music." The view of folk music as music of the people and as an inherent part of the nation's cultural life has been widely propagated by various nationalist movements. Such a view remains potent in the modern world. In Finland, contemporary folk music draws on, and incorporates, elements of traditions from diverse sources, including other European folk traditions and "world" music. It is nevertheless held up and represented, within and outside the nation, as "Finnish." So prevalent is this link between folk music and the nation that art music compositions that draw on folk traditions are still regarded as containing inherently "Finnish" elements.[2] This point is crucial to an appreciation of the ongoing role of folk music in nationalist politics and sensibilities. In setting the scene in this chapter, I shall explore this point further in relation to the importance of folk sources to interpretations of the Finnish composer Jean Sibelius (1865–1957) as a national composer.

"NATIONAL ART": FOLK MUSIC, ART MUSIC

Unlike Bartók and Kodály, who devoted their lifetimes to the cause of musical folklore and were profoundly influenced as artists by their scholarly investigations, Sibelius seemed to delve into folklore only insofar as it satisfied his immediate, individual artistic requirements. Yet, since folk music became an inherent part of national culture during the nineteenth century, any composer who turned enthusiastically to folk sources for inspiration risked being labeled "nationalist." Whereas the perception of Sibelius as a nationalist composer has persisted, any inspiration he derived from folk music has been obscured, since his use of folk sources was governed not by obvious or straightforward quotations of folk melodies, but by the incorporation of folk song texts and by allusion to folk themes, for example, Kullervo, Lemminkäinen, Tapiola, and Karelia. The extent to which Sibelius used folk sources, and the designation of "nationalist" to which such use gives rise, have been problematic issues for later commentators. Matters have been complicated by Sibelius's own ambivalent views of folk music. An interest in the relationship between folk and art music was demonstrated in an early paper, "Some Reflections on Folk Music and Its Influence on the Development of Art Music" ([1896] 1980) in which Sibelius claimed: "An artist who is thoroughly steeped in his country's folk music must naturally have a different view of things, lay stress on certain points, and find his artistic fulfillment in a completely different way from others. And in this lies much of his originality" (cited in Tawaststjerna 1976, 191).

Sibelius undertook at least one field trip to collect folk material, but his main source of inspiration was Elias Lönnrot's acclaimed compilation of folk song texts, the national epic, the *Kalevala* (first published in 1835). It was his use of this text that established his reputation as a "national" composer at a time when nationalist elements were imbued with a special significance. Because of the

Kalevala's symbolic and political importance to the process of nation building and to the development of a national identity, the choice of titles from this work sufficed to link the composer incontrovertibly to the nationalist movement. Despite displaying enthusiasm for the *Kalevala* (which was in any case a general artistic trend in Finland around the turn of the century) and openly acknowledging the inspiration gained through this secondary folk source, Sibelius was nevertheless vague about any inspiration he may have derived from primary folk sources. The date of his meeting with the folk singer Larin Paraske, in particular, seems to have caused the composer some confusion. According to Yrjö Hirn, Sibelius met Paraske in the summer of 1891, and the composer "listened to her with great attention and made notes on her inflections and rhythm" (Hirn cited in Tawaststjerna 1976, 98). Sibelius himself insisted (in 1915, to his first biographer, Eric Furuhjelm) that the meeting took place in 1892. The date assumes significance only because it raises the question of the extent to which Sibelius's knowledge of folk song influenced the process of composing what was to be his first major work, the *Kullervo Symphony* (1892). The assertion of a later date points to a repudiation of the folk influence and of the nationalist label. Yet Sibelius did not spurn only folk influences, for, in claiming creative independence, he also wanted to appear uninfluenced by current musical trends. Being aware of his position on the periphery of European mainstream musical culture—for which he was dismissed by critics as merely a "national" composer with nothing of substance to offer a more cosmopolitan stage and regarded as an incongruous heir to the Austro-German tradition of symphonic discourse which was itself being challenged by new musical developments— contributed to a sense of alienation which expressed itself in Sibelius's wish to be regarded, according to Tawaststjerna, as an "independent phenomenon" (Tawaststjerna 1976, 121), and in the symbolic gesture of distancing himself from the wider cultural arena with his retreat to the Finnish forest.

Sibelius, restrained by the label of nationalist as the Finnish nation secured political independence, wished to assert an individual musical identity distinct from sociopolitical concerns. Earlier works that can be read as programmatic symbols of collective cultural consciousness (with their folk overtones) were superseded by works that displayed an emphasis on abstract, individual creativity, by means of which Sibelius's place on a more cosmopolitan stage was affirmed. He was no longer merely a national composer, then, but still "Finnish," for throughout Sibelius's compositional career the influence of the *Kalevala*, the text so inextricably bound to the nationalist cause, is plainly evident. Several accounts (e.g., Layton 1965; James 1983) suggest that the inspiration he derived from this text shaped Sibelius's distinct musical voice, a voice characterized by accent, temperament, and geographic placement—features which are themselves reminiscent of nationalist constructions in their emphasis on language and territory.

Kalevalaic themes, folk music, landscape, Northerness: these are the elements, then, on which narratives of Sibelius as a nationalist composer have focused. Detailed historical and political contextualization, and consideration of the intricacies and complexities which informed Finland's cultural and artistic as well as political involvement with Russia around the turn of the century, are less common approaches. Nevertheless, the construction of Sibelius as a nationalist was the result of particular historical processes whereby political conviction, the folk, and the presentation of a national art were entwined so that the nation could be held up as a discrete, homogenous entity and used to mark cultural, if not yet political, boundaries.

HISTORY

I was touring around the university area in Helsinki by Tuomiokirkko, the city's Lutheran cathedral, in front of which stands a statue of Tsar Alexander II, when I came across the Karelian and Viipuri Associations of Helsinki University. I rang the doorbell of the associations' building, a twentieth-century *jugend tyyli* (Nordic art-nouveau-style) construction, hoping to arrange a time to get some information about the associations' activities. The door was flung open. "Sisään!" ("Come in!") was the hearty greeting I received. During my field research, Karelia had emerged as a focus in national debates, broadcast through the media, with the dramatic collapse of the former USSR, and questions about reclaiming parts of the region lost in the Winter War (1939) resurfaced in national politics. If Finland was the bridge between East and West during the Cold War period, it is in Karelia where the border struggles have been felt most intensely. My discussion with the association members focused on issues of regional identity and the relation of the region to the nation-state. They pointed to a map to show me how large Karelia is. For them, regional identity is important "on historical and cultural levels," but they emphasized that this is not a struggle for separatism and contrasted Finnish regional affiliations to the (former) Yugoslavian and northern Irish situations. "How can we draw the border?" asked Arto Ahola (an agriculturist). "It is the whole nation that decides, from Rovaniemi to Porvoo. We have strong regional affiliations, but Finns perceive themselves as one nation." Toward the end of the discussion they mentioned Karelian music and gave the example of the new folk group *Värttinä*, who "sing traditional Karelian songs but add new, modern things. This is what makes it interesting. This is what makes the tradition alive," according to Kai Sahala, a computer scientist.

In the Peace of Hamina, the treaty concluded in 1809, Finland was ceded to Russia, having been a part of the Swedish kingdom for the preceding six centuries. Tsar Alexander I granted Finland an autonomous status as a grand duchy of Russia, and it was during this period that the Finnish nationalist movement grew (Paasivirta 1981). It was a movement connected to the general European trend toward national self-determination in the mid–nineteenth century. The leader of the Finnish national (Fennomania) movement, Johan Wilhelm Snellman (1806–81), promoted a political philosophy which arose from a study of classical liberal economics and the ideas of the German thinkers George William Frederick Hegel and Herder. Herder, credited as being the founder of cultural nationalism, whose ideas were influential all over Europe, began with the idea of "a man with a culture and with a language and living in a polity" (Llobera 1994, 166). For him, national differences were the result of differences in language, culture, religion, politics, and art and were determined by geographic environment, education, and tradition. Herder's view of the folk was tied to the importance he placed on language: "Volk and language cannot be conceived of independently of each other. Many things in the life of the Volk can be lost, including its political independence, but if the language is preserved, the essence of the nation will survive" (Llobera 1994, 168). There was no loftier expression of the nation's language than in its folk poetry. For Herder, folk poetry was "the expression of the weaknesses and perfections of a nationality, a mirror of its sentiments, the expression of the highest to which it aspired." He perceived folk poems as "the archives of a nationality," "the imprints of the soul" of a nation (Herder cited in Wilson 1976, 29–30). Hegel (1770–1831) followed Herder's concept of the folk but placed more importance on political frameworks, maintaining that "each Volk had to be a state because the political conditions of the time so demanded" (Llobera 1994, 171). While Hegel's concept of the folk was tied to arguments about political power, subsequent German folklore scholarship can be characterized by a "curious hesitation to target issues of power and politics," all the more marked because of the concrete political aims which centered around the movement toward German unification and which framed folklore research in Germany (Linke 1995, 1). By contrast, Finnish folklorists who were strongly directed by German models and philosophies were more explicitly involved with issues surrounding the collection of folk culture and political power. For many of them, folklore research became synonymous with the pursuit of national power; it was a national science, and research was motivated as much by patriotic sentiment as it was by scientific curiosity (Wilson 1976, 62–66). Snellman asserted that state power was derived from the folk, the people of the nation, and that "the capacity of a nation to withstand foreign aggression or undergo transformation is not dependent on its military strength or on revolutionary violence but on its degree of cultural power, development and unity" (Huxley 1990, 26). In this climate of romantic nationalism, Finnish folklore research flourished and was in fact, as Wilson (1976) argues, to play a significant role in the development of a national identity and in the process of nation building. This was largely due to the publication of the *Kalevala*.

While the nineteenth-century collection, analysis, and representation of a Finnish culture was informed by Finland's position within the Russian imperial power, the notion of a Finnish cultural distinctiveness found a surprising ally in the Russian emperor himself. He promoted the idea of Finns as a distinct and unified people by keeping Russian and Finnish administrations separate. All matters concerning Finland were taken up directly with the tsar and not through the intermediary of Russian ministerial procedures. In the absence of a Finnish military power it was under these conditions that Finland began to assume its own political character. Moreover, reforms implemented under Russian rule (such as the reintroduction of a customs frontier between Finland and Russia in 1812) strengthened Finland's independent position. So important has been Finland's relation to Russia that Huxley goes so far as to state that "Finland as an independent nation has arisen and developed its identity largely through an intricate on-going dialectical process of conflict and resistance and cooperation and accommodation with Russia," a dialectic that "began in 1808 when 'Finland' was conquered by Russia and, a year later, 'Finland' was created by Russia" (1990, 82).

Huxley's assertion accords with current notions of identity as relational. This dialectic is important, too, in thinking about the representation of "Finnish folk" music. In gathering cultural strength to build national identity and ultimately the nation-state, the identities of folk music traditions, from which the *Kalevala* as a national epic was constructed, were transformed in various ways.

Such transformation included the recontextualization of material collected from the present-day border areas of Finland and Russia and also from Russian Karelia. In particular, the interest shown in Karelia by folklorists and artists gave rise to the movement known as Karelianism, which was to be a dominant strand in the construction of a "Finnish" identity.

A national sensibility has been formed also in relation to Finland's alignment to the West, particularly through centuries of involvement with Sweden. In terms of musical practices, while folklorists were "rediscovering" eastern vocal traditions during the early nineteenth century, there were ongoing, coexisting, and lively performance traditions of *pelimanni* (folk musician) repertoires that were broadly related to Swedish and German folk instrumental practices. During the seventeenth century in Finland, rhyming songs (verses consisting of rhyming couplets) such as ballads, broadsides, and cradlesongs had largely begun to replace the runes collected by nineteenth-century folklorists. The fiddle had replaced the *kantele* (a traditional Finnish zither-like instrument), becoming the main instrument in folk music. Many fiddlers played dance music for a solo performer or were accompanied by a clarinetist. The dance repertoires included the *polska*, which came to prominence in Finland with the fiddle in the seventeenth century, the minuet, which has been recognized as a folk dance since the eighteenth century, the waltz, which reached Finland in the early nineteenth century, and the polka, which followed in the latter half. There is evidence of folklore interest in collecting these instrumental dance repertoires. Krohn (1975) refers to collections undertaken with grants from the Finnish Literature Society, for example, by H. A. Reinholm (1848), K. Collan and J. F. von Schantz (1854), I. J. Ingberg (1857), J. Scharlin (1865), and O. A. J. Carlenius (1869). The emphasis was still placed on the "old." Krohn's late-nineteenth-century collection of "old pelimanni compositions" reveals the absence of dance forms—polkas and mazurkas—considered to be too modern (Asplund and Hako 1981, 243). By the late nineteenth century, however, different approaches to the nationalist enterprise were being introduced with the establishment of various cultural and political associations. These were mass movements contributing to the emergence of what has been termed "organizational culture," which recruited large memberships from all sectors of society. Group practices—brass bands, choirs, and theatrical performances—were the associations' main cultural pursuits, and they promoted the political ideology of an independent Finnish nation (Kurkela 1989b). Although these associations were not specifically concerned with folk music, contemporary pelimanni societies can be regarded as a continuation of late-nineteenth-century cultural organization trends (Karinen 2001), as well as following the model of fiddlers' societies found in other Scandinavian contexts (Ling 1997). Rapid urbanization and aesthetic trends from the 1950s onward contributed to pelimanni traditions' achieving a central space in the national imagination during the 1960s folk revival. I return to a closer examination of both kalevalaic and pelimanni traditions and their histories in later chapters. At this stage, the above details provide a general historical framework within which Finnish folk music practices can be read. They point to the ways in which folk musics have tugged at geopolitical borders to both the east and the west even as they are used in the inscription of the "national."

Attempts to understand the differences between musical practices described as either "old" or "new" have led recent ethnomusicological inquiry to a greater concern with the music history of the cultures studied by ethnomusicologists (Nettl and Bohlman 1991; Blum, Bohlman, and Neuman 1993). Understanding the "tradition" of the music culture studied is as important to ethnomusicologists as it is to the musicians who assert that their music is based on traditional practices. Folk music research in European contexts has long been characterized by its emphasis on the past, even though folk materials have been collected in the collector's present. Ling's views on the distinctions between folk music in rural and in urban centers derive from surveying folk music in Europe from the late eighteenth century to the early 1990s in relation to the transition from agrarian to urban industrialized society. From this vantage point, urban culture moves to dominate and assimilate hitherto rural cultural traditions (Ling 1997, 220) so that a sense of folk music authenticity is eroded. It is easy to discern a sense of "loss" here. In discussing more recent transitions with regard to the profound political and musical changes in Eastern and Central Europe, Slobin writes that it is as important "to look for continuities as for disjunctures" (Slobin 1996, 11). He offers, therefore, a more positive view of musical change. Slobin extends the dualistic temporal categories of old/new and tradition/ modernity to three strata—current, recent, and long-term—which delineate the ways in which music is layered into consciousness: "The current is always at the forefront of attention, claiming primacy through policy or persuasion. Everywhere, a turn of the radio dial most commonly yields 'the latest.' The recent is the seedbed of the current. Right now, recent might mean 'since the advent of rock music,' a moment that extended in concentric circles around the globe from its heartland in Anglo-America. The long-term operates at another level of memory in this archaeology of music cultures. It is, of course, just as immediate as the others, since music history is reborn every day as a clustering of available resources. Yet long-term resonance is felt, marketed, and inter- preted as distant echoes of earlier vibrations rather than as the shock waves of the latest hit or the soothing sounds of the songs of our youth" (Slobin 1996, 11–12). Finnish new folk music is indeed at the forefront of media attention and cultural policy decision-making processes. As an urban, popular music that has taken its place as a representation of Finnish identity and culture on the world music stage, it is an insistent reminder of the many ways in which those Finnish traditions that were held up as "folk music" during the nineteenth century have changed. Those "earlier vibrations," however, are powerful and draw us into looking through the historical window. There are three main ways in which "history" forms a frame for my analysis of Finnish new folk music and informs my concern with notions of continuity and change. These are, in Slobin's terms and in reverse order, the long-term, recent, and current strata. First, the links between folk music and nationalist ideology are explored, for the concept of folk music itself is "a speciality of European culture through a part of its his- tory" (Nettl 1991, xv). Finnish folk music is a romantic-nationalist construc- tion, and new folk musicians look to the past and to materials, sound record- ings, and notated sources, deposited in such archives as the Suomalaisen Kirjallisuuden Seura (Finnish Literature Society) in Helsinki and the Kansan- musiikki Instituutti (Folk Music Institute) in Kaustinen in their reinterpreta- tions of folk music. Second, with specific regard to the music on which I fo- cused during field research, I present my understanding of the more recent history of folk music in Finland and of the factors that led to the development of new folk music. This is based on the stories I was told by folklorists, folk mu- sic scholars, and musicians about their involvement with folk music from the 1950s to the 1980s. From the different perspectives of these narratives, I have constructed an account in which I draw attention to general trends and to the role of specific individuals during this folk revival period. Thirdly, in docu- menting my experience of Finnish folk music during the early 1990s my focus is on contemporary practice, but I am already writing history.

CONTINUITY AND CHANGE

Folk revival movements have provided ethnomusicologists opportunities to reflect on musical continuity and change.[3] Contemporary Finnish folk music (or new folk music) is one of these folk revivals, and this ethnography will contribute, I hope, to understanding the workings of such movements. New folk music is associated with tradition, the past, and continuity, but musicians borrow and absorb new ideas and influences from other traditions. Whereas much debate in folk music research during the early part of the twentieth century revolved around the connection between folk and art music (Bartók's essays; Sibelius [1896] 1980; Väisänen 1936; Vaughan Williams 1934), contemporary folk music has become increasingly interconnected with the popular or world music market. Recent studies point to changes in the transmission and performance contexts of contemporary folk musics. Some of the most significant changes have been a response to technological developments such as the tape recorder, long-playing phonograph recordings, electronic treatments of folk song, and experiments with folk-rock discussed by Goldstein (1982) and Lloyd (1982) with regard to British folk song during the revival of the 1960s and 1970s. While the use of electric instruments generated controversy, the British and American revivals were to provide models for revival movements elsewhere, including the Finnish example, contribute to renewed debates about folk music, and pave the entry of folk music into a popular music marketplace. The context and metaphor of the marketplace is explored by Bohlman (1988) in his study of folk music in the modern world. Bohlman uses the metaphor of the musical bricolage of a Middle Eastern bazaar. With its juxtaposition of "old" and "new" sounds, its urban setting, and its commercial orientation, this metaphor serves to illustrate that folk music "has shed any cloak, real or imagined, of isolation" (Bohlman 1988, 124). For Slobin, the commercial popular music based on folk sources that, in fact, has emerged across the world is "a sure sign of modernization" (1982, 21). Whether perceived as commercial popular music based on folk sources or analyzed as a revival movement, these are portraits of folk music which are far removed from the traditional model of folk music as orally transmitted traditions located in rural contexts.

Thus, the concept of change, a major theoretical preoccupation of ethnomusicology in any case, is invariably addressed in studies of folk music that take into account contemporary developments. Such studies also include examination of changes in the organization of musical sound (Cooke 1986, with regard to the fiddle tradition of the Shetland Islands) and changing concepts of the tradition bearer and the different social contexts in which folk music occurs (Ferris and Hart 1982; Russell 1986; Czekanowska 1990). Views like Bartók's, of changes in folk music as a negative manifestation, gave way in the 1950s to an attitude in which "musical material available in a culture is the object to be studied" (Nettl 1964, 7). Not restricting the field of study by trying to find music uninfluenced by other musical cultures has further marked the shift to the current ethnomusicological view of "change and history as natural and expected process rather than the aberrant interlocution of unnatural forces acting on unsuspecting ahistorical societies" (Neuman 1993, 276). As Lloyd remarks, "innovation is nothing new" (1982, 15).

For Finnish contemporary folk musicians, the relationship between continuity and change, between the "old" and the "new," between tradition and innovation, is meaningful and is negotiated in various complex ways. In Rice's study of Bulgarian folk music, the relation between tradition and modernity (the latter generating musical innovation) is one of conflict, and individuals are seen as caught between two opposing forces. If tradition "in the form of rituals, instruments, songs and virtuosic performance practices with deep roots in the past, was revivified weekly in weddings, one of the few traditional contexts to survive the communist transformation of society," the communist state nevertheless "created professional cadres of organizers, arrangers, choreographers, and musicians to execute a centralized vision of Bulgarian culture, recast in a socialist mould" (Rice 1994, 19). Here the element of the new was imposed by the state because of a communist ideology that was committed to changing and controlling all aspects of society and culture. Individuals negotiated tradition and modernity by simultaneously acknowledging the authority of the Party while maintaining and adjusting their relationship to their heritage (Rice 1994, 19). The role of the state in determining representations of national culture is illuminating in the Finnish context, too, but for different reasons. Contemporary Finnish folk music has developed in response to grass-roots initiatives, but without state and institutional ideological and financial support it would not have flourished quite so rapidly.

The discourses of contemporary Finnish folk musicians emphasize creative treatments (in, for instance, arrangements) of traditional repertoires and original compositions that use traditional techniques in innovative ways. Individual musicians or groups therefore emerge as mediators between a traditional music and modernity in ways that take into account aesthetic as well as ideological demands. Slawek's (1993) analysis of Ravi Shankar's rigorous training and his theoretical and historical knowledge of North Indian classical traditions as the prerequisites for introducing innovative musical and performance elements provides an appropriate perspective for considering the learning processes of Finnish contemporary folk musicians. Innovation and the creative impulse of the individual is based on the study of tradition, and it is knowledge of this tradition that both enables the musician to recognize what is innovative and legitimizes creative flexibility. If Ravi Shankar, however, can trace a musical genealogy that reaches into the distant past, the ways in which many Finnish contemporary folk musicians acquire knowledge of folk traditions, perceived as ancient in origin, is yet another marker of change.

In negotiating continuity and change, Finnish contemporary folk musicians often refer (although not consistently) to their music as *uusikansanmusiikki* (new folk music) rather than *kansanmusiikki* (folk music). In my analysis, I too adopt this term and for the same reasons as the musicians I studied—to highlight both the contemporary aspect of folk music and the notion of change. The use of the term "new folk music" distinguishes the subject of inquiry from the musical practices of those musicians who adhere more closely to traditional models of folk transmission and performance. Amid the complex processes of musical flow and representations that characterize the Finnish new folk music scene, I have adopted two principal approaches to the description of new folk music. One approach is to examine who is involved with new folk music, including the networks formed between individuals and the ways in which they operate to bring new folk music to the attention of a wider public. Individuals with interests in this musical genre are often affiliated with educational, research, and state institutions, with record companies, or with the media. This account of new folk music includes descriptions of activity within these spheres of influence. A second approach is to describe people's notions and concepts of new folk music. These include, on one hand, notions of history, of tradition, of the link between the past and the present, of folk music as the expression of the people—of the nation. On the other hand, this music is associated with innovation, originality, creativity: the element of the new. Folk music absorbs elements from other traditions and is always changing. But even when folk music is described as new, it is paradoxically perceived as part of tradition. Contemporary representations of folk music, like those of the nineteenth century, refer, then, to similarities and differences between past and present soundworlds. They are as much informed by images of the past and of continuity as were nationalist projections. If nineteenth-century nationalists looked to a mythical past, current representations of folk music are embedded in the images of the folk that dominated the nineteenth-century Finnish cultural and political scene. The term "new folk music" draws a distinction between contemporary practice and the folk music of the past, but its use rests on an assumption of continuity. "New folk music" follows "folk music." Thus, new folk music can be understood as "a temporal concept, inherently tangled with the past, the future, with history" (Glassie 1995, 399). Considering continuity and change through the prisms of historical perspectives offers significant insights into contemporary folk musical practice. Above all, I have accorded central importance to the discourse of musicians. What I was told about new folk music, as well as my observations and experience of performance practice and of the processes of transmission (through education, performances, and recordings), has been central to my understanding of this music.

IDENTITY AND REPRESENTATION

The identity of a particular music as Finnish or as new folk is linked to the more general question of how music is used in constructing and maintaining a sense of group identity. My analysis rests on the assumption that a sense of a Finnish national identity, as well as the identity of a particular music as new folk, depends upon interaction with others. Indeed, this relational aspect has been highlighted in the recent history of Finland—seen as a bridge between East and West. The point that notions of distinct identities are formed in relation to others has been discussed by a number of writers, including Clifford (1988), who suggests that human identities are mixed, relational, and conjunctural. Honko (1988) emphasizes fluidity and flexibility in conceptual expressions of identity, variation and change in studies of cultural identity as being the rule rather than the exception, and studying identity as a process of ongoing negotiations.

The notion of a national identity, however, implies homogeneity and collectivity. Indeed, nations are held up as discrete, homogeneous entities on the basis of asserting, among other factors, differences in culture, language, religion, and tradition (Lewis 1976; Spencer 1990; Smith 1994). In depicting a world made up of bounded, homogeneous cultures, nationalists and anthropologists share certain concepts and assumptions that, Spencer (1990) suggests, have made the study of nationalism problematic for anthropologists. Spencer's characterization of both nationalism and anthropology as modes of "cultural self-consciousness" (Spencer 1990, 283) is relevant in the context of new folk music, which is a self-conscious reinterpretation of a past "folk culture."

The nationalist enterprise often includes the search for evidence of unique cultural practices and traditions from the past that can be used to signify difference (from other nations) in the construction of present political realities. Traditions from the past are used not only to signify difference, but also to create a sense of continuity. The nation can be regarded as having been culturally distinct in the past even before it self-consciously recognized itself as being so. Sometimes these traditions are "invented" and, although recent, are perceived as stemming from a more distant past (Hobsbawm and Ranger 1983). In the production of cultural identity, new "traditions" sometimes emerge to reinforce political change. An example is the role played by contemporary popular music in the construction of a pan-Yoruba identity. Waterman was told by a juju bandleader, "our tradition is a very modern tradition" (Waterman 1990, 378). This musician drew attention to the way in which the contemporary popular music he played could act as a "medium for the retrospective definition of tradition" (Waterman 1990, 369).

The themes which emerge from discussions about nations and the construction of national identities are closely connected to those I have outlined in relation to new folk music: the relationship between past and present, notions of change and continuity, and assertions of cultural distinctiveness. That the notion of the culturally distinct nation remains potent in a world in which the possibilities for interconnectedness become increasingly apparent (Spencer 1990) is paralleled by the way in which Finnish new folk music signifies a distinct musical category, despite the difficulty in establishing where the boundaries between this music and any other lie and its location in a world music marketplace.

Questions of identity (national or musical) are intertwined with issues of representation. In pursuing a historical perspective the emphasis is placed here on the role of "symbols, myths, values and memories in the formation and persistence of collective cultural identities, and on the way in which such identities can be preserved by often gradual changes in these elements of shared culture" (Smith 1994, 709). New folk music is different from folk music of the nineteenth century (in the use of electric instruments and in the combination of diverse musical elements in contemporary folk music, for example), yet it is still "Finnish." What has endured is the way in which folk music operates as a symbol of identity. By focusing on new folk music, I am attempting, therefore, to describe identity in terms of the symbols and metaphors by means of which a sense of group identity is created. Honko suggests that a description of a group identity entails the selection of symbols and metaphors, which should be governed by the selections made by members of the group being studied (as is the case with folk music). Describing group identity on the basis of individual testimonies, however, raises obvious methodological problems (Honko 1988). The notion of a group identity, moreover, is itself a representation of collectivity that becomes problematized by close examination of the symbols of unity. Thus the notion of a homogeneous group (in this case, "national") identity is questioned by my subsequent scrutiny of the diversity that it encompasses. My analysis focuses on musical diversity within new folk music—that is, within the music that typically operates as a symbol of national identity. Part of the diversity stems from the meeting of different regional traditions that are together represented under the umbrella of Finnish new folk music. Diversity is also evident in the borrowing of fragments of the musical traditions of "others" and in the location of new folk music in a global music space. These borrowings can be read in terms of cultural appropriation (Ziff and Rao 1997) or creative innovations (Meyer 1989) and can be analyzed in relation to the construction of musical difference (cf. Solie 1993). If new folk music extends the conceptual parameters of folk music research, its representational role as a symbol of national identity, which encompasses musical multiplicity and diversity, emerges as a challenge to notions of the coherent and homogenous nation.

Honko (1988), like Spencer (1990), notes the complicity of scholars in representations of homogenous collective identities but observes paradigmatic and methodological changes resulting from the eloquence and fluency of "informants" who engage in scholarly discourse. He writes that "whereas we used to have passive research objects, e.g. groups whose cultural identity could be defined by way of our internal, detached scholarly operations, we may in the future be seeking not objects but partners, whose cooperation is necessary not only in creating the data but also in evaluating and testing the results of our analysis. This kind of symmetry . . . is closer now that many of our 'informants' are well able to use such concepts as 'tradition,' 'culture' and 'identity' and, more important, are actively engaged in the definition of the cultural identity of their membership and reference groups" (Honko 1988, 8). Both the emphasis on individual testimony and the symmetry between "informant" and "scholar" noted by Honko were apparent throughout my experience of fieldwork and in the later processes of analyzing my data and engaging in ethnographic writing. The symmetry lies in the discussions I had with informants, an integral part of this text, who themselves freely used concepts of Finnish "tradition," "culture" and "identity." But "identity" resisted reification. Concepts of identity were fluid, multifaceted, and changing. Perhaps people find music such an appropriate medium for expressing and shaping identities because music too is never static, as Slobin puts it in a memorable description: "music's social and cultural role is always that of shape-changer, if not trickster" (1996, 4).

The focus on individual testimony in examining the workings of Finnish new folk music is accompanied by presentations of individual musical biographies. This focus on the individual is crucial in relation to the tradition of folk music research in which folk music has been represented as collective creative musical expression. For Bartók, the role of the community in folk music making was given priority over individual composition: "pure folk music is the spontaneous expression of the musical feelings of a community" (Bartók 1976, 173). Bartók's research demonstrated, however, that folk music's links extended beyond national frontiers, and he was well aware of the attribution of particular music to particular people as part of nationalist projects.[4] Lönnrot's view is an encompassing one, based on a unity in human expression, but he similarly asserted the instinctive nature of folk art to attribute a particular art to a collective: "folk poems [song texts] cannot therefore be called made. They are not made, but they make themselves, they are born, they grow and form themselves without any special maker's care. The earth that nurtures them is mind and thought, the seeds from which they grow are all kinds of emotions. But since mind, thoughts and emotions at all times and in all human beings are mainly of a similar kind, so the poems born of them are not the special property of one or two, but common to the whole people" (Lönnrot cited in Hautala 1969, 31). Even Brăiloiu, who noted that the question of creativity was a theme which inspired folklorists' "liveliest and sometimes most confused argument" (1984, 6), adhered to the notion of collective composition because of the absence of a musical score (a comparison made to the Western art music tradition). For Brăiloiu, indications of individual creativity in folk music are expressed only through the principle of variation: "Without the help of writing, what is created can only last by the universal consent of those who bear it, itself the consequence of the uniformity of their tastes. The oral 'work' only exists in the memory of whoever adopts it, and only becomes concrete by his will. . . . since no writing stabilizes the composition once and for all, this work is not a 'finished object' but an object that is made and remade perpetually. That is to say that all the individual performances of a melodic pattern are equally true. . . . that is also to say that the 'instinct for variation' is not merely a simple passion for varying but a necessary consequence of the lack of any unchallengeable model" (Brăiloiu 1984, 105). Collective composition as a characteristic of the creative process in folk music is aligned to the homogenizing tendencies of nationalist discourse. A collective creative process is a powerful representation of musical unity that lends itself to the building of an analogous social and political solidarity. The folk, it seems, sing the same song, perhaps in unison as in Sibelius's representation of the folk in the *Kullervo Symphony* (see Ramnarine 1998).[5] Even for Brăiloiu, who introduced the idea of the folk musician as an individual creative agent because of the opportunities for variation, the folk song survives by universal consent.

While scholarly discourse about folk music contributed to ideals of the united and uniform nation, these representations of folk music were equally significant in the ways they influenced scholars in their roles as composers. Discussion about the nature of the creative process contributed to a "discursive" construction of difference (Shepherd 1993, 65) between musical traditions, for the folk composed and preserved their material collectively while the art composer (through processes of transforming folk material) composed as a creative individual and produced new musical expressions.

The Finnish scholar Armas Otto Väisänen, in an account of his first meeting with the Ingrian musician Teppo Repo, gives us an example in which the issues of composition and reproduction, of individual and collective creation, are raised. At this meeting, Väisänen urged Repo to play something "from his own head," which he recorded. Finding the composition "beautiful," Väisänen asked Repo to play it a second time: "'I don't remember,' said Repo. He was a true improviser. This was an interesting occurrence which, during my long career, I had never come across. I thought that this composition should be preserved. I played it many times and said to him, 'listen carefully now and learn *your* own composition.' I do not remember whether I replayed his composition four or five times before it stuck in his mind, so that he would be able to play it in exactly the same way" (Väisänen [1970] 1990, 158; my translation and emphasis). Later, Väisänen was visited by Paolo Pavolini (who translated the *Kalevala* into Italian), and for this occasion he arranged a performance by Repo. Väisänen noted, "I asked him to play *our* first composition. . . . this composition began to be known as Pavolini's tune" (Väisänen [1970] 1990, 158; my translation and emphasis). His request to "play our composition," reveals a self-consciousness about the scholar's influence on the compositional process: Teppo Repo's improvisation becomes a fixed composition (see example 1.1).[6] Musical memory can be short. The possibilities for variation are extensive. In its perpetual making and remaking, folk music not only retains its role as a

Example 1.1: Teppo Repo's improvisation, "Pavolinin Sävel" ("Pavolini's Tune"; transcription from Luohivouri and Nieminen, 1987, 50)

representational symbol but also offers new ways of perceiving, imagining and constructing national identity.

BORROWING FROM THE TRADITIONS OF "OTHERS"

History, continuity and change, identity, and representation are interweaving themes offering various perspectives from which we can contemplate Finnish new folk music. The issue of identity, particularly that of national identity, is prominent because of an abiding preoccupation with the question of how musicians draw inspiration and musical ideas from a variety of traditions yet retain specific views regarding the identity of the musical tradition within which they work and the place to which it belongs. Attempting to grapple with this question takes me beyond the certainties of folk music's association with defined national boundaries and identities.

For Baumann, musical borrowings in the fusion of all kinds of Western musics display "superficial processes of mixing and synthesis," and the "newer, technological form of acculturation overshadows all earlier processes of cultural meltdown." "World music" threatens the existence of music cultures, which may not even have been heard and which may disappear before they have been documented (Baumann 1992, 159). His view of folk music revivals is more positive. The dynamic of tradition lies "in the musical relationship between local and global perspectives, regression and emancipation, and between retrospection and future outlooks" (Baumann 1996, 71). His hope is that traditional music will contribute to "world music" in such a way that the emphasis will be placed instead on "musics of the world" (Baumann 1996, 84). This book will explore how Finnish musicians continue to be engaged with traditional music and to take it into the arena of world music. The paradox in this case is that Finnish new folk music, with its feature of musical "hybridity," nevertheless continues to represent a national identity in a global market place. The dialectic between distinct musical identity (representing a national identity) and musical borrowings can be expressed in the form of the following related questions, which are central to this text: (1) Why is it important for its practitioners that Finnish new folk music continues to operate as a marker of national identity? How is this tradition represented as being both "Finnish" and "new folk"? (2) How and why do musicians draw on musical ideas from diverse sources yet retain specific ideas regarding the identity of their musical tradition? Although interrelated, these questions pull us into different directions. The first appears to stress coherency (as it deals with nationalist projects with ideals of homogeneity), while the second emphasizes diversity (borrowing from others) and recurs in the contemporary context with its unprecedented variety of accessible music, both from a historical and from a global perspective. In posing these questions I delve into the construction of musical boundaries, appropriation, the transformative power of musical borrowings, and creative hegemonies as well as into musical multiplicity and fluidity in identity formation. Through the ethnographic material I discuss how new folk musicians simultaneously experience their practice as both a destabilizing force to notions of national and cultural homogeneity and a means whereby a sense of identity (on multiple levels of nation, region, village, and family) and a sense of belonging are reinforced. The story begins with nineteenth-century nationalist constructions of folk music.

The Folk
and the Nation

I will sing the people's legends, and the ballads of the nation.
Elias Lönnrot

In the *Kalevala*, a mythical hero—shaman and musician—Väinämöinen, emerges from a wide expanse of water into a barren and silent land:

Nousi siitä Väinämöinen
jalan kahen kankahalle
saarehen selällisehen,
manterehen puuttomahan.

Viipyi siitä vuotta monta,
aina eellehen eleli
saaressa sanattomassa,
manteressa puuttomassa.

Then did Väinämöinen, rising,
Set his feet upon the surface
Of a sea-encircled island,
In a region bare of forest.

There he dwelt, while years passed over,
And his dwelling he established

On the silent, voiceless island,
In a barren, treeless country.[1]

(*Kalevala*, rune [epic song or poem] 2, lines 1–8)

Väinämöinen directs a man of the earth to sow the land with trees. Once the man of the earth, Pellervoinen, has sown the land with trees, the land is named Kaleva. Väinämöinen toils in the forest and takes the role of singer:

Vaka vanha Väinämöinen
elelevi aikojansa
noilla Väinölän ahoilla,
Kalevan kankahilla.
Laulelevi virsiänsä,
laulelevi, taitelevi.

Väinämöinen old and steadfast
Passed the days of his existence
Where lie Väinölä's sweet meadows,
Kaleva's extended heathlands,
There he sang his songs of sweetness,
Sang his songs and proved his wisdom

(*Kalevala*, rune 3, lines 1–6)

Later in the epic, Väinämöinen creates an instrument, the kantele, from the jawbones and fins of a great pike (plate 1). Others try unsuccessfully to play the instrument. It is handed to its maker and all living things come to listen.

Jo kävi ilo ilolle,
riemu riemulle remahti,
tuntui soitto soitannalle,
laulu laululle tehosi.
Helähteli hauin hammas,
kalan purstö purkaeli,
ulvosi upehen jouhet,
jouhet ratsun raikkahuivat.

Now came pleasure after pleasure,
As the sweet notes followed others,
As he sat and played the music,
As he sang his songs melodious,
As he played upon the pike-teeth,
And he lifted up the fish-tail,
And the horsehair sounded sweetly,
Clearly sang the strings of horsehair

(*Kalevala*, rune 41, lines 23–30).

No listener remained unmoved by the kantele music:

Ei ollut sitä urosta
eikä miestä urheata,
Ollut ei miestä eikä naista
eikä kassan kantajata
kellen ei itkuksi käynyt,
kenen syäntä ei sulannut

There was none among the heroes,
None among the men so mighty,
None among the men or women
None of those whose hair is plaited,
Whom he did not move to weeping,
And whose hearts remained unmelted

(*Kalevala*, rune 41, lines 171–76).

At the Ateneum Art Gallery in Helsinki I looked at a painting of another kantele performance. The painting, entitled "Kreeta Haapasalo Playing the Kantele in a Peasant Cottage" (by Robert Wilhelm Ekman, 1868), shows the gathering of disparate sections of Finnish society who are united in their attention to the performance. The setting is the interior of a wooden cottage. Kreeta Haapasalo, playing the kantele with a scarf tied around her head, is a peasant woman, indisputably one of the "folk" and the focal point of the painting. Beside her sits an affluent mother with her children, and in front of her a young peasant boy sharpens a wooden stick. On the other side, a fisherman mends a net and a veteran of the Crimean War smokes a pipe. Peasant women prepare coffee in the background. They are united in listening to the performance and by their common cultural heritage, symbolized by the instrument. But Ekman's portrayal of national unity is a dream. In 1868, Finland was still a grand duchy of Russia. The contrast between Ekman's aspirations for the future and the political reality of 1868 is revealed through the artist's addition of Tsar Alexander I's portrait hanging above in a corner of the interior (Levanto 1991).

Despite the accuracy of ethnological details in the work and its significance as a portrait of a well-known folk performer, Ekman's "ardent dream was to illustrate the epic poetry of the Kalevala" (Levanto 1991, 31), a project which was never fully realized. His preoccupation with Lönnrot's epic as a narrative suited to his artistic vision was characteristic of the period. The *Kalevala* as a text and as a national symbol overshadowed the performance traditions from which it emerged during the nineteenth century as well as a host of other coexisting folk music practices. In the pages of the *Kalevala* we do not hear the songs. We read the texts. Ekman's painting of Haapasalo and her audience is a silent image. It is text rather than context. Much folklore research of this period referred to these folk songs as "folk poetry." Today, new folk musicians still speak of *Kalevala,* kantele, Väinämöinen, and Lönnrot in discussions about new folk music history and the Finnishness of their music.

INTEREST IN FOLKLORE BEFORE LÖNNROT AND THE *KALEVALA*

Abrahams notes that it is virtually canonical to relate the growth of folklore studies to the development of romantic nationalistic movements throughout Europe during the late eighteenth and nineteenth centuries. Folklore is thus seen as the "handmaiden of a politics of vernacularity" (Abrahams 1992, 36). Nineteenth-century folklore research in Finland, informed by such movements, focused on the *Kalevala* as the epic embodiment of land, language, and tradition. Yet Abrahams notes that the beginnings of the idea of the "folk" emerge earlier, during the sixteenth and seventeenth centuries (Abrahams 1992, 36), and there are important sources of information about Finnish folklore that precede nineteenth-century scholarship. These were isolated examples, and much of the nationalism that has been attributed to earlier sources has been by implication only (Honko 1979). Nevertheless, they provided a background of folklore research and a sense of continuity that directed nineteenth-century investigations. Mikael Agricola (c. 1510–57), bishop of Turku, mentioned Finnish gods in connection with furthering the cause of Lutheranism. He included Finnish proverbs in his works but denounced the singing of epic songs in which ancient deities seemed to be worshiped. Whatever his views about folk songs, his list of pagan gods suggests that songs referring to them were still widely performed in the sixteenth century (Wilson 1976, 7).

At the time when Sweden was a great power, one of the most notable writers to deal with Finnish folklore material was Daniel Juslenius (1676–1752), a professor at Turku University who later became the Bishop of Porvoo and then of the Skara diocese in Sweden. He was particularly concerned with the people of Finland and the Finnish language, and he was the first of the eighteenth-century scholars to turn his attention to this area. Using the Bible as the basis for his arguments, he praised Finland, its people, their language, and their past. He placed the Finnish language on the same level as the "holy, original languages," Hebrew and Greek, claiming that it was easy for Finns to learn these languages as they are related to their mother tongue. This attitude parallels that prevalent in other parts of Europe, where Greek antiquity was often considered the prototype for folklore research. Greece was conceived as the "source of Europe" and as "having originated European culture" (Herzfeld 1982, 11). The writing of Juslenius differed from Swedish patriotic tracts, as his praise was directed not to the Swedish kingdom as a whole, of which Finland was a part, but specifically to Finland. He used folk song texts (called "folk poetry") as proof of the ancient Finnish civilization, believing, as did many others at that time, that epic song recounted actual historical events. The influence of Juslenius on Finnish folklore research is noteworthy. He drew the folklore collectors and scholars who followed in his footsteps in a patriotic direction.

Another important though later scholar of the eighteenth century was Henrik Gabriel Porthan (1739–1804). With views similar to those of Juslenius, Porthan followed the ideas of the romantic movement awakening in Europe, which looked to "a distant, idealised ancient time, towards a mythical past which was considered more noble than the present" (Hautala 1969, 17). These ideas were leading to the search for and the collection and publication of folklore material throughout Europe. It was understood that folklore material contained messages from a "golden age" (Hautala 1969, 17). This ideological background may furnish a reason why folklore research centered on the study of text. Texts could be interpreted as giving indications of the historical past, in contrast to the music, the melodic line of the song itself, or the instrumental pelimanni traditions, which had no narrative content and could not be interpreted in this way. As Lewis suggests, claiming an ancient history or "inventing" history has been a way of either legitimizing or undermining authority, in asserting "new claims and new arguments, sometimes even a new identity." It was common in European nationalist history, where the "nation" was defined by "language, culture, and origin" (Lewis 1976, 64).

Although Porthan was a contemporary of the German philosopher Herder, who was writing about folk song and poetry as the property of all the people, debate at the University of Turku, where Porthan taught, centered more around Macpherson's *Poems of Ossian.* (Ossian was reputedly a third-century Gaelic bard whose works were "translated" by Macpherson in the 1760s; see Mac Craith 1996).[2] Porthan wrote the first detailed account of Finnish poetry, *De Poesi Fennica* (Porthan [1778] 1983), which included sections on folk poetry (rune language and style). His views were developed by his students and influenced research well into the nineteenth century. One of his students, Eric Lencqvist (1719–1808), anticipated later comparative research that took into account the migration of tradition. In *De Poesi Fennica,* Porthan had begun comparative work, looking at variants of the same song. This approach laid the foundations for future research, most significantly for Lönnrot's work in the compilation of the *Kalevala.*

Nationalistic ideas emanating from Germany spread around university circles in Finland. Porthan set up a literary association, known as the Aurora Society, whose patriotic ideals were expressed in terms of the promotion of the Finnish language and culture. It was active in Turku from 1770 to 1779. Although interested in Finnish history and folklore, Porthan did not write about Finland as a "nation." When he died in 1804, Finland was still no more than a province of the Swedish kingdom; "his nation was largely dormant, unaware of itself" (Honko 1979, 141). It was six decades after his death, in 1864, when Porthan was identified as a national hero and his statue was unveiled in Turku (Honko 1979, 141).

Continuing after Porthan, in the early nineteenth century, Herder's ideas and the *Poems of Ossian* still influenced scholars at Turku University. This period is referred to as "Turku romanticism," and one of its proponents, Gottlund, had conceived the possibility of combining folk poems into "a systematic entity, be it an epic, a drama or whatever" by 1817 (cited in Asplund and Lipponen 1985, 10).[3]

Rheinhold von Becker (1788–1858), a contemporary of the Turku roman-
ticists, though not closely associated with that circle, can be seen, according to
Hautala, as the link between them and their predecessor, Porthan. He established a paper, *Turun Viikkosanomat* (*Turku Weekly News*), in 1820, and in the
paper he published an article about Väinämöinen. His influence on his student,
Elias Lönnrot (1802–84), was substantial, for it was under von Becker's guidance that Lönnrot became familiar with the work of Porthan and Lencqvist. For
Lönnrot's first written research work, published as an academic thesis under
the title *De Väinämöine, priscorum Fennorum numine* (1827), von Becker gave
Lönnrot the poems about Väinämöinen which he had used himself for the article in *Turun Viikkosanomat* and some additional poems which had not been
used for that article. Although the aim of the thesis was simply to collate and
order information on a particular subject, the thesis foreshadowed Lönnrot's
later work. As Hautala explains, "While composing it, Lönnrot had to get thoroughly acquainted with everything written about Finnish folk poetry and with
all publications of poems, and he had to link those songs which followed the
same hero, into one continuous whole. This kind of procedure was in its way
the first step towards the *Kalevala*" (Hautala 1969, 22).

LÖNNROT AND THE *KALEVALA*

Lönnrot became the "greatest figure in the Finnish Romantic movement"
(Hautala 1969, 21). Nineteenth-century folklore research generally focused on
his work, the *Kalevala,* which completely fulfilled romantic nationalist aspirations and which, down to the present day, is still described as the national epic
of Finland. The story of his compilation of the *Kalevala* can be read in terms of
borrowing, appropriating, transforming, forging, and inventing cultural elements: in this case items of folklore, to use as markers of national identity. Indeed, subsequent analyses of the *Kalevala* demonstrate an interest in questions
about the migration and borrowing of tradition that assume significance in
heralding the epic as "national" and as "Finnish."

Lönnrot's studies coincided with a time of change in Finnish intellectual life.
The University of Turku was destroyed by fire in 1827, and its members moved
to the University of Helsinki, newly established under the auspices of Alexander I. Lönnrot, who had begun his studies in Turku (1822) working with folklore material, embarked on a study of medicine at the new university.[4] Shortly
after the University of Helsinki had been opened, the Lauantai Seura (Saturday

Society) was formed. From this informal circle, of which both Lönnrot and Snellman were members, there arose the idea of establishing a society whose object would be to create a national culture, and in 1831, the Suomalaisen Kirjallisuuden Seura (Finnish Literature Society, also referred to as SKS) was founded. The aim of the SKS was to collect, publish, and study folklore material, and one of its first decisions was to award a grant of one hundred rubles to Lönnrot to collect folk poetry. Lönnrot made several field trips, mainly around the Finnish-speaking area and on both sides of the present-day Finnish-Russian border in Karelia. He continued to make field trips and to collect folklore material after beginning his practice as a district doctor in Kajaani (1833) and began to conceive plans to construct a literary epic from this material, for the nation, by 1834. In a letter, he wrote that "a desire to organise and unify them [folk poems] awoke in me, to extract from Finnish mythology something corresponding to the Icelandic *Edda*. . . . I do not know, however, whether the work of linking the mythological poems into one whole should be attempted by one man, because our descendants will possibly esteem such a collection as highly as the Gothic nations regard *Edda* or the Greeks and Romans, if not Homer, at least Hesiod" (cited in Hautala 1969, 24). During this year, Lönnrot worked on *Runokokous Väinämöisestä* (*The Väinämöinen Poems*), also known as the "proto-*Kalevala*." His fifth field trip was made to northeastern Karelia, where he met one of the most renowned singers, Arhippa Perttunen, in Latvajärvi. Perttunen was sixty-five years old at the time when Lönnrot met him. He had learned his songs as a child from his father and had an extensive repertoire. In two days, Perttunen sang over four thousand lines of poetry to Lönnrot, and his repertoire contained nearly all of the narrative elements that were to make up the future *Kalevala*. As a result of this meeting, Lönnrot obtained many additions to his material. *Runokokous Väinämöisestä* was left unpublished while Lönnrot worked with the new material, and in 1835 the SKS published what is known as the "old" *Kalevala*, consisting of 12,078 lines arranged into thirty-two poems.

The Kalevala *and Nationalist Discourse*

The publication of the *Kalevala* had an important effect on the process of nation building. With its appearance, the status of the Finnish language and of Finnish literature was immediately elevated. A major work, demonstrating the richness of the Finnish language, had appeared, and it gave to Finnish literature "what the period held as most valuable in literature: an ancient epic, a national epic" (Hautala 1969, 25). Such was the positive response to the *Kalevala* that Lönnrot expanded the work using his further collections and material made available to him by other collectors, notably D. E. D. Europaeus (1820–84), who collected material in Ingria. A later edition, known as the "new" *Kalevala*, was published in 1849 and contained 22,795 lines arranged into fifty poems. This epic provided the foundation for the presentation of a "national" art. Characters from the *Kalevala* were painted by artists such as Akseli Gallen-Kallela, and titles of musical works were also based on these characters (e.g., Sibelius's *Kullervo Symphony, Luonnotar,* and *Pohjola's Daughter*).

The *Kalevala* profoundly influenced the development of folklore research, which was to focus on Lönnrot's work for over a century, beginning with the study of the epic itself. In the 1870s, Julius Krohn turned his attention to the original poems from which the *Kalevala* had been written, but it was thought that the collections still being made would provide additional material for the *Kalevala*, thus enabling all the separate parts of what had once been a whole epic to be reassembled. Lönnrot was regarded by his contemporaries, and indeed even until the mid–twentieth century, as the writer who had begun to piece together the remaining fragments of an ancient, forgotten, epic poem. The fact that the *Kalevala* had been constructed into a unified whole from disparate elements was later acknowledged, particularly since Lönnrot had been clear about his methodology.

Disparate elements mean that there is a duality in Lönnrot's work. It is a "polyphonic monologue" (Bakhtin 1973)—the work of an individual writer and a compilation of the words of many singers. In the "new" *Kalevala*, Lönnrot departed from the original poems in his collection much more extensively than he had done previously. He assumed the role of a singer himself, explaining this procedure in the periodical *Litteraturblad* (1849): "I considered that I had the same right that, I am convinced, most singers take upon themselves, namely to organise the poems according to how best they fit together. . . . in other words I regard myself as being as good a singer as they are" (cited in Asplund and Lipponen 1985, 27). Lönnrot made this view explicit in the opening lines of the *Kalevala*, thus inextricably linking the work to himself:

Mieleni minun tekevi,
aivoni ajattelevi
lähteäni laulamahan,
saa'ani sanelemahan,
sukuvirttä suoltamahan,
lajivirttä laulamahan.

Sanat suussani sulavat,
puhe'et putoelevat,
kielelleni kerkiävät,
hampahilleni hajoovat.

I am driven by my longing,
And my understanding urges
That I should commence my singing,
And begin my recitation.
I will sing the people's legends,
And the ballads of the nation.
To my mouth the words are flowing,
And the words are gently falling,
Quickly as my tongue can shape them,
And between my teeth emerging.

(*Kalevala,* rune 1, lines 1–10)

Lönnrot was one of the few collectors who mentioned the singers from whom he collected songs, but these are passing references, and only the material from about twenty singers can be identified in the first edition of the *Kalevala.* Collectors of folklore material generally did not mention the singers. They did not seem to be interested in their lives or in the singers as people, but only in the songs they sang, which were collected as products. There is a contradiction here in the perception of folk song, on one hand as the musical expression of people, of communities, and ultimately of the nation, and on the other hand as a product which can be collected and used in a quite different context. In addition to the material collected by Lönnrot from the singer Perttunen, two more examples of material contributed by folk singers can be noted here. In June 1833, Lönnrot heard the singer Ontrei Malinen in Vuonninen (Russian Karelia). One of his songs was the substantial 366 lines about the forging of the *sampo* (a mythical, magical object) which Lönnrot heard from him for the first time, and which was to become one of the *Kalevala*'s central themes.[5] Not many female singers were mentioned, but Lönnrot did write about a widow called Matro in the village of Uhtua (renamed Kalevala by Soviet authorities), who performed lyric poetry and narrative poetry about women and family relationships. One of her songs, which Lönnrot heard for the first time from her, was "The Hanged Maid," about a girl called Anni, who commits suicide when approached by an unknown man. This song provided the basis for Lönnrot's poem about Aino—the girl who is unwillingly betrothed to the hero, Väinä-möinen, and who commits suicide by escaping into water, only to be turned into a fish (see Timonen 1985).

It is clear from the above examples that Lönnrot's *Kalevala* was compiled from the repertoire of many singers, yet it was the work of Lönnrot as an *individual* that was used in the construction of national identity. In a sense, it was the individual's monologue that was taken into the public sphere. The other multiple voices that are contained in the *Kalevala* remain private, hidden from view. Yet the fact that they were contained in the work was one of the main reasons why it was seen as representing the people and capturing the national spirit. The transfer from multiple voices to monologue, from the "folk" to the "intellectual," from the private to the public sphere, was accompanied by a change in idiom, from many spoken (or sung) voices to a written record.

The ways in which an individual's work incorporates that of many other people can also be seen on a broader scale, in connection with the paradox that a work which inspired strong nationalist sentiments, and which seemed to embody the spirit of a particular people, was nevertheless compiled as a result of ideas and trends prevalent among a cosmopolitan elite. Lönnrot was influenced by ideas of the "nation-state" which were current throughout Europe in the late eighteenth and nineteenth centuries. The *Kalevala* fulfilled the conditions enunciated by Herder, who argued that a nation's need for a distinctive identity should be founded on the language and literature of the people. From this perspective, Lönnrot's individual voice (incorporating the multiple voices of his informants) can be seen as one of a multiplicity of voices making up the discourse of nationalism. A polyphony of voices was transformed into a monologue, which in turn became a part of a recontextualized polyphonic discourse.

As elsewhere in Europe, the discipline of folklore studies in Finland provided "intellectual reinforcement for the political process of nation building" (Herzfeld 1982, 4). This leads to another paradox, that folklorists belonging to university circles that were actively involved in promoting an identifiable "national" culture were in some ways separate from the folk culture that was being upheld as constituting the essence of the nation. The case is similar to that of Greek folklorists, who, as Herzfeld notes, "saw their nation's culture as a unity in which they were themselves fully participating members," but whose separation from the folk was marked by their "willingness and ability to think in terms of *studying* folklore" (Herzfeld 1982, 8; my emphasis).

Language

In the case of Finnish folklore research, the distance between the rural folk and folklorists was additionally marked by differences in the languages they used. The language of the folk was Finnish, and the *Kalevala* was also in Finnish. By contrast, the main language of the folklorists and of other intellectuals who worked with folklore material, as well as the language of government and of education, was Swedish. Moreover, much scholarly work was written in Latin. Research writings about folk traditions were therefore largely inaccessible to the folk whose traditions were being studied. Even the *Kalevala*, although immensely influential in furthering the aims of the nationalist movement, attracted only a small readership for several years after its publication. Those most interested in reading the *Kalevala* were the Finns who realized the work's political significance as a "national" epic. Yet many educated (Swedish-speaking) Finns were unable to understand its poetic language, hindered by their lack of competence in Finnish. Despite this separation between folklorist and folk, there were also links between them, as in the case of Lönnrot himself, who was born as one of the folk, the son of a tailor in a Finnish-speaking family. Later scholars were thus able to perceive Lönnrot as being one of the last of the folk singers: "In preserving the original character of the poems," wrote Julius Krohn, "it is most advantageous if the final shaping is performed with as sensitive a hand as possible; and it is most fortunate if the compiler, in poetic matters, is as close to the folk singers as possible. This our Lönnrot has been" (Julius Krohn cited in Wilson 1976, 56).

Until the late nineteenth century, the *Kalevala* was read more widely in translation than in its original language. Parallels drawn between different folk traditions demonstrated that what had been regarded as peculiar to one nation was in fact common to many. It has already been noted how folklorists from all over Europe were eager to make comparisons between the folk poetry of their regions and ancient Greek poetry, with the political motive of establishing an ancient history. Lönnrot had taken Homer as his model, writing in 1883: "I shall not cease collecting until these poems form a collection comparable to half of Homer" (cited in Asplund and Lipponen 1985, 24). But comparisons were made not only with Greek poetry. Julius Leopold Krohn (1835–88) pursued a comparative approach in his search for the origins of folk poems, and Grimm, at a lecture given at the Berlin Academy of Science in 1845, compared the *Kalevala* to Nordic mythology and to German verse epics and fairy tales.

The Origin of the Kalevala's *Folk Songs (Poems)*

Much debate focused on whether the *Kalevala* should be interpreted as myth or as history. Lönnrot himself favored the historical interpretation and adhered to the belief that the poems had been handed down from the ancient Finns. This concern about historical authenticity can be related to subsequent folklore research, which tried to establish whether the poems originated from the West or the East. The songs used by Lönnrot in the *Kalevala* mainly survived in the eastern regions of the Finnish-speaking area (Savo, Ingria, and both sides of the present-day Finnish-Russian border in Karelia). Reasons for the survival of these songs in these areas may include regional isolation from Western European influences and the more lenient attitude of the Russian Orthodox (in contrast to that of the Lutheran) Church toward folk poetry (Branch 1985, xiii). The "preservation" of "Finnish" cultural material within those same imperial boundaries from which Finnish nationalists sought a separation was problematic, and folklorists' concerns with origin were linked to a developing sense of a distinct identity in which Finland was more aligned to the West.

Borenius, for example, concluded in a study published in 1873, *Missä Kalevala on syntynyt? (Where Did the "Kalevala" Originate?)*, that the poems did not have their origin in the places where they were last sung—that is, in eastern Finland or in Karelia: "The poetry has come to Russian Karelia from the West, from Finland, and not spread from there in the opposite direction into Finland" (cited in Hautala 1969, 65). As proof, he pointed to Swedish loanwords, which had been distorted in the songs since these words were unknown in the ordinary language of the song regions. In a later work, Borenius compared *Kalevala* poetry to equivalents in English, German, Danish, and Norwegian to demonstrate that the Finnish poem cycle was linked to the medieval tradition of Western Europe. Julius Leopold Krohn also considered the origins of the *Kalevala* poems. He concluded that the *Kalevala* was the creation of the entire Finnish nation, since the poems originated from Western Finland and partly from Ingria and Estonia too. But in his view, the poems had been developed into the form that constituted the *Kalevala* by the Karelians.

Julius Krohn's research method, which he called local-historical, was developed by his son, Kaarle Krohn, and it became known as the geographical-historical or "Finnish" method. This method, influenced by Darwin's positivistic and evolutionary doctrines, was used to examine the migration, diffusion, and borrowing of tradition. The basic assumption of this method was that all variants of a folk poem are "historically and genetically interconnected" (Honko 1979, 144). In theory it should have been possible to locate the time, place, and language of origin of a folk poem and, by reconstruction, to delineate the original form of the poem. In a study published in 1885, Julius Krohn concluded that by origin Finnish folk poetry was not Finnish at all. As in his earlier study of the Väinämöinen and Lemminkäinen poems, he asserted that *Kalevala* material had migrated to Finland mostly from the West. These conclusions were potentially damaging to the view of folk poetry as the spontaneous expression of the folk. How then did Julius Krohn account for the "Finnish" qualities of the poems? He argued that the materials that migrated to Finland were small units or cells, which, like living organisms, evolved into poetic cycles as they migrated eastward to where Lönnrot had discovered them. His claim was that the Finns had "nothing to fear," then, for "it was not so much the original subject matter as its re-creation by the Finns that had imbued the poems with the Finnish spirit" (cited in Wilson 1976, 54–55).

The theoretical perspectives outlined above indicate the extent to which folklore scholarship in Finland during this period was implicated in, shaped by and in turn shaping, nationalist urges. From 1888, folklore was represented at the University of Helsinki. Kaarle Krohn was nominated its docent, and a permanent chair was established in 1908. One of Krohn's students, V. J Mansikka (1884–1947), docent in Slavonic and comparative folklore research from 1910, was one of the few scholars to examine the links between Finland and the East. He examined the relation between Finnish and Slavonic folklore and published articles in Russian journals. Questioning the origins of Finnish poems and songs and comparing Finnish folklore material to Swedish and Russian material were ways of defining Finnish identity—an identity asserted and constructed in relation to the similarities and differences between Finland and its neighbors.

Comparing Finnish folk expressions with their Swedish and Russian counterparts in probing questions about the distinctiveness of Finnish culture highlights the relational dimensions of identity formations. As Melucci notes, this is a view of identity not as a "thing," an object that can be attained, but as "a system of relations and representations" (Melucci 1982, 68). In the context of a folklore scholarship that emphasizes collectivity in national expressions, Melucci's concept of identity is illuminating, for he pays attention to individual action. For Melucci, identity is linked to the importance of individual action and he asks why any given social actor should appear on the stage at a given moment. Melucci's argument is expanded by Schlesinger to the context of "national identity," where "identity is seen as a dynamic, *emergent* aspect of collective action" (Schlesinger 1987, 237). Schlesinger argues that "national identity" is best understood as a "specific form of collective identity" (237). Together with Bakhtin's (1973) notions of the coexistence of contrary voices, of "multileveled-ness" and "multivoicedness," of polyphony in monologue—these arguments provide a frame through which Lönnrot and his assembly of the *Kalevala* can be seen. As the achievement of an individual on the public stage and as an embodiment and as a representation of collective action, Lönnrot's work was central to the construction of national identity.

Identity as a system of representations assumes qualities of flexibility with the potential for changes and re-representations. Julius Krohn's argument rests on the concept of change: borrowed "cells" are expanded and re-created to become imbued with a quality of "Finnishness." His view allows folklore to be as much subject to re-interpretation as are notions of identity. The borrowed cells that Lönnrot used in a representation of "Finnishness," then, can be re-created today and differentiated by the term "new folk music" in expressing new ideas of this national identity.

Recent folklore scholarship reveals an abiding concern, however, with the question of origin. This concern centers on the development and characteristics of the metric structure of kalevalaic poetry and indicates the extent to which debates continue to treat the *Kalevala* as text. Korhonen, for example, argues against the theory that the Finns borrowed their models from the Balts. He informs us that since A. R. Niemi's study, published in 1918, in which similarities between the metric structures of Latvian folk songs and *Kalevala* meter were examined, the view that the Finns assimilated the meter of their songs from the Balts has been widely accepted. For Korhonen, however, the birth of the *Kalevala* meter "does not require any explanation based on foreign influence" ([1987] 1994, 84). He rejects the theory of Baltic origin or influence and concludes in a truly nationalistic vein that the Kalevala meter "emerged as a spontaneous reaction to the phonetic and prosodic development of Proto-Finnic" (87). In reproducing earlier views on the Finnish qualities of folk poetry to make the same point about its distinctiveness and its spread within national borders, Korhonen provides an example of the ongoing implication of scholarship and the use to which it is put in the legitimization of political (in this case, national) expression.

THE *KALEVALA*, SONG TRADITIONS, AND THE KANTELE

Musicians have sought to rediscover the musical and performance aspects of kalevalaic traditions since the revival movement of the 1960s and have drawn on

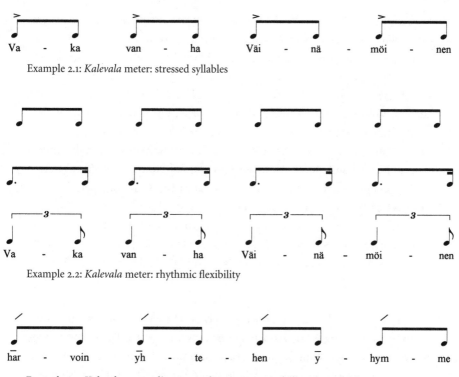

Example 2.1: *Kalevala* meter: stressed syllables

Example 2.2: *Kalevala* meter: rhythmic flexibility

Example 2.3: *Kalevala* meter: discrepancy between metrical (′) and word (–) stress

folklorists' insights and the recorded collections stored in the archives of the Finnish Literature Society. In this section, I wish to indicate some of the musical features of these song repertories.

METER: *Kalevala* songs are described as ancient and differentiated from songs in other traditions such as ballads and rhyming songs on the basis of their narrative content and metric structure—a trochaic tetrameter known as the "*Kalevala* meter" (see Kuusi [1978] 1994, Leino [1985] 1994, Korhonen [1987] 1994). So what are the features of this "ancient" and "Finnish" meter? It is basically an eight-syllable trochaic line, which is composed of four pairs of successive stressed and unstressed syllables (example 2.1). The first syllable of a word is always the stressed one in the Finnish language, but rhythmic variety can be introduced in several ways: through rhythmic flexibility in performance (example 2.2), by avoiding a continuous coincidence of metrical and word stress (example 2.3), and by alternating lines in which metrical and word stress coincide and lines in which they do not.

NARRATIVE CONTENT: The *Kalevala* meter is seen as unifying diverse categories of song, although folklorists have not agreed on a classification system for *Kalevala* material. *Runo* (epic) and *lyriikka* (lyrical) songs, spells, and festive material have often been identified as falling into distinct categories (Asplund 1978, 51). Branch's (1985) categorization is also fourfold: myth, magic and shaman, adventure, and Christian period poetry. Of these various categories, epics (dealing with mythical and supernatural subjects such as the origin of the world, how objects such as the boat and the kantele were made, and the important character Väinämöinen) are generally considered to be the oldest stratum of *Kalevala* songs. Matti Kuusi's ([1978] 1994) theory of stylistic periods demonstrates an ongoing preoccupation with antiquity. He distinguishes four stylistic periods: early (c. 400 B.C.–c. A.D. 500), middle (c. A.D. 500–1100), medieval (c. A.D. 1100–1400), and late (c. A.D. 1500–1800) *Kalevala*. Lönnrot's material is regarded as being derived largely from the early and middle *Kalevala* periods (see Asplund 1978, 52).

MELODY: *Kalevala* melodies are generally syllabic, although some melismas are found, becoming more frequent as one moves eastward. The melodic range is narrow, typically within the range of a pentachord. The intervallic movements are small, moving by a semitone, whole tone, or third. The songs are simple in structure, based on repetition and variation (Asplund and Laitinen 1979).

Many of the features described above can be seen in one of the oldest of transcribed *Kalevala* songs, published by Tengström in 1795 (example 2.4). The melody has become so well known that it is often referred to as the "*Kalevala* melody." In fact, as recently as 1989, the Finnish ethnomusicologist Timo Laitakari told me that a common misconception was that there was only one *Kalevala* melody.

INSTRUMENTAL ACCOMPANIMENT: The kantele is the main instrument associated with the *Kalevala* song tradition, and, just as the *Kalevala* has become the national epic, the kantele has been proclaimed the national instrument of Finland. The oldest versions of the kantele were made from a hollowed-out piece of wood with five strings. The strings are plucked, producing a soft sound, and they are tuned to a pentachord. Music played on the five-string kantele, like *Kalevala* songs, is based on repetition and variation. The kantele repertoire includes *Kalevala* melodies (example 2.5, based on the "*Kalevala* melody"), and the instrument was (and still is) sometimes used to accompany singers. New folk musicians have used Väisänen's (1928) collection of

Example 2.4: The "*Kalevala* melody"

Example 2.5: "Kuokkaisten Ruuki," a kantele piece based on the "*Kalevala* melody" (source: Väisanen 1928)

Example 2.6: "Konevitsan Kirkonkellot" ("The Church Bells of Konevitsa")

kantele melodies as a source; an example is "Konevitsan Kirkonkellot" (example 2.6), a kantele melody that appears in the repertoire of several new folk music groups.[6]

PERFORMANCE PRACTICE: In a pioneering study of folk runes as a performance tradition, Enäjärvi-Haavio (1951) mentions solo, two-part, and group singing.[7] Enäjärvi-Haavio demonstrates how one representation affected later performance practice. She argues that a myth regarding the performance manner (gesture and posture) of epic songs was quite easily established because of the lack of interest in the performance of *Kalevala* songs until the end of the nineteenth century. In 1801 and 1802, two travelers, Skjöldebrand from Sweden and Acerbi from Italy, published separate volumes about their tours around Finland. They referred to Porthan's *De Poesi Fennica* when describing the posture of rune singers in men's two-part singing. They misinterpreted his Latin text, however, and produced drawings of the performance posture based on this misinterpretation rather than on their own empirical evidence. The drawings portrayed rune singers sitting opposite each other with both pairs of hands joined. Skjöldebrand and Acerbi both described the singers tugging each other back and forth and even raising each other from their seats. These images had a profound impact on rune performers, since later artists copied them and they became associated with the *Kalevala*. The images became so widespread that rune singers in the 1940s adopted the posture, and when Rein translated *De Poesi Fennica* three hundred years after the death of Porthan, his translation of the passage on the posture of the singers was inaccurate "since even his imagination was bound by the national symbol which shone from the pages of the illustrated *Kalevala*" (Enäjärvi-Haavio 1951, 164). But during my field research, I saw no new folk musicians adhering to this performance practice. The performance of folk runes by new folk musicians for staged events features solo and group vocal arrangements with instrumental accompaniment.

MYTH, MUSIC, LANDSCAPE, IDENTITY

Since the nineteenth century, the image of a landscape of forests has been important in the formation of a collective Finnish identity (Lehtinen 1991), and "the old values of the forest are still living in the mind of the modern, even the urban, Finn" (Reunala 1989, 55). At the conclusion of a formal interview, the revival musician Seppo Paakkunainen announced "I would like to introduce you to a good friend of mine here." We were walking through a forest toward Ainola (the former home of Sibelius). I looked around. The farmhouses we had passed earlier seemed empty. Seppo stood with his hand placed on the trunk of a large pine tree. "This is my good friend, *iso mänty* [big pine tree]." He encouraged me to feel the warmth of the tree trunk, to see the resin bursting through the bark, and to perceive the tree as a being to whom one confides one's innermost thoughts. Seppo seeks the advice of this tree when he needs inspiration or guidance in his musical activities. Other trees were also friends, but *iso mänty* was his musical mentor, "the king of the forest." This tree was of a venerable age. Contained therein was the wisdom and perception of one who has diverse experiences from a long life.[8]

Seppo Paakkunainen's discourse paralleled that surrounding the composer whose house (now a museum) I was going to see. The Finnish forest to which Sibelius retreated offers further scope for nationalist projections, for a sense of territorial affiliation is commonly found in the construction of nations and of national identities. This is the stance adopted by James (1983, 1989), who describes Sibelius as a leading nationalist composer, a "fervent patriot" who gave conscious expression to nationalist sentiments through his music. James locates Sibelius's nationalist musical expressions in evocations of a northern landscape rather than in any folk inspiration. He writes that in his music Sibelius offered "the harsh voice and reality of the frozen wastes, the burdened forests, the whiplash of winds that strike to kill, the barren expanses of spirit as well as of landscape" (James 1989, 11). James is not alone in finding parallels between Sibelius's music and a northern landscape. Sibelius himself encouraged this notion, claiming from his retreat in Järvenpää that he needed to compose in silence, surrounded only by the sounds of nature, the sounds of the forest. Evocations of nature, with references to "the northland's dusky forests," are to be found in his works as late as the symphonic poem, *Tapiola* (1925), prompting Simpson to describe the poem's precursor, the seventh symphony, as a planet, on the surface of which we also find Finnish forests (Simpson, quoted in Layton 1965, 6). The folk and the landscape of forests and lakes are similarly intertwined. Folk music is habitually described in terms of where it comes from, as it was in Herder's "vision of a folk whose aesthetic creativity sprang from nature" (Bohlman 1988, xix). Nineteenth-century nationalist ideology focused on the construction of the "folk" as rural people, inhabitants not only of particular politically determined spaces but also of specific landscapes. The folk, myths, music, landscape—all of which have been constructed as symbols of identity—are interlinked in manifold ways in Lönnrot's epic. Väinämöinen, as part of the creation myth, can be seen as the mythical embodiment of the nascent Finnish nation. He rises from water and transforms barren land into forest. Only after transforming the landscape does he assume the role of bard and creator of the kantele. The myth of Väinämöinen's rising from the water, transforming the land, and his role as bard can be read as a metaphor in which the spirit of the nation springs from the landscape of forests and lakes and is given a voice (language and literature) through (folk) song. Thus Lönnrot portrayed Väinämöinen as a kind of prototype for the nationalist enterprise: through (political) transformation the true nature of the Finnish nation (as embodied in the *Kalevala*) would be revealed. This is one of my readings of the runes about Väinämöinen. While it may be an interpretative move on my part, folklore research certainly contributed to the development of a national identity by providing materials whereby a Finnish national identity could be asserted in relation to Finland's immediate neighbors. The *Kalevala,* as one representation of folk music in which song traditions were transformed into a literary epic, played a central and complex role in this process.

Ethnography: The Transmission, Performance, and Repertoire of New Folk Music

We are the music-makers,
And we are the dreamers of dreams . . .
For each age is a dream that is dying,
Or one that is coming to birth

Arthur O'Shaughnessy, *Ode*

THREE

The Folk Music Revival in Finland

TOWARD "NEW FOLK MUSIC"

Like improvisations on a motif, a characteristic of revival movements is the continuous re-representation and reinvention of folk music. Even when, as in the Finnish folk music revival, there is an emphasis on the creation of "new" elements, folk musicians' reinventions of their musical activities are made in relation to notions of "tradition." With its "doubtful empirical status and ideological entanglements" (Coplan 1993, 36), it is "tradition," with its appeal to the past, which nevertheless determines the designation of any musical activity as being "folk." How did Finnish folk revivalists during the early period of the revival movement (from the late 1960s) understand folk music as being both "old" and "new"? This chapter charts their various approaches to folk music. During this period, pelimanni instrumental traditions from the western regions of Finland, from Ostrobothnia, caught the public imagination. Vocal traditions of the kind that had been used in the compilation of the national epic began to be treated as formal educational material. Jazz and rock musicians discovered folk materials as sources for musical inspiration. This chapter will explore, in particular, the ways in which musicians, scholars, and political activists turned to folk materials from different regions within the nation-state, since these approaches to Finnish folk music were to shape the development of "new folk music."

REVIVAL, TRANSFORMATION, AUTHENTICITY

In Norway, a revival debate for and against the legitimization of *gammaldans* (old dance) as *folkemusikk* (folk music) centered on folk music authenticity based on how long particular fiddle repertoires had been part of folk music. *Gammaldans* was not accepted by all folk practitioners as "folk music" because its repertoire stemmed from nineteenth-century dances and thus was a "new" addition to the Norwegian folk canon (Goertzen 1997). This debate was coming to an end in the late 1980s (with general acceptance of *gammaldans*), just as new folk music was beginning to be established as the main representation of Finnish folk music as a result of revival aesthetics stemming from the 1960s. In contrast to the Norwegian *gammaldans* controversy and to early-twentieth-century scholars' fears for the loss of traditions, several revival movements of the 1960s and 1970s were characterized, like the Finnish example, by their search for the new. Thus, Levin, in his examination of the role of Dmitri Pokrovsky in the Russian revival movement of the 1970s, writes that the experiences of this particular musician as a cultural activist and folk music revivalist "challenge the chaste image of traditional folk song" (Levin 1996, 16). According to Levin, Pokrovsky transformed traditional Russian music by pointing to a "more complex and demanding musical language that is the true legacy of Russia's folk heritage" (34). The element of transformation is important to Levin's analysis. Moreover, such transformation took the form of overturning previously held views of folk music, in this instance the sanitized Soviet interpretation, and returning to what is construed as representing a more authentic Russian folk soundworld: one which consisted of traditions associated with specific regions. Levin's notion of transformation concurs with folk revivalists' perceptions of their musical activities. Their transformations or reinventions of folk music are made in relation to their predecessors' views of the folk, which seem to offer misinterpretations of the "true" traditions. At the same time as revivalist musicians introduce novel elements to the tradition, then, they paradoxically imagine recapturing a lost folk essence.

Similarly, in an analysis of the Hungarian revival movement (the "dance-house movement" of the 1970s), Frigyesi (1996, 66) claims that revivalists "turned to authentic performance" in their search for new sounds. So finding the new in the old is evident in the Hungarian context, too. The appeals to tradition made by the Hungarian revivalists, in contrast to their nineteenth- and early-twentieth-century forebears, were motivated neither by a nostalgia for the past nor by the search for national identities. Rather, the juxtaposition of the traditional with the innovative created "a new context for folk music" (Frigyesi 1996, 59). Frigyesi locates the origins of this revival in the avant-garde music-theater experiments of the Halmos-Sebo duo and their collaboration with the choreographer of the Bartók Dance Ensemble, Timar.

From Sebo's own testimony (cited in Frigyesi 1996, 61)[1] we learn that his desire to learn about Hungarian folk music stemmed from an interest in the "exotic," from a wish to experiment with novel sounds. Information that Sebo received from the scholar Vikar prompted him to investigate folk music further. Hungarian folk music itself, which had "existed already for centuries," as Vikar suggested, offered the possibility of as yet unexploited sound materials.

The contradictions between the new and the old, which are apparent in several revival movements throughout Europe during this period, are reflected in analytic accounts. Frigyesi's analysis, like Levin's, is informed by revivalists' perceptions. Thus, she argues that the revival movement "created a category of music entirely unlike those previously existing in Hungary" and at the same time claims that the movement took over "genres of peasant music . . . in their entirety, preserving the traditional framework of forms and performing styles and much of the context as well" (Frigyesi 1996, 54).

The folk revivalist transformation of traditional material not only introduces a new folk music tradition but also in reclaiming an apparently authentic perspective is implicated in preserving tradition. Managing to achieve a symbiotic relation between the new and the old has significant ramifications for the representation of the musical tradition as being "folk." The revival movement could be based (and in fact often was) in urban rather than village settings. Its principal practitioners were as involved with state folklore programs and national cultural politics as they were with reclaiming ancient peasant traditions. Thus, Pokrovsky was a folklore specialist, appointed by the Folklore Commission, which was run by the Ministry of Culture, and a performer. While he sought to revive authentic folk traditions, his efforts, as Levin points out, are "the product of an ideology that has as much to do with the values of contemporary transnational urban culture as it does with the intrinsic interest of village art and music" (1996, 34).

The Finnish revival movement of the late 1960s to the early 1980s shares much with its Russian and Hungarian counterparts. Parallels between these revival movements revolve around the institutionalization of folk music, the role of scholars and individual musicians in promoting an interest in folk traditions, the search for new sounds and new concepts of folk music, and the concern with "tradition." By the early 1980s, the claim of folk revivalists that their music was both traditional and innovative established the ways in which new folk music would be differentiated from folk music toward the end of that decade (fig. 3.1):

FIGURE 3.1: THE FOLK REVIVALISTS' CONSTRUCTION OF
DIFFERENCE BETWEEN "FOLK" AND "NEW FOLK" MUSIC

Folk	New Folk
Past	Present
Collective composition	Collective and individual composition
Oral transmission	Oral, written and recorded transmission
Tradition	Tradition and innovation
Rural (local)	Rural and urban (international)
"Preserved" music	"Preserved" and "new" music

The account of the Finnish revival movement that follows is a presentation of the more recent history of folk music in Finland, and of the factors that have shaped contemporary folk music practice. It is a story of complex interactions between individuals and institutional bodies: among scholars, musicians, media agencies, state and regional bodies, and educational institutes. Just as Levin's and Frigyesi's analytic accounts are shaped by revivalists' viewpoints, so too is mine, for it is based on the stories I was told by various informants: folklorists, folk music scholars, and musicians—in particular, those associated with rock and jazz music. They told me about their involvement with folk music during the revival period. From these different perspectives I have constructed an account in which attention is drawn both to general trends and to the contributions made by specific individuals to the folk revival.

From the late 1960s the revival movement drew on British and American folk-rock models and began to overturn perceptions of folk music that had been constructed during the nineteenth century. Earlier constructions of folk music as collective, homogenous expressions gave way to more diverse representations. These were partly informed by notions of the "new." They were also the result of ideas of reviving folklore culture (folklorists' experiments) and of new images of folk music from different regions, especially the pelimanni music of the violinist Konsta Jylhä. The following discussion will focus on three main strands in the revival movement: (1) the establishment of the Kaustinen Festival of Folk Music, the new image of a folk performer, Konsta Jylhä, and a new emphasis on pelimanni music of the western regions of Finland; (2) the contributions of folklorists and folk music scholars to the folk revival movement in recreating the musical dimensions of kalevalaic songs; (3) the contributions of musicians in the fields of rock and jazz music to the folk revival movement.

THE KAUSTINEN FESTIVAL AND KONSTA JYLHÄ

In Finland, the establishment of the Kaustinen folk music festival in 1968 helped to bring folk music to national prominence after a period of neglect, for with the fulfillment of certain political aspirations, there had been less demand for studies of folk culture.[2] Finnish society had undergone a rapid transformation in the 1950s and 1960s, with the emphasis on urbanization, industrialization, and modernization. Rural areas lost population as young people emigrated to the urban centers in search of employment. During this period, folk song traditions, which were already dying out at the time when nineteenth-century folklorists were collecting their folk material, continued to diminish. Many people in Helsinki considered it old-fashioned to sing folk songs, and there was a consumer demand for "modern" music, largely American and British rock music.

While some traditions like *runolaulut,* the epic songs in *Kalevala* meter, mostly survived in archive collections, other traditions were still very much part of local musical activities. It was on the basis of their familiarity with these traditions that some folklorists and musicians set out to examine what other traditions existed in Finland. The folklorist Heikki Laitinen, for example, reminisced about hearing folk music performances "held now and then" and folk chorales in evangelical settings in the 1950s. He began to record them, and on the advice of Erkki Ala-Könni (a folklorist who later became a professor at the Department of Folk Tradition of Tampere University, attended other folk performances (Heikki Laitinen, personal interview, June 25, 1992).

Acting in an advisory capacity, Erkki Ala-Könni was involved with the establishment of the Kaustinen Festival of Folk Music, which did much to overturn the perception that folk music was an outdated form. As Laitinen noted, "In 1968, Kaustinen held the first folk music festival, which proved to be a kind of turning point. . . . When Kaustinen's folk music festival was held, there were about ten or twenty rural cultural festivals in the whole country. Five years later there were seven hundred; that was the beginning of the revitalization of rural culture, and Kaustinen was central to all this just because it had been the first" (Heikki Laitinen, personal interview, June 25, 1992; my translation).[3]

There are some interesting parallels between the nineteenth-century construction of folk music as a symbol of Finnish national identity and the promotion of folk music in Kaustinen during the revival period as an index of local and regional identities within the nation-state. Just as folklore was used to pursue political objectives during the nineteenth century, the more recent promotion of folk music was also informed by political agendas. The folk revival in Kaustinen was interlinked with attempts to promote the region of Ostrobothnia in a climate in which local groups perceived the capital as exerting too much power over local interests. In 1965, Viljo Määttälä, the director of the Association of the Central Ostrobothnian Region, together with Erkki Salonen, the chair of the Association of Finnishness, organized a conference on the theme "The Region in a Changing Society." One of the results of the conference was that the regional newspaper held an essay competition. Readers were invited to contribute ideas on how to promote the region economically and culturally. A local man, Martti Palo, suggested an international folk music festival, an idea inspired by his visit to the Llangollen International Folk Song and Dance Competition in Wales. The idea was pursued. Kaustinen was an area that was already recognized throughout Finland as having rich traditions. Those local folk music traditions, which could be displayed through a festival, were to provide the "cultural capital" for the political aim of promoting the region.

Following the establishment of the Kaustinen Festival, the Folk Music Institute was set up in 1974. This has become one of the most important centers for folk music research and education. While it developed from the festival context, members of this institution now contribute to the festival (in organizing folk music courses, for instance, and in assisting with deciding the festival theme). A committee chaired by Viljo Määttälä continues to be responsible for approving the research and educational projects implemented by the Institute.

The Kaustinen Festival was significant not only because it was the first festival display of folk culture and provided conditions for fostering research and pedagogic projects but also because the local traditions that became nationally famous provided a new representation of folk music. This representation centered on one of Kaustinen's pelimanni violinists, Konsta Jylhä (1910–84), who became an important figure during the 1960s. He was the first folk musician whose record sales earned a gold record, and he appeared on television. In achieving a national prominence he helped to bring fiddle traditions from his village to public attention. Jylhä, as well as the folklorist Ala-Könni, contributed ideas to discussions about the festival. Such was his influence as a performer that the images evoked by the term "folk music" until the early 1990s were "either a white-bearded old man playing the kantele or a pelimanni ensemble (two violins, double bass and harmonium) playing dance music" (Tolvanen 1991, 37). The first image is a romantic construction deriving from nineteenth-century collectors such as Lönnrot, who came across such figures in their quest for folklore material. The second image is mostly associated with Konsta Jylhä and his group, Kaustinen Purppuripelimannit. The kind of folk music played by these musicians, then, became representative not only of regional traditions but also of the nation. Only during the early 1990s, with the success of the group Värttinä, was this image of folk music replaced. Significantly, the repertoire to which Värttinä turned was that which folklorists had been exploring during the revival.

The use of local traditions as the basis for the Kaustinen Festival project confirms notions of folk music as being village based. Kaustinen was well placed to become a focus for local traditions, since this village could already boast renowned folk performers, including the kantele player who was the subject of Ekman's (1868) portrait of national unity, Kreeta Haapasalo. Yet from its inception the aim of the festival organizers was to present music from the local context (Kaustinen) alongside musical traditions from other regions and from around the world. The festival was thus established as an international celebration of folk music, and performers have come from various countries.

THE ROLE OF FOLKLORISTS IN THE
FINNISH REVIVAL MOVEMENT

Erkki Ala-Könni's involvement with the establishment of the Kaustinen Festival is one example of the contributions made by folklorists to the folk revival movement in Finland. Two folklorists (Anneli Asplund and Pirkko-Liisa Rauma) from the Department of Archive Material at the Suomalaisen Kirjallisuuden Seura (Finnish Literature Society, hereafter SKS) were involved in the production of a record of *Kalevala* material, *Pääskylintu Päivälintu* (*Swallow*

Daybird), published in the late 1960s by the Kalevala Seura (Kalevala Society). Reflecting an emphasis on folk text, the record was used in schools by teachers of Finnish language and literature, rather than by music teachers. As part of their school education, all children still study the *Kalevala*, and the record was useful because it contained songs in the *Kalevala* meter. The first song on the record was about the creation of the world and was copied from an archive recording of an Ingrian group of singers. Asplund believes that this was one of the first experiments in using *Kalevala* material. She claimed that the singers' aim was to reproduce the song exactly as they heard it from archive recordings. They were not interested in introducing novel elements.

Issuing a record of Kalevala *songs* was significant in that it marked a change in emphasis, from the *Kalevala* as text only to an examination of the whole song tradition from which the *Kalevala* emerged. However, the trend set in the nineteenth century in the field of folklore research, with its emphasis on the texts of songs and on the study of the *Kalevala* as a literary compilation, remained dominant until the 1980s. The first general text to discuss folk music, *Kansanmusiikki* (*Folk Music*), was published by the SKS as recently as 1981.[4]

Following the initial recording, *Pääskylintu Päivälintu*, Asplund and Rauma formed a group at the end of the 1970s, with Laitinen and Seppo Knuuttila, which was called Nelipolviset. All the members of this group were researchers of folklore and folk culture and at first, according to their own testimony, sang *Kalevala* songs only for recreational purposes, since they were working with that material. By that time, Laitinen had become director of the Kansanmusiikki Instituutti (Folk Music Institute) in Kaustinen, and he was interested in developing ideas about how to re-create these folk songs. Although by the 1970s there were folk music festivals, and everyone had become aware of folk music of the kind played by Konsta Jylhä, some kinds of folk music were obscure. For example, runes of the kind that Lönnrot collected and used in the *Kalevala* were not very well known despite the role that the epic continued to play as a national symbol (Heikki Laitinen, personal interview, June 25, 1992). These folklorists soon formed ideas about bringing neglected song traditions to public prominence: "Nelipolviset was also formed to perform these kinds of songs. It was not a musicians' group but a researchers' group, and in fact it was quite by chance that the group was formed, but it was formed more or less because of the researchers' wish to tell people about the existence of these songs" (Heikki Laitinen, personal interview, June 25, 1992; my translation).[5]

Nelipolviset began teaching, holding a course in Kaustinen, where the group taught songs in the *Kalevala* meter. The main function of the group changed from being a recreational pastime for its members to performing for educational purposes. They produced teaching material for schools in the form of a cassette (Nelipolviset 1979) and book (Asplund and Laitinen 1979), which dealt with songs in the *Kalevala* meter. The book opens with the statement "Kalevala on kansallisen kulttuurimme kulmakiviä" (the *Kalevala* is the cornerstone of our national culture). Epic, lyric and wedding songs and the *Kalevala* meter are introduced. The musical examples presented in the book and on the cassette recording are vocal. According to Asplund this was because of the emphasis on education rather than on the production of music for the commercial market. Once younger people started to sing songs using *Kalevala* material, Nelipolviset ceased to perform, as the members felt that they had achieved their goal (Anneli Asplund, personal interview, November 4, 1991).

Although these folklorists emphasized reproducing examples found in early recordings in their performances of this repertoire, the 1979 teaching book provides a means whereby a more flexible approach to the tradition may be adopted. It presents guidelines on principles of improvisation in *Kalevala* songs. One example deals with possible melodic and rhythmic variations on the line "vaka vanha Väinämöinen" ("Väinämöinen, old and steadfast"; example 3.1).[6]

Example 3.1: Variations on "Vaka Vanha Väinämöinen"

Other examples of *Kalevala* song from this project (see examples 3.2 and 3.3) have become part of the reinterpreted repertoires of new folk music groups, including the group of which the folklorist Hannu Saha is now a member, Salamakannel (Lightning Kantele). I heard example 3.2 at a live performance

kal - li - ol - la   kal - kut - tet   li   sai   ve - ne   vii - men   val - miik - si

Example 3.2: "Vaka Vanha Väinämöinen"

Käin   mi - nä   kau -nis - ta   kang - as - ta   myö - ten   hoi   kang - as - ta   myö - ten

Example 3.3: "Käin Minä Kaunista Kangasta Myöten"

at the Kaustinen Festival, where Salamakannel was singing the stories about Väinämöinen carving a boat on a mountaintop to the well-known *Kalevala* melody, and the group has recorded example 3.3 (Salamakannel 1992, track 11):

Käin minä kaunista kangasta myöten, käin minä kaunista kangasta myöten
hoi kangasta myöten, hoi kangasta myöten
(All lines repeated in the same way)
heliästä hiekkasta rannasta myöten.
Ostin mä saikan syyäkseni
tuopin oltta juuakseni.
Söin minä palan taikka puoli,
aina mä ajattelin armastani.
Armas on pantu paarein pälle,
musta verka kirstun päälle,
terävä miekka kaulan päälle.
Kultan on kuollut ja kannettu hautaan,
paaril on kannettu, paperist on laulettu,
kellol on soitettu, mullal on peitetty.
Itkisin, itkisin armastani,
vaan en saanut naurultani.
Silmäni itkee, syämeni nauraa
silmäni vettä vuuattaapi
jalkani lasta liekuttaapi.

I walked along the beautiful heathland, I walked along the beautiful
heathland
Oh along the heathland, oh along the heathland
Alongside the sandy seashore.
I bought some bread to eat
A tankard of beer to drink.
I ate a piece and half,
All the time thinking of my sweetheart.
My beloved has been laid on a stretcher,
A black cloth as a coffin cover,
A sharp sword laid on his neck.
My sweetheart has died and been taken to the grave,
Carried away on a stretcher, songs sung from the paper,
Bells have been rung, the earth has been thrown for his cover.
I would cry, I would cry for my beloved,
But I could not for my laughter.
My eyes are crying, my heart is laughing
My eyes are streaming with water
My feet are rocking the baby's cradle.
(Asplund and Laitinen 1979, 32)

Laitinen was also involved with another group, Primo (an abbreviation of
"primitive music orchestra"), at his institutional base, the Folk Music Institute.
Other members were Hannu Saha and the instrument maker Risto Nieminen.
They made a record, *Haltian Opissa* (*The Sprite's Apprentice*), in 1984 and were
motivated, like Nelipolviset, by a wish to bring folk repertoires to wider notice:
"At the end of the seventies very few people played the five-stringed kantele;
hardly anybody played the *jouhikko* [a bowed string instrument]; nobody
played shepherds' [aerophone] instruments. We wanted to establish a group
which would work particularly with this *Kalevala* tradition; this was the initial idea in establishing the group Primo" (Hannu Saha, personal interview,
April 13, 1992; my translation).[7]

In addition to performance and recording projects, these folklorists played
a more important role in establishing centers for the teaching of folk music.
Laitinen became the first director of the Department of Folk Music at the Sibelius Academy, leaving the Folk Music Institute to take up that post in 1983. He

worked with a small initial entering class of four students, who were to form one of the first new folk music groups, Niekku, and explored ideas about teaching folk music at the same time as developing the department itself. Whereas Nelipolviset had sung songs that were exact reproductions of specific archive recordings, Laitinen was interested in introducing to his students the element of improvisation, which is an intrinsic part of these folk music traditions, and in creating new music within the traditional framework. The earlier emphasis on recreating folk music exactly as it was heard on archive recordings served the useful purpose of ensuring that whatever changes were made to the music in the course of improvisation had their foundations in the recorded traditions, thus making for a sense of continuity.

Laitinen's interest in the improvisational aspects of folk traditions may well have been influenced by the activities of performers in the fields of jazz and rock music, who also turned to folk traditions during the revival period. The course that folklorists such as Laitinen took, stressing improvisation and creating new folk music, allowed the incorporation of contemporary models of music making. Sharing an emphasis on improvisation and new treatments of folk materials, both folklorists and Finnish folk-rock and jazz musicians have influenced contemporary folk musicians.

THE ROLE OF JAZZ AND ROCK MUSICIANS
IN THE REVIVAL MOVEMENT

In the early 1970s, the musicians who turned to folk material in search of musical elements which they could incorporate into their projects included Seppo Paakkunainen, Ilpo Saastamoinen (who both played in the group Karelia), Sakari Kukko, and Hasse Walli (members of the group Piirpauke). Although they are associated with jazz and rock music, their musical experiences have been eclectic. They contributed to the folk revival movement by offering "new" interpretations of folk material and by making commercial recordings. Taking into account their musical biographies demonstrates how musical activity at the level of the individual calls into question the boundaries that are constructed between musical traditions. The biographical details outlined below indicate a familiarity with folk traditions from familial backgrounds. They reveal too how these musicians have consciously drawn upon diverse musical traditions, fragmenting and juxtaposing them, to construct recognizable individual and group styles.

The early musical environment of Paakkunainen, born in 1943 in Kerimäki in eastern Finland, included folk music, listening to his parents singing folk songs, and learning to play, as his first piece, a *Kalevala* melody on the violin: "my mother was singing and my father was a pelimanni, was playing dance music—waltzes, jenkkas, and polkas—just by ear. Also, whenever the cantor in church wasn't able to do the service, my grandfather, who had a very good voice, acted as the choral singer for the hymns. So music is in my family" (Seppo Paakkunainen, personal interview, June 17, 1992). After seeing the film *King of Swing*, about Benny Goodman's life, Paakkunainen became interested in jazz and started playing the clarinet and saxophone. His subsequent musical training was based in the Western art music tradition, as he studied the flute and music theory at the Sibelius Academy, and continued with jazz studies in Boston. Since then, he has established his reputation as a jazz musician, chiefly as a saxophonist and flautist, playing with jazz musicians around the world, and as a composer who has written for various ensembles—big band, choir, chamber orchestra, and symphony orchestra (plate 2).

Paakkunainen's interest in actively studying folk music, rather than just listening to the folk music that he came into contact with in his daily life, was influenced by meeting an Irish musician in Finland in the late 1960s who introduced him to the music of the British folk-rock group Fairport Convention. In terms of using folk material, this was to mark a turning point. Following the models of British and American folk-rock groups, Paakkunainen, together with Edward Vesala, decided in 1970 to set up the band Karelia, playing folk-rock music using Finno-Ugric folk music material:

My first work using folk music was with a rock band, let's say a rhythm and blues band called Eero Jussi and the Boys. That was in 1965. I made an arrangement of [the song] "Tyttöni Mun" ["My Girl"], which is an old Finnish waltz. It was similar to the Beach Boys. At the beginning of the 1960s there was a period of [the group] Shadows-type music (two guitars, bass guitar, and drums). There was a Finnish group like Shadows called Sounds, and they produced a version of the song "Tyttöni Mun," but it was only instrumental. When I was playing in the rhythm and blues band I was asked to make a vocal version. In 1970 we set up Karelia. Fairport Convention was very popular at that time. A friend of mine, Edward Vesala, and I decided to make electric folk-rock music, and we made two LPs then. We broadened the idea. We imitated [Saami] joiku and used rare instruments like a suitcase.

It wasn't just electric, rock-type music. We also listened to the old singers in the SKS [archive recordings] to find out about the traditions. Our idea was to make old Finnish folk tunes fresh, more contemporary, to make contact with young people. The first Karelia LP also marked a folk instrument making renaissance. When Rauno Nieminen saw the record cover he thought I would be playing a birchbark flute. I was just using an ordinary flute. He decided that he would have to make a birchbark flute that would sound good. (Seppo Paakkunainen, personal interview, June 17, 1992)

Paakkunainen's experience shows that musical trends occurring outside Finland provided the stimulus for Finnish musicians to look for something similar in indigenous traditions. These same models also influenced some folklorists. Saha, the present director of the Folk Music Institute, commented that hearing groups like Fairport Convention as a teenager motivated him to consider Finnish traditions more closely (Hannu Saha, personal communication, 1992).

This kind of musical interaction contrasts with those who take a more "purist" perspective of folk music. Asplund, for example, sees a parallel between the motivations for Lönnrot's work and the aims of contemporary folklorists. If Lönnrot was asserting a Finnish culture in the context of Swedish and Russian dominance, Asplund believes that those involved with the study and performance of folk music today are trying to "re-create the old and fantastic Finnish culture" against the dominance of "international—especially American and British culture" (Anneli Asplund, personal interview, November 4, 1991). Many musicians disagree. Paakkunainen, for example, claimed: "I do not want to be classified as a 'pure' folk musician, or as any other type of 'pure' musician. I'm not a folk musician. I am an all-around musician and my main love is improvisation, all kinds of improvisation" (Seppo Paakkunainen, personal interview, June 17, 1992). Sakari Kukko echoes this attitude. Initially, the group Piirpauke (the name comes from a Karelian word meaning "noise" or "clamour"), of which he has been the only permanent member, was regarded as a jazz group. Now Kukko says that he does not compare his music to anything else, although he thinks that "ethnic" elements are quite prevalent, as are Finnish folk music elements: "All kinds of Finnish music—shepherd songs, children's songs, music of Finnish composers, music from Lapland, Karelia, Swedish folk music, and so on" (Sakari Kukko, personal interview, November 20, 1991).

Kukko, born in 1953 in Kajaani, also in eastern Finland, studied the piano, flute, and guitar as a child and sang in a choir. Later he played the tenor saxophone with the Kajaani Big Band, which was led by Saastamoinen, studied at the Sibelius Academy for a while, and then began traveling around the world to hear and play music. Improvisation has become an important element in his music making. One of the reasons for his focus on improvisation is that it allows him easier access to playing different styles: "When playing with musicians from all over the world, I try to adapt and learn. But you cannot learn a new style immediately. It takes a lifetime. So I improvise to get the mood, the feeling" (Sakari Kukko, personal interview, November 20, 1991). Kukko, like Paakkunainen, has diverse musical interests. He has had some classical training, has played dance music—tangos, waltzes, and so on—in *tanssilavat* (open-air dance pavilions) in the countryside, and has become well known as a jazz and as a "world" musician.

Hasse Walli, too, has had a varied career. He was born into a musical family in 1948, in Helsinki. As a child he heard his family engage in diverse musical activities. His mother is a singer, and two of his maternal uncles played in a jazz band. His maternal grandmother was born in St. Petersburg, and she sang both Russian and Finnish folk songs, accompanying herself on the guitar. His maternal grandfather was a violinist and a choral singer. His father plays the piano, accordion, and guitar, and his paternal uncle is a drummer. It was this uncle who first taught Walli the drums, with which he began his musical career before changing to the guitar. Walli's musical career has been as eclectic as the influences from his family background. He collected jazz records of Louis Armstrong, Count Basie, Duke Ellington, and Benny Goodman and played as a schoolchild in various bands, which were inspired by rock musicians such as Elvis Presley, Buddy Holly, and groups like the Shadows and the Beatles. His musical activities during the 1960s, while he was still at school, reflect the influence of American and British rock music in Finland. In 1966 he became the lead guitarist in a Finnish band called Jormas, and a year later he started playing with the blues band Blues Section. Following his meeting with Kukko, he joined Piirpauke in 1974 and became interested in the folk music of other countries. In 1977, Walli left Piirpauke to research the music of Jimmy Hendrix. He heard Bob Marley perform in Sweden and became interested in reggae. In 1978 Walli and Kukko were in Cuba for a festival and they "got in touch with African-Cuban musicians there and went jamming every night" (Hasse Walli, personal interview, December 8, 1991). Kukko introduced Walli in 1979

to Senegalese music, by playing some recordings that he had made while traveling around Senegal. Walli set up a band that experimented with these various
influences—reggae and Cuban and Senegalese music. He traveled to Senegal
himself in 1982, returning to Finland via Paris, where he played with Toure
Kunda's band. Walli, like Paakkunainen and Kukko, is interested in different
kinds of music and has played with a variety of bands.

Kukko met Walli at a jazz music course held in Kajaani in 1969. They collaborated, recruiting Saastamoinen (who also played in Karelia) into the group
Piirpauke, which was established in 1974. Walli explained that members of the
group became interested in folk music because they were bored with their rock
and jazz performances and wanted to find another way of "approaching the
public." They researched traditions from around the world, becoming more interested as they found "fantastic things," and also explored Finnish folk music,
which was well received by their audiences: "One song we played was from a
kantele song called 'Konevitsan Kirkonkellot.' This became a hit song and the
album sold very well. Piirpauke went to the top of the charts with that LP. The
gigs we performed were well paid. We had a new approach, which no one
else at the time had, and we also mixed jazz and blues in our music too. In
'Konevitsan Kirkonkellot,' Sakari Kukko played the kantele melody on the piano. The guitar also played the kantele melody, and the acoustic bass played it
on the bass strings. Many people didn't know this kind of folk music or this folk
song before Piirpauke played it. Now this song is quite widely known because
of our version. It was widely played on the radio and in films. We also had some
improvisation with me on the guitar, and I think that people really liked that
too" (personal interview with Hasse Walli, December 8, 1991).

From Walli's comments it becomes clear that other motives direct the incorporation and use of Finnish folk traditions besides familiarity from childhood
experiences and inspiration from American and British folk-rock movements.
These musicians were motivated also by the search for new and different musical material and the wish to produce distinctive sounds that would be recognized as the music of a particular group. Hence, Piirpauke used "not only
Finnish folk material, but also material from other cultures with which audiences were unfamiliar. On that same LP, Piirpauke's first one, there is a Chinese
song with Kukko playing a Chinese flute, and a Balinese song" (Hasse Walli,
personal communication). Even the use of Finnish material was perceived as
something "new," not only because audiences were no longer familiar with the
Finnish folk music traditions, but also because those traditions were being used

in different ways, within the context of jazz and rock idioms. These motives are related to the commercial aspects of creating interesting music that will sell, and that will attract a larger audience. The eclecticism that characterizes these musical biographies, then, carries with it the sense of "collecting" cultural elements, which can be used in different contexts. As such, it is not unlike the collection of folklore and the construction of national art around the turn of the century. Collectable elements become movable property and can be re-represented as one's own, in these cases, in the international marketplace.

INSTITUTIONALIZING FOLK MUSIC DURING THE REVIVAL

The establishment of the Kaustinen Festival, folklore research and education projects, and the commercial production of folk-inspired recordings, which were important features of the revival movement, were conscious moves toward the institutionalization of folk music that would culminate in the establishment of the Department of Folk Music at the Sibelius Academy (discussed in chapter 4). Other projects, such as the transmission of folk music on the radio and educational initiatives in the school curriculum, supported this institutionalization for they were informed by specific notions of folk music and enforced through state policies, often through the efforts of individuals who were active in institutional networks:

RADIO: The official categorization of music in Finland, in terms of media agencies, state cultural policies, and educational institutes, centers around polarized modes: *kevyt* ("light") and *taide* ("art") music. Although some objections have been raised to this mode of categorization, all music is identified as belonging to one or the other of these categories. Folk or new folk music is "light" and related to popular music, and its categorization as such has ramifications for its funding, transmission, and performance. "Light" music in Finland denotes a commercial viability.[8] Although folk music is placed in this category, it is perceived as a minority interest, which needs support from the state and other organizations. The national radio broadcasting company has had a policy of including folk music programs since its inception. One of these programs was the series presented by Väisänen from 1933 until the late 1940s, in which some well-known folk musicians appeared, including the Ingrian woodwind player Teppo Repo and players from Kaustinen like Konsta Jylhä, Friiti Ojala, and Eino Tulikari. The program did not reach a wide audience, but was significant to the musicians, since by performing on the radio they achieved greater local esteem (Asplund 1981a, 236).

FOLK MUSIC IN THE SCHOOL CURRICULUM: Although it was perceived as the "national" instrument, the kantele was played by only a few people before the folk music revival. In 1975, Laitinen stated that the kantele "is seriously encumbered by prejudice, misplaced reverence and uncalled-for ridicule. The kantele must therefore be liberated from its role of national instrument to be played only by people in national costume" (Laitinen quoted in Saha 1988, 22). As a result of these kinds of perceptions, the Folk Music Institute in Kaustinen inititated an educational project in 1982. Known as the Kantele Project, it had the aims of, first, making the instrument familiar to everyone in Finland and, second, introducing the kantele alongside other instruments already in use in music education. These aims have been achieved by including the five-string kantele in the music syllabus of all comprehensive schools. The Folk Music Institute also published a guide to playing the kantele as a teaching and learning aid (Laitinen and Saha 1988). This guide includes instructions on technique (fingerings, ways of producing sounds besides plucking the strings), an introduction to the kantele repertoire, and hints on providing harmonies and on improvisation. A principal aim in providing kantele tuition is to introduce the main elements of *Kalevala* music, which is regarded as the oldest stratum of Finnish folk music, to schoolchildren. The elements of this musical tradition, which some music teachers consider to be particularly suitable for young children, include a small melodic range, variation, and improvisation. The project set a precedent for the more ambitious task of introducing folk music into the sector of higher education.

INSTITUTIONAL NETWORKS: The institutionalization of folk music has depended on networks of people who extend an influence over policy-making processes as well as on folk music specialists such as folklorists or performers. The successful implementation of the Kantele Project was due to the endeavors of certain individuals who played an active role within committees which had been established to promote folk music and to the provision of instruments, teaching materials, and training for teachers—made available because of the value that the state continues to accord to folk music. One committee in particular, the Central Music Association, was influential because links had been established through its members with the Kaustinen Festival Organization, the

Folk Music Institute, and the Ministry of Education. These links partly revolved around Viljo Määttälä, who has been chair of various organizations including the Kaustinen Festival Organization, the Folk Music Institute, a state music committee, and the Central Music Association. As chair of the latter committee he successfully argued that folk music education should be made available at the very highest level of music education in Finland: at the Sibelius Academy and that a department of folk music with a professorship should be established at Tampere University. Mediating between various organizational, institutional, and state bodies, and handling policy matters in classical, rock, and jazz, as well as folk music, Määttälä's influence has thus extended from the local to the national (Viljo S. Määttälä, personal interview, August 22, 1992). Although such activities do not necessarily attract a public profile, these institutional links play a vital role in the transmission and performance of contemporary folk music.

Paakkunainen commented on a sense of musical and national "belonging": "When I am performing something which is authentic, old Finnish music, or my compositions, arrangements or compositions which are influenced by old Finnish folk music, then I think that I am at my best. Like, I can play jazz, I can play different types of jazz music, but I am not so successful in it [he has actually had a distinguished career in jazz].[9] I can give more to people playing my own music, which is folk music or based on folk music" (Seppo Paakkunainen, personal interview, June 17, 1992). Such revival attitudes, implemented through institutional bodies, have shaped contemporary folk practice. The contributions of revivalists can be summed up in terms of new representations of folk music, promotion, education, and performance. Folklorists produced recordings and teaching materials for schools, ran music courses, initiated projects, and held positions within the educational sphere which allowed them to influence the ways in which folk music was taught at institutions like the Folk Music Institute and through the school curriculum. They revived the musical aspects of a tradition—songs in the *Kalevala* meter—that were no longer widely known although they survived, or took on a different kind of life, in archive recordings and in a literary form. Folklorists were interested in becoming familiar enough with the musical traditions to be able to reproduce them precisely before they began to experiment more with the aspect of improvisation in folk music. Some performers were interested in how they could use folk music in other idioms such as jazz and rock, emphasized improvisation, expanded their repertoires by listening to archive recordings at the SKS, and incorporated music from other parts of the world. Their efforts were directed toward producing commercial recordings and were linked to other folk-rock movements. There was considerable overlap between scholarly, performance, and institutional perspectives. Nelipolviset and Primo used performance-based research methodologies to explore archive materials. Jazz and rock musicians turned to folk archive materials in seeking novel and creative expressions that would inform their performance practices. Performers like Konsta Jylhä collaborated with scholars (see Austerlitz 2000, 201–4, for further examples of overlapping scholarship and performance approaches during this period). While change, including attention to the individual folk performer, modes of transmission, composition, and contexts of performance, emerges as an intrinsic feature of the Finnish revival movement, notions of continuity are maintained because of village-based activities (including the Kaustinen Festival and the establishment of the Folk Music Institute in Kaustinen) and concerns with authenticity. Although some new folk musicians invoke tropes of authenticity through connections with local, regionally based traditions, they express a corresponding wish to use these traditions to create "new" sounds, "collecting" and incorporating musical ideas from myriad sources in doing so.

FOUR

New Folk Music
in the Urban Center

In 1916, Ivana Širgo from Karelia (Impilahti) told the musicologist Väisänen how he learned to play the kantele. As a young man, Širgo went on Saturday nights to sit on the sauna stove and by the crossroads. In both of these places he played what he was able to. His mother had told him that people learned to play from a spirit but it was regarded as a great sin to do so. Širgo wanted to learn to play, however, and an invisible teacher came to him whom he named *tuohihattu* (birchbark hat). Väisänen asked whether Širgo meant a "bad spirit." "The bad spirit knows whatever," admitted Širgo. After three weeks, his courage failed him at the crossroads. He ran home, blessing the house with a prayer so that *tuohihattu* would not be able to pursue him. He justified his "cowardice" by telling Väisänen about a jouhikko player who had been trapped into learning his instrument. This jouhikko player went to learn in the sauna. At midnight on the third night, he heard a voice that frightened him. He hid by crawling under a water pail. *Tuohihattu's* sons came looking for him. "There is no player here," they told their father. *Tuohihattu* himself went to the sauna, and he found the player. This jouhikko player is still there to this day, learning from *tuohihattu*. "I didn't want this to happen to me," concluded Širgo (see Pekkilä 1990, 204).

Širgo's story is offered as a prelude to the themes of transmission and performance in the urban center to be explored in this chapter. His experience of musical learning processes provides a dramatic contrast to early folk musical encounters described by musicians at the Department of Folk Music at the

Sibelius Academy. A variety of responses were offered in relating how they began to play folk music:

> Just before applying for a place at the Sibelius Academy. I got bored with other music. (Pia Rask)

> By chance. My interest gradually broadened from playing the kantele. (Minna Raskinen)

> Father made me play. (Arto Järvelä)

> I began to play the kantele at a kantele course in Ilomantsi [1973], and to play folk music at the Department of Folk Music in the Sibelius Academy [1983]. (Liisa Matveinen)

> Music was not played at home. I went to a music group with my friend. Folk music and old dance music belong essentially to the tradition of the accordion repertoire. I only began to play the two-row accordion when I joined the academy. (Pekka Pentikäinen)

> At home I sometimes played. I listened to a lot of folk music and began to learn from records. (Anonymous statement)

THE SETTING: THE SIBELIUS ACADEMY

A formal strategy for the transmission of folk music has been implemented at all levels of the Finnish state education system, ranging from national programs such as the Kantele Project directed at young school children, to the establishment of the Department of Folk Music at the Sibelius Academy, operating at university level.[1] At this level, the aim is to produce professional folk musicians and teachers who compete with others for audiences, contracts, and resources in national and global markets.

The Sibelius Academy was established in 1882, in Helsinki, as the Helsinki Music Institute. Sibelius studied composition and violin there from 1885 to 1889. With the expansion of the institute, its name changed, in 1924, to the Helsinki Conservatoire. The name Sibelius Academy, after Finland's most well known composer, was adopted in 1939. The first rector, Martin Wegelius, believed that musicians should have a broad musical education, including the study of music history and theory, in addition to solo performance and composition. Despite this apparently holistic approach to music education, the establishment of various departments has had the effect of dividing music into particular categories. A Department for Military Music was established in 1926, and was followed by a Church Music Department in 1951 and the Department of Music Education in 1957. Within this latter department, the kantele player Martti Pokela began teaching folk music as an optional subject in 1975. Departments for Folk Music and for Jazz Music were introduced in 1983, after some initial controversy. Despite Sibelius's own interest in folk music and the transformation and incorporation of folk traditions in art music, some critics asserted that there was no place for "light" music education within the institution that bore his name and represented the highest level of education in the field of serious or "art" music. The departments were nevertheless established and have expanded since 1983. As I was finishing my fieldwork in 1992, a new building housing the Folk, Jazz, and Music Education Departments had just been opened.

The Department of Folk Music has become a point of convergence for folk musicians from all over Finland, and the influences that have shaped folk music both in the urban center and throughout the nation are seen clearly here. A focus on this department provides an opportunity therefore to consider what constitutes "folk" music today, in the urban environment, and how it is actually practiced, transmitted, and performed by a particular group of people. New folk music at the Sibelius Academy, just as in the city, Helsinki, coexists with a variety of musics, all competing for audiences, for financial support, and for recording and performing opportunities. Although there seems to be an opposition in the way in which music is categorized as "art" or as "light" by the institution itself as well as by, for example, state funding bodies, people can be involved with all kinds of music. In fact, when the Department of Folk Music was first established, there was a requirement that folk music students be trained in "art" music too. Heikki Laitinen believes that the major part of his work as director of the department was to increase the amount of study time devoted to folk music, to the extent that current students are not obliged to also study art music (Heikki Laitinen, personal interview, June 25, 1992). The Kalevala Year celebrations of 1985 (celebrating 150 years of the national epic) assisted in focusing public attention on the activities of folk music students at the department. The two groups formed by the department's students, Niekku and Pirnales (plate 3), gave several performances during Kalevala Year (Sinikka Järvinen, member of Pirnales, personal interview, July 13, 1992).

LEARNING FOLK MUSIC AT THE SIBELIUS ACADEMY

What kinds of teaching methods are used in the new context of a music academy? Folk music at the Sibelius Academy is transmitted mainly through individual instrumental and vocal lessons, group work (including writing original compositions and arrangements of material found in scores and archival collections), and lectures. This approach, particularly the provision of individual instrumental and vocal tuition and the presentation of lectures, is that traditionally offered by conservatories or music colleges. Anneli Asplund, a folklorist who teaches at the department noted: "We are living now in a modern culture, not any more in a peasant culture, and so it is necessary to teach the folk culture" (Anneli Asplund, personal interview, November 1991). This view is echoed by Hannu Saha, the director of the Folk Music Institute in Kaustinen, who is also involved with teaching at this department. He writes that folk music "no longer leads a very authentic life in the small country community. Instead it is a cultivated form of music, influencing general musical culture on the one hand and absorbing influences from all the music surrounding it on the other" (Saha 1984, 1).

Here, then, are views in which the perceived necessity for developing strategies for the transmission of folk music is linked with notions of change. Yet these are not the somewhat despairing attitudes of an earlier generation of folk enthusiasts, for whom ancient heritages seemed to be on the brink of extinction. Rather, it is the recognition that the contexts in which folk music has been transmitted have changed that has prompted initiatives in the field of state education, catering to new needs that include the training of musicians at advanced levels of performance.

The approach pursued by folk music educationalists is twofold. First, there is an emphasis on "re-creating tradition" by imparting practical, theoretical, and historical knowledge. Second, students are actively encouraged to use the knowledge acquired as the basis for reinterpreting tradition in new ways, and to produce original compositions that combine "traditional" techniques with "new" ones. Knowledge of traditional practices is a prerequisite for introducing innovative elements. Such knowledge enables musicians to recognize what is innovative and also legitimizes flexibility in introducing the "new." Finnish educationalists are not interested in transmitting musical artifacts. On the contrary, new ideas are welcomed and are considered to be an essential part of the creative process. Educationalists and students alike agree that folk traditions can only be maintained if they are relevant to contemporary audiences.[2] Specific examples of the teaching methods that I observed at the Folk Music Department are given in the following ethnographic descriptions, in which the ethnographic present is used in referring to the period of my main field research (1991–92).

An Instrumental Lesson, Influences from the West

Arto Järvelä, brought up in Häme in Central Finland, is from a family of folk musicians in Kaustinen. He teaches the violin in the Department of Folk Music and focuses on the instrumental repertoires mostly associated with the western regions of Finland. During my field research he was himself a student at the department and was preparing his final examinations. Before he began learning the violin at the age of fourteen, he played drums and bass. His early violin training was in the art music tradition, but he subsequently concentrated on folk music when he went to study at the music school in Kaustinen. Today he is one of the most active violinists in new folk music, playing with ten different bands, including JPP, Koinurit, Salamakannel, and Pinnin Pojat. Arto has started to play the *nyckelharpa* (a Swedish influence) and uses this instrument (a keyed fiddle) in performance and in teaching.[3]

Arto explained that one of his main aims was to teach his students to play by ear, to develop aural skills. The ideal that folk music is an oral tradition is certainly maintained in some teaching contexts, evident from my observations of Arto's violin lessons. At one lesson Arto was teaching a polska. He repeated each phrase several times until the student was able to reproduce it. At first he played with the student, but as she became more familiar with the phrase, Arto listened to her rendition, correcting inaccuracies. At this stage there was no improvisation (a feature of Finnish folk music which many musicians stress), the phrase had to be reproduced precisely, and once the student could do so, Arto played a second line with her, providing harmonization. The whole polska was learned in this way. By the end of the lesson the student was able to play the polska, but Arto recorded it onto a cassette so that she would be able to practice it during the week. The recording was a safeguard—if the student could not recall the polska after the lesson, she would be able to listen to it during the week until her next lesson.

In this instance the polska was taught following the transmission models of oral tradition. Arto, as the player who knew the polska, provided the example for another player, who learned it aurally by imitation and repetition. It was

also learned visually, for the student observed how Arto played the piece—
where he placed his fingers on the fingerboard and how he used the bow. At another lesson I observed how Arto's pedagogic style might be influenced by his
own early classical training. He asked one student to practice a technical exer-
cise of descending scale patterns and to focus on playing with a straight bow.
Although Arto stressed learning by ear, he had asked this student to provide
different bowings to a notated piece, and at the lesson they discussed which of
these were the most effective.

One of the main findings of my field research is that teaching and transmitting folk music through notated examples is common (see examples 4.1–4.4,
which reveal the use of different types of notation). The extensive use of written materials is an important difference between the methods of transmission
in the past and the methods of the present. It is a difference that also points
to the changes in the contexts of folk music performance. Arto recorded the
polska as a safeguard for the student, but the provision of a recording is a modern strategy that, like reliance on notation, encourages standardization and di-
minishes aspects of folk traditions such as variation and improvisation.

Arto Järvelä is an example of a musician who has moved to the urban environment, where regional traditions meet and are combined. He is connected
with new folk music in diverse capacities—as a performer, composer, student,
teacher, and shareholder in a record company—yet he comes from a family
whose members played fiddle music from a particular region, from a background in which local traditions were predominant. It can be briefly noted here
that it is precisely this background of local tradition which allows many contemporary folk musicians to feel a sense of continuity between past and present
practice and to continue to imagine their performances as geographically situated even as they borrow diverse musical ideas and enter global music arenas.
The sense of detachment that arises from "studying" past traditions (cf. Herzfeld 1982, 8) is mitigated by a sense of delving into a personal heritage. I shall return to the Järvelä family in Kaustinen and their music in chapter 7.

A Voice Lesson: Songs from Estonia

An Estonian researcher, Anneli Könt, was working in the department during
my year of fieldwork, and she gave some classes in which she taught Estonian
songs and some simple dances (two lines moving forward and backward). Only
female students attended the class in which I took part. The repertoire that
was studied came from the Setu area in Estonia, which is also referred to as the

Estonian Karelia because, like Finnish Karelia, it was an area in which traditional music and dance continued to be practiced after disappearing from other parts of the country. At one class, a film of women performing songs and dances from the region of Setu was shown. The students discussed the performance style and the women's costumes before rehearsing from notated copies of some of the songs (with song texts and melodic lines notated separately). The melodic lines are quite short and are repeated with different verses. What was particularly striking in the interpretation of one song, in which the melodic range ostensibly consisted of a whole tone (example 4.1), was the variation in pitch. A lead singer introduces a statement, which is answered by a chorus. At the beginning of the lead singer's line the pitch can be altered in any way desired. The pitch variation extends from microtonal adjustments to leaps of a fifth or even more. The chorus must adjust its pitch accordingly, and it was precisely this adjustment of pitch that these contemporary students of folk music rehearsed.

Example 4.1: Excerpt from an Estonian song, "Sinimani Seele"

Neit-su lää-me si-ni-ma-ni see-le
neit-su lää-me pill-il-il-li hää-le
neit-su lää-me tso-tso-pu-ja lee-lo . . .

Let us go maiden, blue-hemmed skirts
Let us go maiden, the joyous sounds of whistles
Let us go maiden, *tso-tso*, the boy's songs . . .
(*The chorus joins in during the second half of the line.*)

(My translation)

A feature of Setu songs that makes them similar to some of the songs from the eastern regions of Finland which were compiled as the *Kalevala*, is the alternation of a lead singer and a chorus. The parts are arranged heterophonically: the lead voice sings the upper part, the middle part is called the *killo*, and the lowest part is the *torro*. In the past, these songs were sung primarily by women in rural contexts, and the song texts deal with the everyday life of women in these contexts—songs to accompany grinding wheat, for example, by hand, work songs, wedding songs, songs for Easter, and so on. Learning and performing the songs in the context of the department is quite different. They are studied because they were once prevalent in the oral traditions, but they are learned in an urban setting, from films and recordings, with the direction of a teacher, and in an institution, rather than as part of everyday rural life. Yet in this instance, gender distinctions remained, with women's songs being studied by female students.

Lectures

Students attend lectures about the history and aesthetics of folk music traditions from all over Finland. They also become familiar with archival materials from the Finnish Literature Society, and with published collections of folk music. These materials can be understood in their historical context and also provide sources for reinterpretation and performance in new contexts. The folklorist Anneli Asplund and the ethnomusicologist Erkki Pekkilä gave some lectures to second year students about folklore research in Finland, discussing the work of figures such as Lönnrot, Väisänen, and Borenius. At one of these lectures Asplund talked about the compilation of the *Kalevala*, and we compared extracts of the opening lines from Lönnrot's proto-*Kalevala* (1833), old *Kalevala* (1835), and new *Kalevala* (1849). At other lectures we compared variants of the first lines of well-known song texts and looked at a map of Finland, which folklorists had divided into regions in attempting to formulate classificatory systems of the kinds of traditions found in particular places.

I thought about Armas Otto Väisänen's story, as told to us in Pekkilä's lecture, in relation to current perceptions of Finnish folk music history and the boundaries of "Finnish" practice. In May 1912, Väisänen made his first field trip (funded by the Finnish Literature Society). He went to Tallin (the capital of Estonia). On his outward journey, the ship foundered and his phonograph was destroyed. Väisänen spent two months in Estonia, where he collected about five hundred folk tunes from over one hundred folk singers and players. He transcribed these and sent copies of them to Tallin. Every subsequent summer he went on field trips, going to different places with his phonograph and camera and taking ethnographic photographs of musicians, instruments, buildings, and clothing. His collections of melodic materials from Estonia are significant and are the largest of that era. He collected material from Ingria, described by Pekkilä as being like a Finnish island in the midst of the Russians where old traditions had been preserved. During the early twentieth century, Finland was part of the Russian Empire, and Väisänen held a Russian passport, which facilitated his access to areas like Estonia and Ingria. He worked at a critical time. The Russian Revolution and the Finnish war for independence lay ahead, and by 1917 Finland had proclaimed itself independent. After this it was impossible to undertake that type of fieldwork and to collect materials from related Finno-Ugric peoples. His collections are valuable because they provide a comparative perspective on Finno-Ugric traditions in the early twentieth century.

Väisänen did not get a university position until shortly before his retirement (an emeritus appointment in the music department of Helsinki University in 1956), but he was active in the Kalevala Society and in the promotion of folk music performance. He organized performers for the *Kalevala* centenary celebrations (1935) and promoted folk players through his radio program. His organological research, particularly into the construction and repertoire of the kantele, was vital to the 1960s folk revival. He also recorded in Karelia examples of jouhikko playing, an instrument and performance practice that had almost died out. Today, his purchase of a jouhikko lies filled with nails in the attic of the National Museum. Pekkilä views Väisänen as the most important figure in Finnish folk music research and compares him to Bartók. Both scholars undertook field trips among Finno-Ugric peoples to gain greater insights into Finnish and Hungarian music, respectively (Pekkilä 1990).

By learning something about historical context, performance practice, and the aesthetics of folk music, students at the Department of Folk Music at the Sibelius Academy gain a broad understanding of folk traditions and are motivated to reproduce and reinterpret them in their own ways. Through formal teaching situations like the instrumental lessons and lectures dealing with different aspects of folk traditions, and through the use of archival material, published collections, notated examples, films, and recordings, what was hitherto the orally transmitted music of rural areas continues to be self-consciously reinterpreted, adapted, and represented today as "folk culture." Such specialized training has led not only to a reinterpretation of folk culture, but also to the notion of professional folk musicians—people who earn their living by performing and teaching folk music, and even by composing "new" folk music.

Finnish Folk Music for Foreign Students

Self-conscious representation of what constitutes Finnish "folk" music was evident, too, in the introductory classes that the department offered to foreign students in Helsinki. These students attended lectures about folk music and started learning the kantele, as part of a course entitled "Finnish Society and

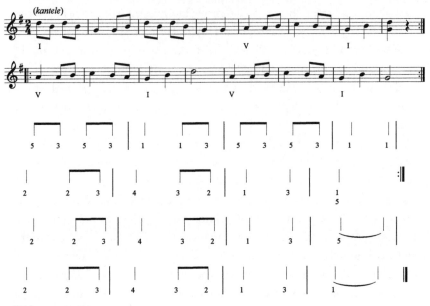

Tablature notation

Example 4.2: "Vanha Sodessi," a kantele piece used as teaching material

Culture." One of the students of the department, Minna Raskinen, taught the course following the model of what first-year folk music students are taught, introducing rune singing, instrumental traditions and dance music from West Finland, Saami and Rom music, and Finnish aerophone instruments. The class listened to many examples and discussed questions of aesthetics such as the issue of musical change and whether or not contemporary folk musicians should adhere strictly to the musical conventions preceding them. For the foreign students, participatory action rather than theoretical considerations proved to be most rewarding. Listening to the music, learning to play the kantele, and using the teaching material as the basis for improvisation rather than focusing on historical and aesthetic issues yielded their greatest insights into Finnish folk music, albeit at an introductory level (see examples 4.2 and 4.3, two pieces used as teaching material, in staff and tablature notation).

Cuban Drumming

The study of folk music in this department entails (for the students who are interested) the study of music traditions from other parts of the world as well as

Rissakka: tablature notation

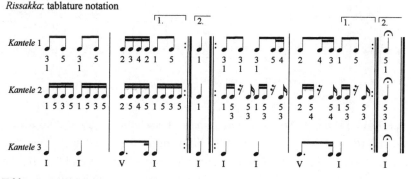

Tablature notation

Example 4.3: "Rissakka," a kantele piece used as teaching material

Finnish traditions. A Cuban musician, Jimeno, gave workshops in Cuban drumming, in which he explained some of the historical aspects of the music he taught and demonstrated how various instruments are played. The students played as an ensemble, following rhythmic patterns that were first demonstrated and rehearsed and then notated (example 4.4), and participants tried various percussion instruments.

Reasons for exploring other musical traditions are manifold, but two of these are simultaneously pronounced and contradictory. On the one hand, ideas can be gleaned from other musical traditions and applied to Finnish musical mate-

Example 4.4: Notation used in the Cuban drumming workshop

rial. As one student, Arja Kastinen, remarked, she enjoyed the Cuban drumming class because it was music different from the Finnish kantele music on
which she focused. The rhythmic patterns were more complex and diverse, and
by studying these she gained inspiration and ideas that could be applied to her
kantele playing. Becoming aware of some Cuban rhythmic patterns allowed her
to perceive and use rhythm in Finnish music differently, and she was in the
process of reinterpreting, in terms of rhythmic structure, some of Väisänen's
transcriptions of kantele music. Her comment points to the second reason for
exploring other musical traditions, which contradicts the first, namely, that it
allows Finnish folk music to be recognized, compared, and more explicitly
defined in opposition to other music. The incorporation of other musical elements can eventually lead to the identification of these elements as belonging to
Finnish traditions.

Professional Folk Musicians, Style, and Difference

Contemporary folk music education at the Sibelius Academy overturns the
representation of a rural, village-based musical practice. Finnish new folk mu-

sic is not just a revamping of village styles to suit urban audiences, for it is both rural and urban based. Neither is it necessarily "newly composed," as many other contemporary folk musics are (see Slobin 1996), although new compositions certainly are a feature. New folk music in Finland is as much new arrangements of old material as it is new compositions. Although new folk music is both an urban and a rural practice, music in the urban center raises specific questions to which Nettl draws our attention in asking "what is it that sets urban musical culture off from that of villages, small towns, and nomadic life?" (1978, 6). Many of the factors in his response maintain their relevance in contemporary contexts: "It is wealth, power, education; it is specialization in professions; it is the interaction of different and diverse population groups, rich and poor, majority and minorities, recent migrant and long-standing urbanite; it is the ease of rapid communication, the mass media, literacy; it is crowding and enormous divergencies in living standards and styles. Translated to musical culture, it is in many cases—though by no means in all cities for all repertories—the patronage of wealthy aristocrats and of government agencies. It is the specialization of the professional musician. It is Western musical notation, recording, radio, television. Perhaps most of all, it is the coming together of different musical styles and genres from many sources" (Nettl 1978, 6). The ethnographic description above has explored the "specialization" of professional folk musicians and "the coming together of different musical styles and genres from many sources."[4] To extend Nettl's latter point, Finnish new folk music, characterized by the ways in which it draws on diverse styles, provides an apt example of his suggestion that it is most of all as a meeting place for different musics that urban musical culture can be distinguished from other musical cultures. Since so many musicians have converged at the Department of Folk Music at the Sibelius Academy, this institutional framework presents a microcosm of this diversity. While a familiarity with and use of musical diversity has been crucial to the development of new folk music, it is, however, in the urban center in which the meeting of different regional styles has been facilitated that differences between musics are emphasized and regional, musical, and social identities are asserted. Thus, during the period of my fieldwork, new folk musicians could study, for example, Karelian, Ostrobothnian, and Saami traditions as well as Irish or Estonian song traditions, and Cuban or Senegalese drumming.

Although contemporary folk music in Finland with its self-conscious reinterpretations of folk music reveals a profound institutional involvement and influence, the discursive representation of folk music returns us to the subjects of musical differences and individual definitions. In the class for foreign students, Roma and Saami music was presented as music of minorities in Finland that contributes to Finnish folk traditions. When I asked new folk musicians at the department whether they thought of Roma and Saami musical traditions as "Finnish," they expressed a variety of views regarding their place in the national space:

Yes.

Joiks are; the roots of Rom music are further afield, but in a way it also belongs to Finnish folk music. It depends on the definition!

Joiks are Saami folk music and Rom music is Rom music. One can define Finnish folk music in different ways, whether joiks and Rom music are considered part of Finnish folk music depends on the definition. In my own opinion Finnish Rom music is nearly Finnish because the language in which the songs are performed is often Finnish.

Just as much as Karelian, Ingrian, Finnish-Swedish, Ostrobothnian, and so on. What is Finnish folk music?

Without doubt.

Yes, it depends on what one means by the word "folk music."

Of course. The joik has been an ignored part. . . . Saamis are a part of us, a part of Finland; they are a terribly important part of Finnishness, because not many nations in the world have these kinds of minorities as we do. We have Roma, and we have Saamis, but they have always been treated in a very outrageous manner, so that it has been a bit like in the Soviet Union. . . . Saamis have been forced to speak Finnish, just like in Russia, where all the Ingrians, Setus, Karelians have been forced to speak Russian.

Recurrent themes in these responses are the students' appreciation of the difficulties in defining the terms "folk music" and "Finnishness." These themes are related, for the historical processes whereby the music came to be self-consciously redefined as "folk" were also the processes of constructing a distinctive Finnish nation with an identity transcending regional and ethnic particularities. The musics associated with marginalized peoples such as Saamis and Roma are, nevertheless, a reminder of musical "hybridity" and competing interests within the nation-state. That such discourses about whether or not these musics properly belong to the category of "Finnish" folk music are at all evident reveals the peripheral positions of Saamis and Roma within the nation-state and highlights questions about ethnicity and national belonging (cf. Gilroy 1987).[5] Questions about musical repertoires and national belonging are exacerbated by the introduction of musical elements so evidently perceived as "other," as in the Estonian song and Cuban drumming classes. These questions will be explored further in chapter 8.

PERFORMING FOLK MUSIC IN THE URBAN CENTER

The model of folk music as the orally transmitted musical expression of rural communities is challenged by new folk music performance contexts just as it is by the transmission of contemporary folk music in the urban center. One main performance context is the music festival. The Kaustinen Folk Music Festival is the largest one of its kind in Finland. Here, four examples—a performance for specialists in a private context, a festival attended by an interested audience, a performance for the general public in which some members of the audience were merely passers-by, and performances at the midsummer celebrations— will illustrate the variety of modern folk music performance contexts in the urban center.

An Examination

In a dimly lit hall a spotlight falls on the performers on stage. Sitting in the balcony, examiners are making notes on the performance. Students from the Department of Folk Music listen silently to their peers. As a center for new folk music, the Department of Folk Music at the Sibelius Academy is obviously a place that provides many contexts for performance including rehearsal and teaching performance spaces. Department parties (such as pre-Christmas celebrations) provide informal and private performance opportunities. The kind of music performed at one such festive event was that which is studied at the department: Finnish folk music, music of related peoples (Estonian and Karelian examples) and music from other parts of the world (in this instance performances given by musicians from Senegal and Cuba). If these are performance contexts which are in some sense a part of everyday and informal musical activity, folk music performance for examinations presents a highly structured context far removed from the idea of folk music being performed as an integral part of daily activities. Whereas competitions for folk musicians have been organized at least since the early twentieth century, I suspect that the examination as a performance context has emerged only recently. What competitions and examinations have in common is the judging and evaluation of performances against the judges' or examiners' expectations and notions of what constitutes a suitable performance. Competitions or examinations are thus contexts in which clear value judgements are expected. The examination as a context for folk music performance has probably emerged as a result of the recent incorporation of folk music tuition within an institution that focuses on the Western tradition of art music, in which examinations, as a way of assessing performance, have been long established. Sinikka Järvinen compared the assessment criteria for classical and for folk musicians: "Folk music has not been a taught tradition and although it is performed a lot, people think that it is not 'good' because they equate it with simple music and with untrained musicians who play as a hobby. Classical music is not always a hobby. The technique for performing folk music may not have been so high, but it is improving all the time. In folk music, talent lies in being able to make arrangements, in composition and in playing many instruments. Not just playing one instrument to a very high level as in classical music" (personal interview with Sinikka Järvinen, July 13, 1992).

Students at the Department of Folk Music take examinations in solo and group performance. All students in the same year form a group, playing together and taking examinations as a group. In the examination, students must demonstrate that they are familiar with a variety of folk traditions, and they must show evidence of bringing new ideas to these traditions. I heard a group performance examination taken by fifth-year students. The instruments played included various types of kantele, fiddles, contrabass, accordions, harmonium, electric keyboard, and voice. Most of the pieces were in the idiom of new folk music—combining different traditions and using modern, electric instruments. The duration of the examination was two hours. The repertoire illustrated the different Finnish traditions and musics from around the world that have influenced and produced new folk music, including a song about emigrants to America, which was sung by the character of a "widow"—a woman left behind in Finland, and an arrangement of a Latin American song.

Group performance assessment is an important part of the curriculum and stems from notions of folk music as collective activity. Within the group, individuals are identified as arrangers or composers of particular pieces. The establishment of groups for learning and assessment has led to the proliferation of new folk music groups from which individuals emerge as soloists (often "accompanied" by other group members). Niekku, for example, was the first new folk music group formed at the Department of Folk Music, and one of its members, the accordionist Maria Kalaniemi, is establishing a solo career in which she is often joined by her colleagues as "accompanists" on stage and on record.

Etnosoi Festival

The Etnosoi Festival was established in 1988. Hannu Tolvanen, who was at that time working part-time at the Kansanmusiikin Keskusliitto (Central Union for Folk Music) and is now the administrator of the Department of Folk Music, was asked whether he would be interested in initiating a winter festival for "ethnic" music. Only Finnish bands appeared in the first festival, but of these groups only one performed Finnish folk music—Niekku. The rest performed music from other parts of the world such as the Javanese gamelan and Bulgarian folk music (played by Slobo Horo, a band from Tampere). The festival has been expanding since its inauguration, and more Finnish folk bands have participated (e.g., JPP, Pohjantahti, Värttinä, and Koinurit). The groups that appeared in this festival in 1991 were Maria Kalaniemi & Co, Tuulenkantajat and Happy All the Time from Finland, Lars Hollmer & Band from Sweden, 3 Mustaphas 3 from the Balkans, and Ethio Stars from Ethiopia.

The last night of the Etnosoi festival took place in a jazz club in an underground shopping center near the main railway station. Other performances had taken place in Café Adlon (a smart hotel bar), and Vanha (the Helsinki University student union building). Yamar and Papp Sarr, who had been teaching at the Department of Folk Music, began the evening's proceedings with a performance of their drumming (Senegalese talking drum—*tama* and *sabar*). They then joined Happy All the Time, who played arrangements of pieces from different parts of the world (e.g., Belafonte's "This is My Island in the Sun"), and called themselves an "ethno" band. Finally, a band from Addis Ababa, Ethiopia, Ethio Stars, performed. The audience was diverse and included members of the Department of Folk Music, some of the Ethiopians who live in Finland, some of Helsinki's Senegalese musicians, and other Finnish musicians who are interested in musics from around the world. Strains of music and conversation blended in this dim, small club decorated in black, and the smells of beer and cigarette smoke floated through the air. Happy All the Time urged the audience to participate by dancing. One person in the audience commented: "I do not like this kind of organization—all these different bands put together and called

world music. I have only come to hear Ethio Stars." A musician from the Department of Folk Music said that he had not heard music from Ethiopia before,
and that it sounded a bit strange and not really "traditional."

"Helsinki Day"

It was a sunny June day. Musical performances were given in the open air at various locations and many of the bands that participated performed in several
of the locations, moving around from one to another. The performance areas
were all in the city center where there would be many passers-by: in the markets, outside a large department store (Stockman), and in a park (Esplanadi)
near the harbor where performances took place throughout the summer. The
music played was diverse. The Helsinki Philharmonic Orchestra played in the
park, rock and folk bands (including Koinurit, shown in plate 4, and the "Irish"
group Korkkijalka) played in all of the performance sites. In the park there was
also a bazaar where vendors were selling arts and crafts, flowers, sweets, pastry
and ice cream, second-hand books, balloons, and other items. The stalls lined
the path from a statue of Johan Ludvig Runeberg (1804–77, Finnish national
poet and a contemporary of Snellman) at one end, to the performance stage at
the other end, near the harbor. Members of evangelical groups urging the public to join their cause preached by the statue of Runeberg. Families with young
children, people taking their lunch break from work and other inhabitants and
visitors to the city strolled around these venues, looking at the merchandise,
sunbathing, and listening to the music. A military parade marched around the
center too, attracting much attention. In this context, the musical performances
were one part of a festival day, heard by all of those who were in the city center.

Midsummer Celebrations at Seurasaari

Seurasaari is one of the islands of Helsinki. It is the site of an open-air museum
with a collection of old wooden buildings and farmsteads from different parts
of Finland, which are displayed in a forest setting. For the midsummer evening
celebrations, extra buses had been provided to transport people to the island,
but even so, they were brimming to capacity. Arriving on the island, the pre-
dominantly urban audience was to witness the reconstruction of past rural traditions, and the juxtaposition of different traditions, past and present. Handi-
craft stalls with plant dyeing, lace making, and basket weaving lined the island
pathways. Stall owners were dressed in traditional costumes from Uusimaa (the
southern region of Finland), as were dancers and musicians who demonstrated
and taught some folk dances. As the visitors walked on through the island the

aromas of grilled sausages, sweets, pies, and drink filled the air. A few Roma offered to read palms.

Further into the island a main stage had been set up. There were demonstrations of folk dances and a dance (polka) competition (plates 5, 6). Much of the folk music performed during the evening was in accompaniment to folk dances. There was, however, some concentrated attention to folk music performance: kantele pieces played by the *mestaripelimanni* (master folk musician) Toivo Alaspää in collaboration with Minna Raskinen (who had been teaching kantele at the Sibelius Academy to foreign students), Estonian folk songs, and a Vietnamese song. Raskinen's collaboration with Alaspää demonstrated her knowledge of traditional music performance and her ability to conform to established folk music aesthetics and linked the kantele traditions of Ostrobothnia with new folk music practice in Helsinki. If the Etnosoi Festival highlighted the innovative, the contemporary, and global musical exchanges, the Seurasaari celebrations emphasized the traditional, the past, and the "Finnish."

One of the highlights of the evening was the "staging" of a traditional wedding. A couple held a private wedding ceremony in the wooden church, one of the preserved buildings in the museum, and then danced a waltz on the main arena, having entered under a traditional wedding canopy. Toward the end of the evening's celebrations a bonfire was lit. In the past, the lighting of the bonfire was intended to provide ritual protection from disease and to ward off malevolent spirits (Reunala 1989), but these meanings have long since disappeared. The newlyweds embarked on a wooden boat toward the bonfire and lit it as members of the audience opened bottles of champagne.

This midsummer celebration is both a representation and an affirmation of a Finnish identity, drawing upon notions of the past and upon past traditions that encompass ideas about "folk music." The staging of a traditional village wedding, the lighting of the bonfire, the emphasis on folk music, the performance on the national instrument, and the traditional handicrafts and costumes are diverse elements that have been put together in the urban context in this representation. Yet, even if it is a conscious reconstruction of past traditions (the vast majority of people no longer go through the kind of wedding ceremony which takes place on Seurasaari every year), it is a celebration that has relevance and meaning in the present. Ideas about the forest and folk traditions, and the link with patriotic sentiment, are part of a comprehensive nationalist ideology. The idea, too, that people go to the forest to re-create themselves, forging a link with their ancestors through being in the environment of their ancestors' everyday life and by listening to musical expressions from the past

(Väinämöinen's tale, chaps. 1 and 2), is part of the ideology of modernity. Here, in the midsummer festival, people set the present off from the past even as they emphasize the link with their ancestors, and the forest has been incorporated into the twin myths of nationalism and modernity which provide the ideological foundation for the contemporary Finnish state.

One can note that within the context of the affirmation of a Finnish identity, there were two performances—of the Estonian folk songs and of the Vietnamese song—which were apparently unrelated to this purpose. Like the Finns, the Estonians are a Finno-Ugric people, and there are close links between the two. Thus, the performance of Estonian folk songs evoked a tradition that is much akin to Finnish ones. This was not the case with the Vietnamese song, which contributed a novel and exotic element to the evening's performances. The inclusion of this song can be interpreted in several ways. It can be perceived as an attempt to acknowledge the arrival and settlement of "new" populations in Finland. Until relatively recently, barring the Swedish-speaking minority, the small and scattered Roma population, and the Saami in the far north, Finnish society was characterized by its ethnic homogeneity. By the 1980s, Finland had begun to accept refugees, following international trends. The inclusion of the Vietnamese song may denote an awareness of the presence of Vietnamese people in Helsinki. It could even be seen as an attempt to include these new populations within the ambit of Finnish society. More likely, though, within the context of a celebration in which Finnish identity is reinforced, this performance could be interpreted in terms of its contribution to the aesthetics of the exotic and novel. Putting the exotic "other" on show as a curiosity with novelty value reinforces popular stereotypes, and indeed, one short performance was a fleeting moment in an evening's events in which multiple invocations of "Finnishness" were evident.

Organizing Performance

All four examples of urban folk music performance contexts reveal well-planned organization strategies, the effects of which have been described by Wallis and Malm: "The development towards performance in concert form . . . involves a departure from some of folk music's spontaneity. Concert performances require a greater degree of organization and discipline. Pieces of music are linked together to form a programme, where every item has a defined length. In each piece, the music tends to be arranged in a particular fashion (according to series of norms that develop based on, for instance, the acoustics of the halls, the demands of the audience, the organizers, and sometimes the sponsors, the technical abilities of the musicians etc)" (Wallis and Malm 1984, 13). The audiences for these performances ranged from specialists to people who do not necessarily choose to listen to the music at all. In the first example the audience consisted almost exclusively of people who were themselves involved in the production and performance of new folk music, and the performances were situated in the department in which they studied. In the second example, the location was a club for the general public, and the audience consisted of people who had either come to hear specific performers, or who were interested generally in "world" music. Many of the members of the audience were either "specialists" themselves—performing musicians—or had connections to Ethiopia. The performance stage was in the open-air city center in the third example. Passers-by, who may or may not have been interested in listening to this music, nevertheless heard it as the musical performance mingled with other city sounds. In the first two examples, members of the audience were predisposed to enjoy the performances, whereas in the third example the musicians had to attract the attention of the general public. Toward the end of the time allotted to Koinurit the musicians were told they had time to perform only one more song, so the singer instructed the group to play one of their most popular songs ("Progelaulu"), indicating the ways in which audience responses influence performance presentation. Audiences may also expect to hear versions of pieces that they have become used to from recordings. While the discourse of new folk musicians includes improvisation as a feature of folk music, their improvisations are often prearranged.

Whereas changes in tradition and the commercial success enjoyed by some folk musicians have inspired heated debates in other contexts, Finnish new folk musicians promote the view that it is through change that tradition lives. These are the musicians who attract the largest audiences. The latest developments at the Department of Folk Music include the formation of more new folk music groups, reaching out to wider audiences through the organization and promotion of more folk music festivals and clubs, the launch of the department's own series of recordings in collaboration with commercial labels, plans to provide better facilities—a new building in the center of Helsinki, for example—and the use of new technology (communication systems, computer and recording technologies). Not only do these initiatives in the field of folk music education take into account processes of change already undergone, but they also represent preparations for the continued transmission of folk music in the new millennium.

FIVE

Värttinä

WOMEN'S SONGS FROM THE EAST

One of the groups that emerged from the Sibelius Academy during the early 1990s was Värttinä (although it has had a changing membership). It achieved a huge public prominence and was arguably the most well known folk music group at this time. Its members can be properly described as professional folk musicians. Värttinä is a group of female singers and instrumental backing (acoustic bass, guitar, saxophone, accordion, violin, bazouki, and tin whistle). Although many of the members of this group were students at the Department of Folk Music, they gave so many performances that they were hardly seen in the department in 1991 and 1992.

Why did this group become so popular in the early 1990s? How do the vocal timbres of the group's female voices articulate a position of power? How does the practice of this new folk music group throw into question the notion of "folk" music as an expression of nationness and national belonging? While contemporary folk music is represented under the homogeneous label of "Finnish new folk music" it is in fact a composite of several regional styles. Sometimes these are promoted as belonging to specific regions. Värttinä is an example. Within the national arena the group promotes itself, and is perceived, as coming from the region of Karelia, even though several musical influences can be traced in its work.[1] Notions of regional practice are important to some of the group's members because of the repertoire they sing and their musical backgrounds. The public association, too, of Värttinä with Karelia proved to be important on political, social, and individual levels. Public association of the group with a specific region during the early 1990s was interlinked with political processes and with assumptions about the nature of folk practice—traditional modes of transmission, in particular—which were, as it transpires, somewhat incommensurate with the actual formal educational strategies which the group went through.

This chapter explores new folk treatments of Karelian repertoires through the practice of Värttinä (plate 7). I want to show that while this group is associated with this eastern region of Finland, it nevertheless draws on a variety of musical elements that make the task of attempting to describe musical practice in relation to bounded areas difficult, even impossible. Yet the region remains significant to interpretations of this new folk music group's performances. The analysis looks at the mixture of individual experiences, ideological strategies, and political circumstances that inform Värttinä's music. Since the group mainly sings songs following the models of Karelian women's traditional repertoires, I also want to uncover some of the complexities of gender formulations in these song narratives. The song texts of this group deal with women's relations to particular landscapes, the seeking of partners, the changing status of women as they enter marriage, and the leaving behind of the childhood home. These texts point to gendered experience and evoke and reinforce specific landscape images. Gender and region, then, join the discursive categories of "tradition" and "innovation" in discourses on contemporary folk music practices. I begin with the discourse of the leader of the group and one its principal media figures, Sari Kaasinen, who provides insights into Värttinä's musical practice.

AN INTERVIEW WITH SARI KAASINEN: MAKING THE MUSIC

Värttinä draws on the same body of folk music material from the eastern regions of Finland that Lönnrot turned to in compiling the national epic and that folklorists (in groups like Nelipolviset and Primo) sought to revive as song traditions in the 1970s. Lönnrot identified the parish of Rääkkylä (among others in northern Karelia) as an area rich in folk songs in the 1840s. This is the area, around sixty kilometers from the Russian border, from which Sari Kaasinen comes. Like other new folk musicians, she has a sense of certain musical practices as being significant to her from historical, regional, and familial perspectives. Evident in an interview with Kaasinen were the ways in which musical experience is embedded in the individual's total experience of "tradition":

I am from a farm; we had cattle, cows—and I have lived, so to speak, with
them; it has been that sort of country life where all these traditional things
have been a very strong part of life. It was not intentionally recognized as a
tradition as such, but it was a part of life that was a normal way of life. And
not like, that when I now bake these Karelian pies they are Karelian pies,
they are traditional things, but they were as we learned them a quite natural
way of life. Then my mother has more or less pushed me, and my sister
Mari, who also performs in Värttinä, to sing and play. They, our mother and
father, gave us the opportunity to study music. We went to have music lessons in Joensuu, about fifty to sixty kilometers from Rääkkylä. Mother and
father took us there and back every Saturday for about six years. I played the
kannel [kantele] and still play, and my sister Mari played the harmonium.
So that is the way my music interest started. And then my mother led a
recital group giving recitals; poetry, singing, drama. So I performed from
childhood with my mother's group. Then mother asked me to play the kantele, to accompany a song. I did not know how to accompany, I had never
learned these kinds of things; nobody had ever taught me; I had only played
kantele pieces. So I started to teach myself gradually, to play myself, to experiment myself. After that mother told me to add another voice to the
song. What voice? I had never even heard of such things, so I added another
voice, which sounded good to me, and that is how it all started, largely self-
taught before I went to the Sibelius Academy. All this background to the beginning of Värttinä and to my childhood, all this has been sort of found and
tried by ourselves, and learned that way.[2] (Sari Kaasinen, personal interview,
August 5, 1992; my translation)

In the personal musical history contained in this narrative, musical choices are
described as emerging from processes of experimentation pursued in a familial
environment. Kaasinen's account resonates with the Herderian model of orally
transmitted traditions, and she emphasizes the oral aspects of her musical
training together with her own attempts at composing countermelodies. Her
account is framed, however, by beginning and ending with reference to the formal dimensions of her musical training: to kantele lessons in Joensuu and to
her studies at the Sibelius Academy.

   Kaasinen specified that she felt a closer affinity to traditions from her region
than to other ones performed in Finland: "In Finland people were interested
in pelimanni music only, which comes from the west side, from western Fin-

land. So I also played the violin; I tried it, but it did not feel good; I did not recognize it as my own at all. Somehow singing and starting my career through songs seemed to be my own straight away. Probably also for the reasons that in Karelia the song tradition is the tradition that has lived, whereas in western Finland it is more instrumental music—we have been singing, so it is more natural" (Sari Kaasinen, personal interview, August 5, 1992; my translation).[3] In addition to Karelian traditions, Värttinä's repertoire and vocal techniques come from areas neighboring Finland's present day borders. They sing mostly runes (epic songs) of the Mordva, Hanti, Udmurti, Ingrian, Mari and Setu peoples. Värttinä's members were influenced by the song traditions of Finno-Ugric peoples that they heard at a song festival in Petroskoi (in Russian Karelia) in 1989. The group made audio-visual recordings that they then studied carefully for the following few months. Kaasinen's enthusiasm for these repertoires is evident in her statements about the festival: "We performed at a song festival on the island of Kiz to which Finno-Ugric people had been invited from Ingria, Setumaa in Estonia, and the Mari Republic. The Mari song and dance ensemble called Maribamas made a tremendous impression on us. On the last evening we played and sang and danced together on Petroskoi railway station, and even though we couldn't understand a word the Mari were saying, the atmosphere was quite crazy" (Sari Kaasinen cited in Pietilä 1992, 47).

In part singing, the intervals between the voices change according to the area from which the song comes. A feature of Setu songs is the juxtaposed intervals of the second and of the fourth, whereas Ingrian part singing is based on the triad. In Petroskoi, the group first heard Ingrian *röntyskä* (roundelay) songs with onomatopoetic lines made up of words without meanings such as "kiiriminna kaariminna kiiriminna kaaraa, kiiriminna, kaariminna kaara" (Pietilä 1992). Värttinä include these different features in their repertoire. They do not reproduce the songs exactly as they have heard them. They change the words that are in dialects and that are hard for them and their audiences to understand, often replacing the original dialects of the song texts with a Finnish dialect, or just adding their own song texts to the melodies (Sari Kaasinen, personal communication). Another conscious difference from their sources lies in the instrumental accompaniment, which shows the influence of rock, blues, and pelimanni styles in which some of the musicians have their musical background. Indeed, Pietilä (1992) suggests that the more recent membership of professional instrumentalists has set the singers higher standards. As Sari commented, "We almost never sang in parts in the old Värttinä songs, but we do on the *Oi Dai* record [1991], and we're trying to develop and add to the number of parts all the time" (Sari Kaasinen cited in Pietilä 1992, 48). Reasons for adapting musical materials include the freedom of individual interpretation inherent in these song traditions and performing music that is considered relevant today. As Kaasinen explained:

> It has always been thought that Finnish folk music is boring, the reason for this is that people believe that only old men have played it, and inevitably because we in Finland have always admired anything American and anything that comes from abroad, so it has been, after all, boring to hear what sounded to us like out-of-tune melodies, and all these sorts of things. So, in that sense it has been difficult to create music that would have appealed to people. People have always thought that it is only folk music and it does not interest anyone, especially as it was not directed to young people. As we are young ourselves, we make music to appeal to the youth, so that has for sure been an influence that now people have been getting interested in folk music in Finland in a renewed fashion. Folk music must expressly live with the people; now we are living in the year '92, so folk music must also live in the year '92, it cannot be fifty years behind us. This is the way we have thought in Finland, that folk music must be something dignified, old, dusty, and that it should not change at all. On the contrary, that is how folk music lives, it changes, it goes forward with people, it changes with people, that is when it lives.[4] (Sari Kaasinen, personal interview, August 5, 1992; my translation)

As well as listening to other singers, Värttinä finds and uses musical material from collections published at the turn of the century. I traced an example of such early-twentieth-century source material in the sound archives of the Finnish Literature Society. It was a 1906 field recording made by Armas Launis (SKS, A 300/42a; II 532–66). The solo performer was a thirty-two-year-old woman called Ustenja Miikkulant. Chorus singers were not named. Both the chorus song text and a transcription of its two-part vocal lines are provided in the archive holdings (example 5.1). Värttinä's interpretation is recorded in an early album (1989, track 6) and adheres closely to the archive source. It can be compared to the treatment of the chorus by the Swedish-Finnish group Hedningarnar (1992, track 3). Both groups retain the two-part vocal texture but add different kinds of instrumental accompaniment and verse texts and choose different performance tempos.

Example 5.1: "Vot I Kaalina": archival material

In rehearsing, Värttinä's singers combine text and melody and rehearse their vocal parts before adding the accompaniment with the instrumentalists. Their language is often a mixture of the Rääkkylä dialect and words from published texts, which they themselves do not always understand. One problem they face is that sometimes texts and melodies have been published separately (Sari Kaasinen, personal interview, August 5, 1992; my translation). Yet the separation of melody and text has encouraged the group's efforts in composition. Kaasinen commented that she had always composed melodies as a child but that original compositions were now beginning to be featured in the group's recorded canon. Another consequence of separated texts and melodies is that the sense of having to recombine source materials to re-create folk songs can be easily extended to combining musical elements from increasingly diverse sources and styles.

GENDER AND REGION

Värttinä's song texts are multireferential, and the text of the title song of one of the group's best-selling recordings, *Oi Dai* (1991), is one such example (see example 5.2). The main themes of this text are commonly found in Karelian folk song repertoires: allegiance to a particular environment—to one's "own land, fir-trees and pine-trees"—and grief and nostalgia on being in "strange lands." The text deals with the imagery of particular landscapes and of the subject's situatedness within them. In the spirit of Tarkka's (1998) analysis of nature, particularly forest symbolism, and gender in Karelian oral poetry, "Oi Dai" can

Example 5.2: "Oi Dai": principal melodic material and harmonic outline. (The transcription is based on the recording [Värttinä 1991, side B, track 3].)

be understood as a text that refers to landscape imagery in the "cultural processes of organising selfhood" (Tarkka 1998, 94):

OI DAI

Kuin oisin omilla mailla
Oman pellon pientarilla,
Oi dai oman pellon
Oman pellon pientarilla.

Toisin lintu laulelisin,
Toisin kukkusin käkönen,
Oi dai toisin . . .
Omat kuuset kuuntelisi,
Omat oppisi petäjät,
Oi dai omat . . .

instrumental interlude based on a descending bass line

Verse 4, embellished with an instrumental countermelody

Saxophone

Voices

Nyt oon mail - la   vie - ra - hil - la   ...

Verse 4, embellished with voices in thirds

Voices

Oi dai   tui - ki   ...

Nyt oon mailla vierahilla,
Tuiki tuntemattomilla,
Oi dai tuiki . . .

Miss ei lennä meien linnut
Eikä vaaku mein varikset,
Oi dai eikä . . .

Mihin jouvun mie polonen,
Jouvun joutsen-joukostani,
Oi dai jouvun . . .

Haihun hanhiparvestani,
Haihun hanhiparvestani,
Oi dai haihun . . .

Tok mie lintu laulelisin,
Sekä kukkusin käkönen
Oi dai sekä . . .

OI DAI

If I were on my own land
Beside my own field
Oi dai my own field
Beside my own field.

Another way would sing this bird
Another way would call this cuckoo
Oi dai another way would call
Another way would call this cuckoo.

My own fir trees would listen
My own pine trees would learn
Oi dai . . .

Now I am in strange lands
Altogether unknown
Oi dai . . .

Where our birds do not fly
Neither crow our crows
Oi dai . . .

Where did I end up poor me
End up a swan from my own crowd
Oi dai . . .

I vanished from my flock of geese
Vanished from my flock of geese
Oi dai . . .

Surely this bird would sing
And this cuckoo call
Oi dai . . .
(My translation)

The processes of "organizing selfhood," commented on in these song texts, revolve around women's social roles. At the turn of the century, 90 percent of Finland's population still lived in the countryside, and even into the mid–twentieth century, agriculture continued in Finland as the major source of livelihood. One of the main celebrations held in the countryside was the wedding, and wedding songs were widespread. For women, weddings were the most significant celebrations in their lives. Marriage affected a woman's occupational choices, her way of life, and her status within the community. Songs were an intrinsic feature of the wedding ceremony and were performed over a period lasting many days. They were performed during the proposals, the engagement, and the preparations for the wedding—including the brewing of beer and the baking of the wedding bread. The longest and most varied songs were sung on the wedding day. These included songs sung at the home of the groom while he was preparing himself for the day and while he was traveling to the bride's home. At the bride's home, songs announcing the arrival of the groom and greeting songs followed. As the bride later arrived at the groom's home, arrival songs and a series of praising, mocking, advisory, and thanking songs were performed (Asplund and Laitinen 1979). These songs have been analyzed as channeling the "emotional charge, fears and anxieties associated with this rite of passage" and also of regulating "communication between kin groups," in which what is depicted above all are notions held by the groom's family of the ideal daughter-in-law (Ilomäki 1998, 167).

The songs associated with the wedding ceremony mark a change of environment (described in relation to the landscape) and articulate the socially defined traditional roles of women as daughters, brides, and wives. During the ceremony, the groom comes to the bride's house and then the bride is taken to her future home—the groom's house. The change of environment from childhood to marital home is highlighted by the performance of various songs at specific moments in the ceremony that mark the changing role of the bride. Since the bride's new home was often near her former one, the emphasis on a different landscape signifies not so much the distance involved as the change in the woman's social status and her transformation from cherished daughter to subordinate daughter-in-law. Wedding laments expressed in terms of leaving familiar surroundings sung by the bride and by her mother reflect on the woman's transformed social status.

The songs, then, describe and are patterned by the sequence of events during the wedding ceremony. They indicate social expectations regarding the marriage and contain an evaluative and instructive dimension. As Ilomäki notes,

Example 5.3: "Tumala": principal melodic material and harmonic outline. (The transcription is based on the recording [Värttinä 1994, track 2].)

"during the leave-taking ceremonies celebrated at the bride's home, the girl, soon to be detached from her home, was assured of the finality of her separation and was made ready for the reality of the life which lay before her. . . . Elements of the festival celebrated at the groom's home included the reception of the bride and the evaluation of her, the mutual comparison made by the two kin groups of each other, and praise for the marrying couple" (Ilomäki 1998, 150).

Instrumental interlude (following the third repetition of the chorus)

Accordion

Ascending ostinato bass line

Instrumental interlude (following the fifth repetition of the chorus)

Saxophone

Bass

While traditional Karelian song texts point to the restrictions in women's so-cial spaces, Värttinä present these narrative and musical conventions in a rein-terpreted fashion that overturns previous expectations of women and resonates with contemporary gender relations. Värttinä's texts portray women as mak-ing their own choices; marriage is no longer a principal aim. The following two examples (examples 5.3, "Tumala," and 5.4, "Mie Tahon Tanssia") illustrate the subtleties of the group's recontextualized narrative treatments. There are three

Example 5.4: "Mie Tahon Tanssia": principal melodic material and harmonic outline. (The transcription is based on the recording [Värttinä 1994, track 5].)

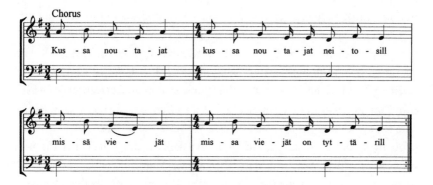

Chorus

Kus - sa nou - ta - jat   kus - sa nou - ta - jat nei - to - sill

mis - sä vie - jät   mis - sa vie - jät on tyt - tä - rill

points I would like to emphasize with regard to "Tumala." The first point concerns the manner in which the narrator, in this case the unmarried girl, describes herself in the song text. She "has never played a lady," "combed her hair," or "enticed other boys." She has cows and sheep and pigs and is therefore able to work on a farm. Her self-description corresponds to the desirable characteristics featured in women's traditional instructional songs to their sons. As Timonen notes, such instructional songs may be delivered in terms of prohibition: for example, "do not get engaged on the way to church" (for the girl will be dressed in her finery, not in her everyday apparel). They also include positive models: "choose your wife near the barn, busy at work." Diligence is the most desirable characteristic of the daughter-in-law. Undesired characteristics include ostentatiousness, physical attractiveness, promiscuity, and merriment (which refers to a woman's sexual desire). The "laughing woman" is therefore to be avoided (Timonen 1998, 210). A second point about "Tumala" is the reference to the cottage. The cottage is a dominant image, "a key symbol" (Timonen 1998) with multiple meanings in northern Karelian traditional song texts. In a literal sense, many nineteenth-century northern Karelians were landless, without their own cottages. The cottage on one level, then, is an image of "everyday living space," a symbol of "a good life" and of "security and happiness." But there are deeper levels of meaning to this image, including its mythical dimensions: offering spaces of another reality as "the sacred beginning" (childhood home) and sacred end (the grave; Timonen 1998, 226). The third point I wish to make about this song text concerns the ways in which Värttinä uses a traditional narrative song medium with traditional imagery to overturn traditional gender concepts and social expectations. While the narrator conforms to self-descriptions that conform to desirable female qualities and evokes traditional imagery, she nevertheless takes the initiative in proposing to the man and ultimately asserts her own independence. If the man will not "give his heart to her" she will work on her own. This is a perspective that departs from the sentiments expressed in traditional marriage song material that deals with the theme of "waiting for a husband" and the prohibitions on women's actively making their own choices. The second example, "Mie Tahon Tanssia," further illustrates this female positioning. In this song, the young women seek dance partners. Their open invitations are in contrast to traditional dance codes, still evident for older women, in which men, who issue invitations, determine which women will dance. In studying pensioners' dance scenes, Vakimo observes that women of this generation are still reluctant to be seen as taking the initiative to dance and disapprove of those who are seen as "too eager," and "chasing the men" in asking them to dance (Vakimo 1998).

Reconceptualized gender relations in Värttinä's song texts also interface with their "new" treatments of folk music material. The "modern" sounds of Värttinä's performances reinforce the group's representations of contemporary gender relations and authoritatively center the female voices as singing from a position of power that is based on equal social standing.

TUMALA

Olis mulla poika sulle
Hiukan sanomista.
Sen mie kuiskin kahen kesken,
Jos se on mahollista.

Tokkopa tohit miule tulla
Talonpitäjäksi,
Pienen mökin iloksi
Ja karjanhoitajaksi.

Chorus:
Tumala, tumala, tumala ko kolena
tumala, tumala kolena.

Hiukan se mökki ahdas lie,
Ja tiekin on pitkänlainen,
Silti se meijät yhteen vie,
Vaikk onkin vajavainen.

Chorus

En oo koskaan rouvastellu
Lankkisaappahissa,
Vaan tallustelu virsuissa, ja
Sarkavaattehissa.

En oo päätäin kammannu,
En liikoja silitelly.
En oo liioin muita poikkii
Viereen vikitelly.

Chorus

Mull on lehmät nutipäitä,
Sarvekas on mulli,
Läävä täysi lampaita, ja
Pässin nimi Julli.

Sika sekä porsaita,
Ja pari vasikoita.
Eikö syki sydämesi
Aatellessa noita?

Chorus

Jollet sä usko sanojain,
Ja sydäntäs et anna,
Itseppä sitten mullit syötän,
Elä huolta kanna.

Chorus

TUMALA

To you boy I would have
Something to say.
I'll whisper it alone to you
If it is possible.

Wouldn't you come to me
To keep house,
For the joy of a little cottage
And tending cattle?

Chorus:
Tumala, tumala, tumala ko kolena
Tumala, tumala kolena.

Small that cottage may be
And the way there longish,
Despite that we'll get on together,
Although it is incomplete.

Chorus

I have never played a lady
In polished boots,
Just walked in
Birchbark shoes and
In frieze clothes.

My hair I have not combed,
Not too much smoothed.
Nor have I other boys
By my side enticed.

Chorus

My cows are pollards,
The bull is horned,
A cowshed full of sheep, and
The ram's name is Julli.

Swine and pigs,
And a couple of calves.
Doesn't your heart beat
When thinking about those?

Chorus

If you don't believe my words,
And don't give your heart to me,
Then by myself the bulls I will feed,
Do not trouble yourself.

Chorus
(My translation)

MIE TAHON TANSSIA

Oi tänä iltana tahon tanssia
tänäpä iltana tahon tanssia.
Oi missä oisi viejät tyttärille,
Oi missä oisi viejät tyttärill.

Oi tänä iltana tahon tanssia
tänäpä iltana tahon tanssia.
Oi kussapa oisi noutajat neitosill,
Kussa oisi noutajat neitosill.

Oi tänä iltana tahon tanssia
tänäpä iltana tahon tanssia.
Oi onko tanssittajia tasaisille,
Onko tanssittajia tasaisill.

Chorus:
Kussa noutajat,
kussa noutajat neitosill?
Missä viejät on tyttärill?

Oi tänä iltana tahon tanssia
tänäpä iltana tahon tanssia.
Liekö kulettajia kaunehille,
Kulettajia kaunehille.

Oi tänä iltana tahon tanssia
tänäpä iltana tahon tanssia.

Oi onko saattelijoita somaisille,
Saattelijoita somaisille.

Oi tänä iltana tahon tanssia
tänäpä iltana tahon tanssia.
Oi löytyisikö kylästä tästä,
löytyisikö kylästä tästä.

Chorus

I WANT TO DANCE

I want to dance
Oh this evening I want to dance
This evening I want to dance.
Oh where are the partners for these maidens,
Oh where are the partners for these maidens?

Oh this evening I want to dance
This evening I want to dance.
Oh where are the escorts for the young girls,
Where are the escorts for the young girls?

Oh this evening I want to dance
This evening I want to dance.
Oh are there like minded dancers,
Are there like minded dancers?

Chorus:
Where are the escorts,
Where are the escorts for the young girls?
Where are the partners,
Where are the partners for the maidens?

Oh this evening I want to dance
This evening I want to dance.
Might there be escorts for these beauties,
Escorts for these beauties?

Oh this evening I want to dance
This evening I want to dance.
Oh are there companions for the pretty ones,
Companions for the pretty ones?

Oh this evening I want to dance,
This evening I want to dance.
Oh do we find from this village,
Do we find from this village?

Chorus
(My translation)

RECEPTION, AESTHETICS, POLITICS

The challenge to traditional gender roles and the reflection on contemporary relations offered in Värttinä's songs were perhaps reasons why the group achieved popularity. The group was able to present contemporary sentiments within traditional frameworks. Värttinä commanded substantial and positive media coverage and attracted an audience of all ages with all kinds of musical tastes. The *Oi Dai* album sold so well it became a gold record. Since the Ostrobothnian folk fiddler, Konsta Jylhä, these were the first folk musicians to have achieved this kind of popularity, but their success was not representative of interest in folk music generally. The music critic Waldemar Wallenius summed up public understandings regarding the group's success: "Things were right for them, it was the right time, they had the right image, they are women singing women's songs" (Waldemar Wallenius, personal interview, October 4, 1991). Other factors included the ways in which Värttinä expressed a reimagining of the national musical self: "Dance musics with small bands, accordions, and tangos have been marketed as Finnish tradition. Finns have been led to believe that they like melancholic, romantic, sentimental music. It is the image of Finnish people as a resigned nation, resigned to their fate. Actual traditions have been forgotten. Truths that are not truths have been accepted. Everyone seems to believe there has been no traditional music in Finland, or they have a mistaken view of what Finnish music is. Värttinä's music comes as a complete surprise to most Finnish audiences, and this adds to their success. Värttinä is a contrast to this melancholic, sentimental view. They are straight talking, bold, positive.

Now we know that Finnish traditional music is not what it is said to be" (Waldemar Wallenius, personal interview, October 10, 1991).

Some of the straight talking referred to the group's presentation of bold young countrywomen seeking partners (as in "Tumala" and "Mie Tahon Tanssia"). For Wallenius, one of the most important reasons for the group's success was the new representation of Finnish folk music that it provided. Yet Wallenius, like other commentators, believed that this was a representation that revealed an authentic tradition that had been overshadowed by other musical practices. Audiences generally believed that they were "rediscovering" authentic Finnish traditions: "now we know that Finnish traditional music is not what it is said to be," claimed Wallenius. Värttinä filled a musical space in the popular imagination by showing that there was a continuing folk tradition and by providing an alternative image of folk music that, until the 1990s, had focused on the fiddle traditions of West Finland. They were widely regarded as being musicians who had embraced their local folk traditions following the traditional models of folk transmission—a perception that Sari Kaasinen was keen to promote. That the group was in some senses also a product of the training they were undergoing at the Folk Music Department of the Sibelius Academy was neither widely known nor generally advertised. Nevertheless, notions of folk music authenticity joined audience appreciation of "new" sounds. The group's music came as "a surprise." As in the revival movement of the late 1960s, the element of the novel contributed to the group's success.

Although Värttinä's repertoire was drawn from vocal traditions of specific regions, they became an icon, embodying the general view of folk traditions, just as Jylhä's instrumental dance music was representative of folk traditions in the 1960s and 1970s. The group's iconicity can be understood in terms of a mixture of aesthetic judgments and ideological viewpoints. In 1991, Finland was negotiating its relationship with the former USSR, which collapsed in that year, and was suffering from economic difficulties as a result of changes in its domestic economy and the general recession in the West. There were many debates, too, about whether or not Finland should apply for European Community membership, and, if so, under what terms and conditions. This political transformation—the replacement of a neighboring superpower by a Europe of new or reborn states—led to radical changes in Finnish foreign policy. As Häikiö and Pesonen note, a foreign policy based on postwar East-West confrontation was now of little use (Häikiö and Pesonen 1992, 42). This political context contributed to Värttinä's success, since people's musical choices were affected by their awareness of general social processes. Conversely, the music of this group had some bearing on social processes. "Straight talking, bold, positive," Värttinä sing with strong voices and with authority, from a position of power. In their performances, perceptions of self, identity, and relations to others were altered, experienced, and interpreted through sound in a different way. Värttinä epitomized "real" folk music, the real music of the people that had been previously hidden. "What other influences?" retorted Sakari Kukko when I asked about his perceptions of this group. "I don't hear influences in their music. This is pure folk music" (Sakari Kukko, personal communication).

Whereas, according to Wallenius, Finns had formerly thought of themselves as liking "melancholy" music and being "resigned to their fate," this self-image was now regarded as a misconception. Through hearing "real" folk traditions, the attributes and self-images that came to the forefront were those of strength, self-determination, and boldness. Yet this "real" folk music consisted of the incorporation of traditions that are geographically positioned along the eastern frontier.

Värttinä's repertoire of Karelian music was also significant in the context of the debate which took place during the early 1990s concerning whether Finland should reclaim those areas which had been ceded to Russia in the Winter War (1939) and in the Continuation War (1943). This was a public debate in which other musicians, Finnish and Russian, also participated publicly. In the national newspaper, *Helsingin Sanomat,* the music critic Seppo Heikinheimo contributed an article about the views of the Russian cellist Rostropovich, who was undertaking a concert tour, on this issue. The headline announced Rostropovich's comment: "Finland will get Karelia back yet" (Heikinheimo 1992; my translation). Given this political climate, the success of Värttinä provides a striking example of the interplay between aesthetic and ideological considerations. Since the song texts often express a woman's sadness in leaving familiar home landscapes behind, revolving around major themes found in the folk repertory of sorrow and loss, they can be understood as a metaphor for the loss of other kinds of homelands and territories (example 5.5, "Korppi"):

KORPPI

Mikä suuren äänen sorti
Äänen mahtavan makasi
Joka ennen jokena juoksi
Virtana ennen vieri.

Example 5.5: "Korppi": principal melodic material and harmonic outline. (The transcription is based on the recording [Värttinä 1996, track 4].)

Päivä pääskyille tulevi
Varpusille valkenevi
Ilo ilman lintusille
Laulain lentäville.

Chorus:
Laulan suurella surulla
Äänellä alakulolla
Kanna lintu kaihojain
Musta lintu murhettain."

Mikä suuren äänen sorti
Äänen mahtavan makasi
Joka ennen jokena juoksi
Virtana ennen vieri.

Kanna korppi huoliani
Murhettain musta lintu
Oksalle osattomalle
Varvulle varattomalle.

Chorus

Laulaisin taitaisin
Kuin oisin omilla mailla
Suvilinnun suusanoilla
Kesälinnun kielellä.

Laulaisin taitaisin
Kuin oisin omilla mailla
Maassa heinänä helyisin
Kukkana kukoistaisin.

Chorus

EAGLE

What has broken your mighty voice,
What has ravaged your calling

That once flowed like a mighty river
Gushing down toward the sea?

Summer has come for the swifts and swallows,
Dawn risen on the sparrow's nest,
Bringing joy to feathered fledglings,
Causing birds on boughs to sing.

Chorus:
But I, poor creature, sing with sorrow,
In a croaky, creaky voice.
Please, bird, come and take my longing
Black and with a heavy heart.

What has broken your mighty voice
What has ravaged your calling
That once flowed like a mighty river,
Gushing down toward the sea?

Take my sorrows, dearest raven,
Black and with a heavy heart,
Fly them to a distant treetop,
Leave them on a lofty twig.

Chorus

I would sing were I but able,
Were I safe at home again,
Chorus like the birds in springtime,
Sing with tongue like summer birds.

I would sing were I but able,
Were I safe at home again,
Singing like the breeze-bent rushes,
A flower in all my finery.

Chorus

While Värttinä achieved widespread critical acclaim both within Finland and in the world music market, the group's amplified sounds, rock backings, vocal experimentation, and the singers' dynamic range, with an emphasis on the loud, "like the child who was always being told not to sing quite so loud" (Sari Kaasinen cited in Pietilä 1992, 48), have also been critiqued, particularly by those who take a more "purist" view of folk music expression and those who challenge the "authenticity" of new folk music practices. Austerlitz reports that at a Värttinä concert in Michigan, several Finnish-American audience members left early: "the heavy amplification and Värttinä's style, strongly influenced by Balkan music, is a far cry from the Finnish folk music that they came to the concert expecting to hear" (Austerlitz 2000, 183). The group has also been described as "neo-folk" (Järviluoma 2000, 53), as effecting a "neo-Karelianist movement" (Van Elderin 1993, 373), and as a form of neo-Karelianism that is "exoticized and re-cloaked as transnational pop culture" that presents "time-honoured symbols of Finnishness in garb that appealed to post-Cold War urban youth, weaned on hippie interpretations of non-western cultures" (Austerlitz 2000, 197). Many of the Karelian refugees who relocated westward in Finland would disagree with such musical assessments. So too would the group's Finnish "urban youth" listeners, who would not recognize themselves in the above description as having been weaned on "hippie interpretations," and the Finnish audiences of all age groups that I have observed at Scandinavian events in Britain. If Värttinä has been "strongly influenced by Balkan music" (Austerlitz 2000, 183), combine Karelian allusions with Balkan vocal techniques (Van Elderin 1993), and "have taken advantage of very complex rhythmic arrangements mixed with hard nasality which have nothing or little to do with Finno-Ugrian style" (Leisiö cited in Austerlitz 2000, 199), this is part of the new folk music aesthetic that encourages musical experimentation and exchanges, and is also a "reclaimed" singing style that dismisses the more recent vocal production techniques favored by the Lutheran church (Sari Kaasinen cited in Pietilä 1992, 48). Kaasinen insisted on placing the group's musical practice within Karelian and more widely within Finno-Ugric vocal traditions. Following this perspective, I have tried to show in this chapter how Värttinä's repertoires, vocal techniques, and textual imageries are understood by the group and by their audiences and can be analyzed, in relation to traditional expressions from the eastern regions of Finland and from neighboring peoples, even as they draw on a wide musical vocabulary. Interestingly, with regard to reception among Finnish audiences in different contexts, while some Finnish-Americans and Finnish-Australians have felt estranged from Värttinä's style because the group does not conform to their expectations of Finnish folk music (Austerlitz 2000, 199), Finnish-British audiences have greeted this new folk group with the same enthusiasm that had been extended to the folklorist-based group, Nelipolviset in the 1970s.

Within traditional frameworks, Karelian song texts have been understood as both interpreting models of collective experience and of shaping them. Timonen observes that the world described in these songs "provides an outline of the way in which northern Karelians comprehended reality. And conversely: since the lyric songs focus on the self and on fundamental questions of emotional life, the lyric songs carry, in a more direct manner than most other folk genres, messages concerning even the unique experiences of individual singers and their ways of interpreting these experiences" (Timonen 1998, 202). Timonen's comments in relation to nineteenth-century examples, that the contributions of individuals to the songs in the context of broader social changes might influence others' way of experiencing, holds true in the case of the new folk music group Värttinä. The institutional processes of producing specialized folk musicians in the case of Värttinä were overlooked by the group's audiences. In general they were perhaps not important to public understandings of the group. Its performances, rather than the processes of transmission whereby the group's members learned their repertoires, came to the fore in shaping audience reception of Värttinä, in constructing images of folk music, and in reflecting on contemporary political and social realities.

Plate 1: A kantele played by a young musician.

Plate 2: Seppo Paakkunainen playing a *virsikannel* (a bowed kantele used in the accompaniment of church hymns).

Plate 3: The group Pirnales.

Plate 4: Koinurit performing the song "Progelaulu" on "Helsinki Day," 1992.

Plate 5: Dancers at the midsummer celebrations in Seurasaari, Helsinki.

Plate 6: A polka competition at the midsummer celebrations in Seurasaari, Helsinki.

Plate 7: Värttinä. Sari Kaasinen is in the front row on the left.

Plate 8: Interior of Pelimannitalo (the Folk Musicians' House), Folk Music Institute, Kaustinen.

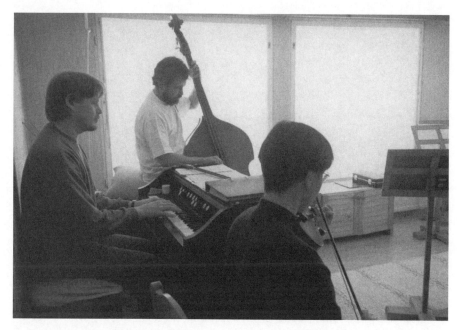

Plate 9: Members of Tallari in rehearsal.

Plate 10: A lecture recital given by Mauno Järvelä (violin) and Timo Alakotila (harmonium) at the Ala-Könni courses, 1992.

Plate 11: Young fiddlers from Kaustinen performing at the Ala-Könni courses, 1992. They are joined by JPP (to the right).

Plate 12: Toivo Alaspää and his grandson demonstrating kantele playing styles at the Ala-Könni courses, 1992.

Plate 13: The main performance arena of the Kaustinen Festival, 1992.

Plate 14: A folk music and dance performance at the Kaustinen Festival, "Roots in Finland," 1992. At the back of the stage is an artwork in two parts representing the disparate branches of Finns around the world (*left*) that have been joined at the festival celebrations (*right*).

Plate 15: A rehearsal of the ballad "Velisurmaaja." *Left to right:* Kimmo Pohjonen, Arto Järvelä, Eric Peltoniemi.

Plate 16: JPP.

Plate 17: A Saami drum.

Plate 18: Badu N'diay (*left*) in performance.

New Folk Music
in a Rural Context

Ennen se oli semmosta ja ny se on tämmöstä
[Before it was like that and now it is like this].
Arto Järvelä

The rural context discussed in this chapter is the village Kaustinen. The importance of the Kaustinen Festival to the revival movement of the late 1960s has already been noted in chapter 3. Folk music activity in this village continues to be significant in arenas extending beyond the region, for, like Helsinki, Kaustinen is a center for new folk music. Any ethnographic account of Finnish new folk music must, therefore, consider folk music making in this context.

There are other reasons, however, for looking at contemporary folk music in the village. Despite the possibilities afforded by access to diverse musics, we have seen how a new folk music group is associated with a specific region although it has developed in the urban center amid, and drawing upon, a variety of musical styles. The links between place and music remain significant in representing folk traditions. Rice relates how he went to Bulgaria with an interest in folk music, which he believed to be the product of "an illiterate or semiliterate rural population" (1994, 21). This was not an unusual view, for folk music has been regarded as a village-based practice. Yet his experience did not match his expectations. He too provides a comparison of folk music in the city and in the village: "In the city I experienced transplanted versions of the village tradition when I watched Gypsy clarinettists and accordionists at hotel weddings and danced to home-made village instruments in restaurants with traditional decors. But I also bought records of Turkish music played by Bulgarian Turks, attended the opera and the symphony, heard English rock bands at stadium concerts, and saw Bulgarian popular singers and jazz musicians on television. The villages, it turned out, were no haven from this modern musical Babylon: all these styles could be heard there on the radio" (21). The village, then, is a musical Babylon just as is the city. Kaustinen is a village in which there are opportunities to hear diverse musics but in which there is also an emphasis on local traditions. This chapter thus examines the continuing significance of the village context to the representation, transmission, and performance of folk music. The interwoven themes of musical continuity and musical Babylon in the rural context to be knitted in this chapter are directly related to one of the central themes of this book: music as a marker of identity where musicians draw on musical ideas from diverse sources.

In the following sketch of my encounter with Finnish new folk music in the village, I first discuss the transmission of folk music at courses organized by the Kaustinen Folk Music Institute. This discussion points to similarities in folk music transmission between the formal educational contexts of the Folk Music Institute and the Sibelius Academy's Department of Folk Music. The focus is then on the 1992 Kaustinen Festival and on one specific performance event: an interpretation of a well-known ballad by Eric Peltoniemi and Hannu Saha. Taking this ballad and the Kaustinen Festival theme for 1992 ("Roots in Finland"), I discuss the ways in which boundaries defining the "local" are stretched and demonstrate that this rural context is as much a meeting place for different musical styles as is the urban center. The Peltoniemi-Saha collaboration stands at a crossroads. History, Finnish identity, and Finnish folk music were invoked by this performance. So too were musical exchanges, shifting identities, and global music trends. In taking this performance event as a point of departure, I explore at a micro level some of the issues that will be developed in later chapters.

FORMAL FOLK MUSIC EDUCATION IN THE VILLAGE OF KAUSTINEN

I first visited Kaustinen on a three-day winter trip, to see the Folk Music Institute and interview those who work there (plate 8). The snow was high. The journey from Helsinki was long. I took a train to Kokkola and then an almost empty bus to Kaustinen. I arrived in the village center, one main road, and booked accommodation on a farm. After dinner, I was given a moonlit tour of the farm and surrounding forest on a horse-drawn sledge.

The following day, I set off for the institute. The Folk Music Institute is a center for Finnish folk music activity: teaching, research, and performance. A database computer system stores all of the archival material held by the institute. This material is substantial. Folk music is notated and put into the archives, sound and video tapes are produced, copies of all articles published in Finland on any theme connected with Finnish folk music are sent to the institute (which held around fifty thousand such clippings in 1992), and information about folk music festivals and recordings is stored there. The institute also publishes studies on folk music and releases commercial sound recordings. It is housed in a traditional wooden building called *Pelimannitalo* (the Folk Musicians' House). In the front room, copper kettles stand by the fireplace, boots hang from the ceiling, and brightly colored rugs adorn the wooden floors.

When I returned to the farm, I asked about life in the village. "You must come during the festival" I was urged. "Kaustinen is completely different." "Are you involved with the festival?" I asked the farm inhabitants. "Oh yes, everyone in Kaustinen has something to do with it." I admired the cows on the farm as I left to return to Helsinki.

Music Education: The Ala-Könni Courses

A few months later, I made the same journey to Kaustinen—this time with my violin in hand. I was joining other hopeful folk players in music courses organized by the Folk Music Institute. Four kinds of courses (named after the folklorist Erkki Ala-Könni) are arranged every summer. These are instrumental courses (kantele, violin, harmonium, and two-row accordion); courses for teachers from nursery school to college level who are often sponsored by their local council or school, designed to give some insight into folk songs and instruments; courses on the construction of instruments; and courses on different musical cultures. In 1991, the courses arranged in the last category gave tuition in French and Swedish accordion music, Scottish Gaelic music (described as "English" and taught by Andy Cronshaw), Cuban music (this was the largest course, with fifteen teachers and around one hundred students), *mbalax* drumming (taught by two Senegalese musicians from the group Asamaan), Estonian music and Russian-Karelian kantele music (Antti Kettunen, education officer of the Folk Music Institute, personal interview, February 26, 1992).

I attended the Ala-Könni courses in June 1992 in the dual role of instrumentalist and researcher, and the following description is presented on general and specific levels to reflect my engagement in the process of learning folk music at the Folk Music Institute courses. The description is interspersed with comments on the teaching methods to illustrate the similarities between the meth-

FIGURE 6.1: ALA-KÖNNI PELIMANNI COURSES
AND ATTENDANCE NUMBERS

Instrument	Number of Students
Folk song	21
Ten-string kantele	19
Two-row accordion	14
Violin	12
Five-string kantele	12
Big kantele	7
Harmonium	6
Mandolin	5

ods of transmission of folk music employed in the Department of Folk Music in Helsinki and the Folk Music Institute in Kaustinen. In both contexts, people from all parts of the country meet in specific institutions for the purpose of "learning" folk music. Whereas the courses offered at the Sibelius Academy are aimed at producing professional performers and teachers, the short courses at the Folk Music Institute are taken for a variety of other reasons, including as a leisure pursuit. Participants commented that they had come to the Ala-Könni courses with the following aims (see fig. 6.1 for musical activity and attendance numbers):

I have been learning the violin at school for eight years but we do not learn folk music. I want to learn to play folk music because I think it is wonderful [*ihana*]. (A twelve-year-old girl from Savo)

I have been to these courses before and I am interested in all aspects of folk music and dance. I began singing folk songs and now I am learning the mandolin. My eldest daughter studies violin at the Sibelius Academy and my second daughter plays the flute, so there is always some music at home. I listen to different kinds of music—world music and opera, too. (A mandolinist from Helsinki)

It is fun to come here and learn how to play some folk music, and it is a holiday at the same time. (A violinist from Helsinki)

It will be useful at work [in a music school] if I can also teach the five- and ten-string kanteles. (A piano teacher from Kotka)

Example 6.1: "Kolan Oskan Polska"

Although the repertoire taught was from different regions, some of the pieces, especially in the violin class, were examples of local styles, and some of the teachers were local musicians who had grown up with these traditions. When we arrived at the Folk Music Institute, an introductory lecture and a concert by Tallari, the state-supported folk music group, were immediately presented (plate 9). After this opening all the students went to separate rooms according to which instrument they played. I joined the violin group, which was taught by Ritva Talvitie and Risto Hotakainen, the violinists of Tallari. Risto Hotakainen is the son of a renowned folk violinist from Ostrobothnia, Otto Hotakainen (1908–90), who was one of the first musicians to be accorded the status of *mestaripelimanni* (master folk musician) at the Kaustinen Festival (together with Konsta Jylhä, Kustaa Järvinen, and Tuure Niskanen).

Sitting in a semicircle with music stands in front of us, we were a group of mixed ability. The first piece we played was "Kolan Oskan Polska" (example 6.1). It was played at a slow tempo, two bars at a time, until everyone could play the notes. We discussed playing as an ensemble and listening to each other, rhythm, bowing styles, phrasing, and ornamentation. Later on, each student had short individual sessions (of about fifteen minutes) with both Talvitie and Hotakainen. At these sessions they were able to give attention to those with technical difficulties, and to discuss some more elaborate notions with others. The bowing style—playing in the middle of the bow and using very small movements—was stressed above all. The way in which the bow was used helped to maintain rhythmic consistency and unity for the group.

My initial reaction was that this class was not dissimilar to group work which I had undertaken in my training as a "classical" violinist, in terms of the attention and discussion devoted to technical and musical aspects, reading from the musical score and writing phrasings, bowings, and fingerings. The biggest dif-

Example 6.2: "Rahapolska"

ference was in the use of the bow. In "Kolan Oskan Polska," we were not asked to play with smooth, legato movements, but to feel rhythmic accents with each slur marked.

Bowing style was an important focus throughout the course. Talvitie talked about different playing styles in relation to bowing techniques. Hotakainen demonstrated how the same "piece" could sound different using a variety of bowings and ornaments. He commented that notation can look "cold" (*kylmä*) and that each player must approach the music with his or her own style. Experimenting with such violin techniques, we gained insights into the various playing methods developed by "master fiddlers" that have come to define individual and regional styles (Ling 1997, 154). One piece with which we tried different bowings was "Rahapolska" (example 6.2). The performance style we practiced was from a village fifty kilometers from Kaustinen. The bow had to be kept on the string all the time and we were told not to use any left-hand vibrato.

As well as practicing violin techniques and rehearsing repertoires played on this instrument, the violin groups collaborated with other groups, which gave everyone an opportunity to see what was taking place in different classes and to play with different ensembles. I joined Talvitie, who was coaching as well as playing with three singers and a harmonium player in a session of sight-reading. One of the scores from which we worked was the song "Halikon Markkinat" (example 6.3). It was learned through repetition of short phrases, with attention being given to achieving balance between the parts (for example, a solid harmonium bass foundation), rehearsal of individual parts, and attention to ensemble coordination.

Other joint activities included attending a lecture recital given by Mauno Järvelä and Timo Alakotila (of JPP; see chap. 7), for participants in the violin,

Example 6.3: "Halikon Markkinat"

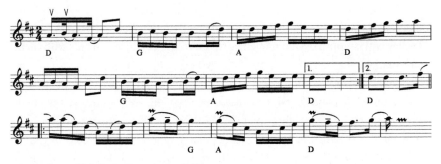

Example 6.4: "Maalarin Franssin Sottiisi"

harmonium, accordion, and mandolin courses (plate 10). The violinists' lessons that morning were then taken by Mauno. A piece, "Maalarin Franssin Sottiisi," was learned first by ear, with rehearsal of bow articulations, and then from notation (example 6.4). In the evening the violin group joined Mauno's violin students from Kaustinen (plate 11) in a performance of some of the pieces we had studied during the day (examples 6.5 and 6.6). Other groups that performed that evening were Tallari, Salamakannel, Pinnin Pojat (Arto Järvelä and Kimmo Pohjonen), and JPP, who ended the evening's performances with a dance session. All of them have a connection to Kaustinen. All of them play new folk music. Their repertoires are "new" but also deeply rooted in local traditions.[1]

Visiting the mandolin and folk song classes, I noted that the teaching methods were similar to those of the violin class—repetition, working from notation, and playing or singing together as an ensemble. Heikki Lahti's mandolin group worked on a Greek piece and then played some Finnish violin pieces.

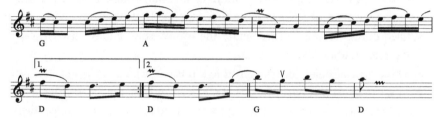

Example 6.5: "Johanneksen Polkka"

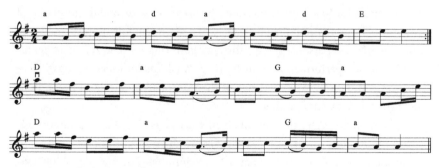

Example 6.6: "Schottis från Övermark"

Example 6.7: Fragment from an Ingrian folk song

Lahti told me that they play many violin pieces because the strings are tuned to the same pitches. Anna-Kaisa Liedes was working on an Ingrian folk song as I joined her class (example 6.7).

Hannu Saha gave a lecture about different kanteles and playing styles. He talked about the history of the kantele but emphasized that these were "living traditions." Several players gave demonstrations, including the *mestaripelimanni* Toivo Alaspää and his grandson (plate 12). Discussions about the aesthetics and history of folk music traditions, as well as advice about aspects of performance, were features common to all the classes. Other highlights of these few days included visits to a workshop with the kantele group to see the construction of kanteles, to Konsta Jylhä's house, and to the museum of folk instruments and an end-of-course concert demonstrating what kinds of repertoires had been studied during the week. Throughout the course, connections between past and present traditions were stressed.

Three general points in relation to folk music teaching at the Folk Music Institute in Kaustinen can be made here. First, if we compare the teaching material (examples 6.1–6.7) to the examples presented in chapter 4, it is clear that the transmission of folk music and the teaching methods at these courses in Kaustinen are similar to those of the Folk Department in Helsinki. The specialized contexts for folk music education, the use of notation and the ideal of oral tradition, the bonds described between past and present folk music activity, the addition of one's personal stamp (through performance style and ornamentation), and the performance contexts (in formal, institutional settings), were features common to my experience of the transmission of folk music in both the urban and the rural setting.

Second, in the violin class, as much emphasis was placed on local traditions as on innovations in contemporary practice. Questions of interpretation and technical aspects of local performance styles dominated my individual folk violin sessions ("a long sound," "no gap between the notes," "bow on the string," "in the middle of the bow," " a little accent," "no stopping," "a short first note," "more speed"). So important is the question of style that Hannu Saha identifies this as one of the principle areas in constructing musical difference: "The style is maybe the most important thing when we are talking about folk music. We have different styles—regional, local, personal, and so on. If we look for the 'Finnish' element in music, we must research style. It is not so much those tunes and so on, but playing styles. Not deep structures but surface structures—embellishments, decorations, those kinds of things" (Hannu Saha, personal interview, April 13, 1992). Despite the emphasis on different playing styles and the attempt to transmit these differences in the violin class, the methods of transmission, with notation, group, and individual work, and the combinations of different instruments produce changes. Cooke's observation with regard to the fiddle tradition of the Shetland Islands that "stylistic differences belong today to the older fiddlers" (1986, 128) is pertinent to the example discussed here. The different styles that are learned by students at the Ala-Könni courses are likely to be personal only in that they are individual interpretations of the formal folk music learning experience.

The third point is that the similarities noted here between the two institutions (the Sibelius Academy and the Folk Music Institute in Kaustinen) center on the provision of a formal folk music education. Yet there is also an important difference between the two contexts that marks out "new folk music" as a sphere of "professional" music making. The courses offered at the Folk Music Institute are open to any interested participant. The levels of ability vary from those at beginning stages to those who may wish to use their acquired skills in a professional capacity. The courses offered at the Sibelius Academy are open to students only on the basis of competitive selection through auditions. The tensions that arise from distinctions such as "amateur" and "professional" and between "folk" and "new folk" have been played out further at the Kaustinen Festival. The festival provides new folk musicians with one of their biggest platforms outside Helsinki, and they attract a lot of media attention. Nowadays, the older festival musicians feel marginalized with the rise of young new folk music practitioners, commenting to me that ten to fifteen years ago there were not so many young players. Aware of the trends toward privileging the musical experiences and activities of new folk musicians, one journalist covering the 1992 Kaustinen Festival decided to highlight the music making of those who do not usually gain media coverage (Pirkko Kotirinta, personal communication, July 1992). She wrote a feature on a ninety-two-year-old singer, Martta Pulli, who had been to the festival twenty-two times. Her showpieces are long ballads that she had learned from her mother. Usually she sings for herself, not for an audience, claiming, "And I am glad of that . . . when I sing at home I do not disturb others!" (Pulli cited in Kotirinta 1992; my translation).

THE KAUSTINEN FESTIVAL:
"ROOTS IN FINLAND" 1992

Background

In Helsinki, an involvement with new folk music is largely determined by individual choice. Most of Kaustinen's inhabitants (approximately forty-five hundred), by contrast, are involved, through the Kaustinen Festival, with this particular music. Involvement with the festival takes the form of either performing or working on running it and providing accommodation for visitors.

The festival is important to the every day life of the village in terms of economic as well as artistic returns. The festival season generates more income than the Christmas season. The revenue generated by the nine-day festival is twenty-five million Finnish marks in Kaustinen alone, and eighty million Finnish marks in the district—an income largely derived from the use of public services such as food shops, markets, and restaurants. The commercial success of the festival has been an important factor in the decision to continue staging this event. While a small state grant is awarded to the project, such is its current success that 65–70 percent of the festival budget is generated by ticket sales (Jyrki Heiskanen, festival organizer, personal communication, 1992; the figure is for the 1991 festival).

Individual patronage, state support, audience attendance, administrative efforts including publicity, funding, and the provision of facilities for performers and audiences have all contributed to strengthening the Kaustinen Festival's position as a focal point for folk music activity. The festival is therefore as important as a new folk music performance context as it is to general village life. It provides one of the main forums for the performance of new folk music, and the interest that is raised in this contemporary genre is indicated by the sales of the magazine *Uusi Kansanmusiikki (New Folk Music)*, which increase twofold during the festival. Five thousand copies are sold during the festival, compared to half that number for each usual issue (Martti Heikkilä, managing editor, personal communication; figures from 1991).

Bohlman's analysis of the folk festival as an example of a setting in which folk music "is most actively nurtured" but in which "the juxtaposition of style and ethnic group [is] most dramatic" (1988, 124) is an apt description of the

Kaustinen Festival, which attracts performers (many of whom go on a voluntary or expenses-only basis) and audiences from all over Finland and elsewhere. Performers are invited so that a roughly equal number represent "traditional" Finnish folk music, Finnish "new folk" music, and "world" music (Jyrki Heiskanen, festival organizer, personal communication). This is a policy that accords with ideas about what the festival should be from its inception—as an "international" celebration of folk music (Viljo Määttälä, personal interview, August 22, 1992). While a vast array of musics can be heard, the festival has given Kaustinen a reputation as a village in which rich musical traditions also continue to be performed. They are, moreover, local traditions whose performers are ranked on a par with those of musical traditions worldwide. The festival context invites such comparison. In bringing together musics that are categorized as stemming from local, national, or global arenas, the boundaries between them are explored in a public music display (plate 13). As well as distinguishing between Finnish traditional music, Finnish new folk music, and world music, Heiskanen's categorization is one that draws a boundary between "our" and "their" music, highlights nationalist associations, and furthers dualistic us-versus-other representations of cultural activity and identity.

Performers are invited according to the specific "theme" of the year's festival, which was "Roots in Finland" in 1992 (plate 14). Working with this theme, the Kaustinen Festival contributed to a wider national celebration of seventy-five years of Finnish independence and of Finnish identity around the world. Several festivals nationwide explored the theme "Roots in Finland" and offered "Finns" outside of Finland an opportunity to express and display their sense of affiliation with Finland, and for Finns to recognize their compatriots abroad. In Kaustinen, while the 1992 festival theme apparently focused on "Finnish" music, it was nevertheless "our" music around the world. Some of the performances that were given under the rubric "Roots in Finland" thus held an ambiguous status between the categories of "ours" and "theirs" and were illustrative of the dialectical relationship between the local and the global. One such performance was Eric Peltoniemi and Hannu Saha's rendition of the ballad "Velisurmaaja." Focusing on this performance event is an exploration of the boundaries between local and nonlocal. Notions of "folk" and "world" music are rendered problematic. Despite the role it plays in celebrating a specific cultural identity, Finnish new folk music in the musical mosaic of the Kaustinen Festival is revealed as conforming to global trends and borrowing from the traditions of "others" as much as it maintains a distinctive character.

Roots in Finland? Exploring Musical Boundaries
in a Performance of "Velisurmaaja"

Eric Peltoniemi is an American musician. He was one of the performers at the festival who had been specially invited as part of the "Roots in Finland" theme. He was joined by the folklorist Hannu Saha for a performance of the ballad "Velisurmaaja" ("Brother Slayer"; example 6.8) on the stage of Suomi-talo (Finland House), in front of an audience consisting mainly of Finnish-Americans. Saha's role was to improvise on the kantele, along with Peltoniemi's rendition of the ballad with guitar accompaniment.

Example 6.8: "Velisurmaaja": transcription of voice melody. (The transcription is based on Eric Peltoniemi's recorded performance [Peltoniemi 1992, side B].)

VELISURMAAJA

Mistäs tulet,
kustas tulet,
poikani iloinen?
Meren rannalta,
meren rannalta,
äitini kultainen.

Mitä sieltä tekemästä
poikani iloinen?
Hevostani juottamasta,
äitini kultainen.

Mist'on miekkasi
vereen tullut,
poikani poloinen?
Pistin veljeni kuoliaaksi,
äitini kultainen.

Minne nyt sinä itse jou'ut,
poikani poloinen?
Muille maille vierahille,
äitini kultainen.

BROTHER SLAYER

Where are you coming from,
Whence do you come
My cheerful son?
From the shore of the sea,
From the shore of the sea,
Mother dear.

What were you doing there,
My cheerful son?
Watering my horse,
Mother dear.

Where did the blood
On your sword come from,
My poor son?
I stabbed my brother dead,
Mother dear.

Where will you betake yourself now,
Wretched son?
To foreign lands abroad,
Mother dear.

Ballad themes appear all over Europe and are said to have begun to arrive in Finland toward the end of the fifteenth century. The ballad plot often unfolds as a dramatic dialogue (between mother and son in the case of "Velisurmaaja") that ends tragically, usually in the death of the protagonists. "Velisurmaaja" is one of the best-known folk ballads in Finland and has a wide distribution, having been published in nineteenth-century broadsheets (the earliest in 1809), in the *Kanteletar* (1840), and in songbooks of the twentieth century. It is a folk ballad sung in Britain as well as in Scandinavia whose origin is unclear (Asplund 1981d).

Due to the popularity of this ballad in Finland, and to Saha's interest as a researcher in folk music, it is not surprising that he is familiar with it. Peltoniemi, a fourth-generation Finnish-American, has also been involved with this ballad from a young age. Describing how he became interested in Finnish music, he said:

> I began playing guitar. I was visiting my grandmother's house and she had been a string band musician back in the early part of this century in Minnesota [she was from Edinburgh and used to play "Scottish-American" music]. She had not played for years, but I was looking under her bed one day and I found the guitar. She gave it to me and I began to play, I guess regular American music [country and western, rock, blues]. But the community I lived in was half Finnish, and the music store in town imported records for them. I was down there one day and listened to a record from Finland. It was a popular Tapio Rautavaara, and it had a great cover on it, so I bought it and immediately loved it and began playing it. I suppose I was about twelve years old—I had had some exposure to Finnish music beforehand through a song book . . . where I learned the song "Velisurmaaja" . . . "Velisurmaaja" was the first Finnish song I ever learned to sing. Then I began to learn other songs in that book. It was really when I heard that Tapio Rautavaara that I really began to get an interest. Then my brother and I would, every time a new record arrived in town, we would buy it. (Eric Peltoniemi, personal interview, July 20, 1992)

In front of an audience mostly of Finnish-Americans, the song text of "Velisurmaaja" was poignant, narrating the tale of the son who must travel to foreign lands. Until recently, Finland has been a country of emigration rather than immigration. There were two waves of emigration, before (1880s–1930s) and after the Second World War. From the 1880s to the 1930s, Finns moving to America formed the largest group of emigrants, and many of them originated in Ostrobothnia. About 120,000 Ostrobothnians migrated to America, and although nearly one-third returned to Finland, the migration figures for this region were higher than for other Finnish regions.[2] It was thus appropriate that the International Festival of Folk Music in Kaustinen, central Ostrobothnia, should explore the 1992 theme of "Roots in Finland." The event was significant in the local context, since the festival itself was celebrating its twenty-fifth anniversary. Many expatriate Finnish performers, mostly from America, had been invited to appear at the festival, and the Suomi-talo was the main venue for their folk music and dance performances. These performances demonstrated the extent to which Finnish traditions (including music, dance, costume, and language) had been maintained by people settling across the Atlantic. The connection to Finland felt by Finnish-Americans through aspects of their cultural heritage was one apparent feature of these performances.

Despite the emphasis on the preservation of tradition, the kinds of traditions that Finnish-Americans presented on the stage of Suomi-talo provided a useful comparison in also examining change. New folk musicians, with their emphasis on musical creativity, producing one's own original compositions, and arranging material from the folk canon in different ways, were more interested, in contrast to some of the migrant communities, in hearing how musical traditions have changed than how they have been preserved. Eric Peltoniemi drew attention to the differences in the reception to his interpretations of Finnish folk music:

> When I have played Finnish folk music in the U.S [to Finnish-American communities] it hasn't been very well received—for the same reason the language hasn't changed much. They really don't like to see you shaking the tree too much. It is a feeling of security when you hear the songs exactly the same every time and it's sort of sacrilegious to change these songs too much. I guess I had a sort of inferiority complex about singing them. When these guys [the Finnish research team—see below] came on the trip and asked me to sing, I was very wary of doing so. I'm sort of in a state of shock that they really loved it and they kept asking me for more. . . . It sort of validated my experience. (Eric Peltoniemi, personal interview, July 20, 1992)

Arto Järvelä and Kimmo Pohjonen were also interested in Peltoniemi's performance. They improvised with him in rehearsals and performances which included "Velisurmaaja" and remarked that what they really liked about his version was his harmonization of the ballad, different from the one with which they were familiar (plate 15). Peltoniemi had arranged his own harmonies to the ballad, since the songbook from which he learned it presented only the melodic line and the accompanying text. His performance of the song was a reconstruction based on incomplete knowledge of the tradition. In most of the songs he plays, however, he does see models of harmonic procedures, for a piano accompaniment is usually provided. Yet he claims that he consciously tries not to use these harmonizations. He takes elements of the song, those which are perhaps most easily recognizable, such as the melody and text, and adds other parts. This way of working gives him a sense of creating something and not just reproducing it:

> When I play I just relate to the text and the melody. I want to take the melody and harmonize it myself and I begin to change the melody a little bit too because I figure it's the only way I can make anything my own. (Eric Peltoniemi, personal interview, July 20, 1992)

For Peltoniemi, a sense of affinity with Finland has grown through his involvement with Finnish music. His knowledge of Finnish folk musical traditions, however, has not been gained in community performance contexts in which these traditions continued to be transmitted. He has learned by listening to records and by playing from songbooks. He developed an interest in Finnish folk traditions through coming into contact with Finnish popular songs (especially those sung by Tapio Rautavaara). Many of those songs were composed by Toivo Kärki and informed by his interest in folk traditions:

> Our family is originally Laestadian, which is a strict [religious] sect from the north of Finland, and they were against dancing and music unless it was spiritual music. So there wasn't a lot of Finnish folk music at the grassroots level where we grew up. The only people who played any instruments were a group who were communists, not religious, so they were the only musicians—communists and socialists of various types. We didn't hear too much firsthand, we got it all from listening to records and then we started playing from song books, learning songs. . . . It was kind of the popular music of Finland in the late fifties and early sixties. Although Toivo Kärki was pretty influenced by folk music, especially Karelian folk music. There was a folk element to everything he wrote. Tapio Rautavaara mostly sang Toivo Kärki's songs, so it kind of gave us a good feeling. I mean, some songs, which later became popular here in the folk music movement, Tapio had actually sung years before. So we got a pretty good education from those records. (Eric Peltoniemi, personal interview, July 20, 1992)

New folk musicians regard the way in which Peltoniemi performs as being completely within the tradition. Folk musicians have always added their own personal stamp, by adapting and rearranging the songs and texts, and by improvising. Peltoniemi's personal stamp on his interpretation of Finnish ballads has been influenced by his work with an American blues singer, and by the way in which he learned ballad singing from a Scottish grandmother. He thus interprets a ballad in Finnish by drawing upon a knowledge of ballad traditions from different European sources. Although he performed at the Kaustinen Festival as a Finnish-American, Peltoniemi spoke about different strands, "adding another piece of meat to the family stew," which have shaped both his musical development and his sense of identity. He talked about his Finnish father and Swedish mother; the way in which his sister identifies more closely with her Swedish "roots" while he and his brother feel more affinity with their Finnish ancestry; his interest in Saami culture and his suspicions that some of his grandparents were Saami rather than Finnish, since they have traced their "hometown" to Kemijärvi, in Finnish Lapland; his Scottish grandmother, from whom he believes he inherited his musical ability; and overshadowing all these considerations, his interest in American folk, blues, and rock music and his role as an American musician.

The performance of Peltoniemi and Saha at the festival was given after a short rehearsal but was not based on only a brief collaboration. Saha had been part of a Finnish research team that undertook fieldwork in the United States looking at the development of Finnish traditions in Finnish-American communities. It was during this research trip that he first met Peltoniemi and heard him sing. He was so enthusiastic about Peltoniemi's performance that it was later recorded in Finland for Eino, one of Finland's small record companies (see chap. 9) and circulated to different radio programs. The research team in the United States had three principal aims. First, they wanted to examine the history of Finnish musical traditions in America. In some cases these traditions are quite new and are connected to the history of the recording industry. Records from Finland began to be circulated in America during the 1920s and 1930s, and much Finnish-American music is a reflection of what has been learned from records and is therefore in the style of this recorded music. Records from the 1950s and 1960s and singers such as Tapio Rautavaara in particular were influential. Peltoniemi's introduction to, and experience of, Finnish music is thus shared with others. The second aim was to study "music as folklorism," which describes how Finnish-Americans study and reproduce old traditions, forming instrumental groups for kantele and jouhikko and learning folk dances. The third aim, and the one which some of the researchers considered most interesting, was to look at the creative use of symbols of "Finnishness" in the composition of entirely new works. Peltoniemi is an example of "a creative artist with his own musical thinking" (Hannu Saha, personal communication). He has an interest in his Finnish roots, and as a musician he expresses this through his own songs using "strong" symbols such as "sauna" and "*Kalevala*." Peltoniemi himself spoke of the significance of these symbols:

> My father pretty much raised my brother and I . . . with the *Kalevala* and *Kalevala* tradition. Even though it was in English, we were very conversant with everything from the *Kalevala*. We knew all the stories, names of the heroes, and all the things that they did. My father didn't really speak Finnish but he was very proud of the *Kalevala*. (Eric Peltoniemi, personal interview, July 20, 1992)

Saha perceives Peltoniemi's original compositions as "American music, which have a symbolic connection to Finnish culture" (Hannu Saha, personal communication). Several layers of difference, then, are perceived in the repertoire of an individual performer. If Peltoniemi's own compositions are regarded as being "different" (American and nonlocal) but having a symbolic connection to Finnish culture, his interpretations of well-known songs in the Finnish folk canon are considered to be in accordance with traditional practice despite any "changes" he may have introduced.

The 1992 Kaustinen Festival provided a venue for Finnish-Americans to express their Finnish identity, to celebrate their connection to their ancestral land, and to demonstrate the ways in which they still continue to receive influences from Finland. Such celebrations are also held annually in the United States, known as "Finnfests." In Finland, in the festival context, the "Finnish" part of their identity was brought to the forefront even though individuals may operate with a number of alternative, coexisting identities, as was seen in the case of Peltoniemi.

The process of receiving influences has not been unidirectional, from Finland to America. Peltoniemi is one of the Finnish-Americans who can be heard through records and on the radio in Finland, and his Finnish counter-

Example 6.9: "Lännen Lokari" (extract)

parts have critically assessed his performances with enthusiasm. Songs written by the Finnish-American songwriter Hiski Salomaa (1891–1957) have also exerted an influence on Finnish folk music performances. Some of his most popular songs are reinterpreted and performed by one of the most prominent of the Finnish new folk music groups, Koinurit. Thus, Finnish-American compositions have become an integral part of the Finnish new folk music recorded canon. One of Hiski Salomaa's songs, "Lännen Lokari" (example 6.9), was performed both by Koinurit and by Finnish-American groups at the Kaustinen Festival.[3]

One of Koinurit's most successful songs, "Progelaulu" (Koinurit 1990, track 13) addresses the experience of Finnish migration to America and can be regarded as being closely related to Hiski Salomaa's texts although its source lies in the repertoire of Finnish *rekilaulut* (sledge songs). Sledge songs were usually four-line verses with rhyming endings of two syllables. The genre is said to be

based on German song repertoires and to date from the late seventeenth
century in Finland, flourishing during the eighteenth century (Asplund 1981b,
95). Arto Järvelä commented on how the band worked on this song: " 'Progelaulu' is Koinurit's own piece (stolen a bit from tradition really). It stems from
an old sledge song from Kauhava: "Has your paper got soaked . . ." In the sledge
songs there has always been the habit of mixing old with new lines. The text is
Rantanen's, the vocal soloist's, own. The majority of the text is really also found
in songbooks of Kauhava. 'Progelaulu' (Koinurit's version) does not have a musical score because the arrangement was conceived in playing" (Arto Järvelä,
personal communication).[4] "Progelaulu" is built on a series of ostinato patterns
introduced first on the accordion. With the entry of the voice a bass figure is
added, and then guitar and mandolin stabs elaborate the harmonic outline (example 6.10). An instrumental bridge with mandolin solo and walking bass part
builds to the climax by introducing more syncopation and increasing dynamic
levels. A sudden and dramatic pause leads to the return of the voice. The song
is one of the longest (5 minutes, 22 seconds) in Koinurit's recorded repertoire
and is an exploration of textural and rhythmic repetition and contrast in ternary form.

PROGELAULU

Amerikkalaisen laivan pääll on lippu liehuvane,
ja hulivilipojan luonto on kuin koski kuohuvane.
Ja onko sinun paperisi kastunu vai miks et ole kirjoittanu,
vai onko sulla muita salatuita friijareita joit et ole ilmottanu.
Kulkuri poika se vierellä tietä näki aukeevan orvokin kukan,
sitä kattella vaan ei omistaa oli kulkuri poijalla lupa.
Ja suru on syrämmessä syvemmällä vaikka iloselta mä näytän,
ja maailman tähren ja flikkojen nähren näin rennosti itteni käytän.

Älä sinä flikka sinisiä silmiäsi itkulla rasittele,
älä sinä tälläsen haljun perähän vuosia voivottele.
Olut on kaikki ryypätty ja lasit on lyöty rikki,
ja taisimpa elää hurjasti kun heilaniki itki.
Kyllä minä rinkissä retkuttelen vaikka oon näin saatanan pieni,
ja lyökää nyt perkele puukolla selkään jos teidän tekee mieli.

Example 6.10: "Progelaulu": transcription of musical features

PROGELAULU

On the ship to America there is a flag flying
And this rascal boy's character is like a surge of the rapids
And have your papers got wet or why have you not written,
Or do you have other secret lovers whom you have not declared.
Rascal boy by the roadside saw a violet blossoming
Only to look and not to own rascal boy had permission.
And sorrow is deep in the heart although I look happy,
And because of the world and in front of the girls in this casual way
    I move.

Do not you girl your blue eyes strain with crying,
Do not after this sort of fool for years moan.
The beer is all drunk and the glasses are broken
And I must have lived wildly since my girlfriend cried.
In a circle I am tramping so although I am so damn small
And you devils stab me with a knife in the back if you so desire.

(My translation)

FROM FIVE STRINGS TO ELECTRIC MODELS

The kantele operates as a powerful symbol in representing "identity." When Hannu Saha joined Eric Peltoniemi for the performance of "Velisurmaaja" on the stage of the Suomi-talo, his use of the five-string kantele contributed multiple layers of symbolic resonances for both the Finnish and Finnish-American audience. The musical instrument as a material object with particular sonic qualities, rather than song texts with their overt references, evoked a sense of Finnishness in this case. Symbols like the kantele forge a link with a collective and personal past and retain their contemporary relevance through a constant reinterpretation and reconstitution of the meanings that are attached to them. While the use of the guitar in Finnish folk music is recent, the appearance of the kantele in Peltoniemi's and Saha's performance could be read as a reminder of an ancient heritage and, in the context of the Kaustinen Festival, of acclaimed local exponents such as Kreeta Haapasalo. The timbral combination of kantele and guitar therefore seems to be a juxtaposition of the old and the new. Yet the kantele, as used by Saha in this performance of "Velisurmaaja" as a symbol of an ancient heritage, has itself been reinterpreted. During the 1920s, for example, Paul Salminen developed a modern kantele, with a lever mechanism so that accidentals could be played. This instrument generally has thirty-six strings.

Since there have been many different structural changes to the instrument, Rahkonen has identified the concept of kantele as problematic: "This problem is much more complex than it appears on the surface because the kantele does not exist in one form, rather, it exists in a number of different forms. . . . The concept [of kantele] grew to include the new styles as they were invented, while at the same time the old styles continued to be recognized as kanteles. The changes which occurred in the structure of the kantele produced a smooth and continuous broadening of the kantele concept" (Rahkonen 1983, 239). Rahkonen turns to the notion of ultrastability ("the capacity of a system to adjust to a changing environment and at the same time remain a unique, coherent entity"; 239) to account for variation in the structure of the instrument but stability in the kantele concept. At the time he wrote, it seemed to Rahkonen that the kantele had reached its limit of ultrastability. He noted the most recent changes in kantele structure but remained unsure of whether these latest variations would be incorporated into the kantele concept: "changes just on the horizon are electric kanteles and fully chromatic kanteles which were seen for the first time this summer at the Kaustinen Folk Music Festival. It remains to be seen if such changes will be eventually accepted into the kantele concept, thus broadening it further, or if they remain outside the kantele concept as experimental" (1983, 241).

The electric kantele to which Rahkonen refers has indeed become accepted in the kantele concept and is played by the new folk music group Salamakannel (Lightning Kantele), loosely based in Kaustinen. The group plays "new wave folk music," according to its publicity material. It experiments with new constructions of the kantele and was formed in 1982 to test the invention, the electric kantele, of one of its members—the guitarist (acoustic and electric) Jussi Ala-Kuha. Other members of the group are Hannu Saha (who plays the five-, nine-, ten-, and thirty-six-stringed kanteles, harmonica, and tin whistle), Kimmo Känsälä (bass), and Arto Järvelä (fiddle, mandolin, and five-stringed kantele).

Rahkonen's concern with variation in instrumental structure but stability in concept is closely related to issues of musical continuity and change in Finnish new folk music. To what extent can either the kantele or Finnish folk music change yet remain recognizable and acknowledged as belonging to a specific tradition? In his study of the changing kantele, Rahkonen argues that there are limits to the ultrastable system and that discontinuous or abrupt change can lead to breakdown and the formation of a new system. It is difficult, nevertheless, for the observer of contemporary developments to assess when a sense of continuity will be lost. The electric kantele seemed as if it might go beyond the boundary of the kantele concept, but it did not, and it has been comfortably accommodated within the tradition of Finnish (new) folk music.

Salamakannel's publicity material specifies that they are not a band for "purists," and in their recorded arrangements of Finnish folk melodies the influence of American folk, bluegrass, and string band music is accentuated by the inclusion of the banjo, played by a guest member, Seppo Sillanpää (Salamakannel 1989). These are musical ideas that stem in part from interest in folk-rock movements of the 1960s, from the global influence of African-American music, and from the domination of the American music industry (Small 1987). But musicians do not always consciously search for musical ideas from external sources. As Saha noted, "We are not trying to get influences at all. We play Finnish folk music and we play Salamakannel music. Those musicians have been playing many kinds of music in their careers—rock and folk. When we make arrangements for Salamakannel, we just play. We try to play folk music and Salamakannel music. As you know, I have been interested in late sixties folk-rock and the folk revival. I have also been interested in American folk music. In my first band, Mummi Kutoo [Granny is Knitting], we played our own music with a lot of influences from American folk music. If you have played those kinds of musics before, I think that some elements of course remain in your musicianship" (Hannu Saha, personal interview, April 13, 1992).

Saha's comment is indicative of widely held views. New folk musicians generally regard influences from other musical sources as inevitable, and indeed to be encouraged. For Saha, changes in the transmission and performance of folk music with each generation make this a "living tradition." Such reconstitution is affected by the prevailing notions and trends of each era, and the production of new folk music is shaped by contemporary influences: "by global pop norms and values" (whereby the boundary between folk and popular music must be reassessed) and "by the way in which the twentieth-century mass media (the electronic means of musical production, reproduction and transmission) have created a universal pop aesthetic" (Frith 1989, 2).

Once a symbol of an ancient, shared heritage which would draw people together and shape a nation, the kantele, as the "national" instrument is now established as one of the symbols of "Finnish" identity. Changes in the construction of the instrument itself, and differences in its use (as an accompaniment to a solo voice, or as part of a band), reflect the adaptability of the kantele as a symbolic vehicle in changing contexts, and the ability of people to attribute different meanings to the instrument. It is not just the transient nature of musical sound that lends itself to reinterpretation. In the case of the electric kantele, it is the musical instrument itself, as a fixed material object operating as a symbol in representing a Finnish culture or identity, which is subject to reconstitution.

That successive generations reconstruct the past as well as symbols of the past is a process of revision that Yung (1987), adopting a diachronic and intra-cultural approach to the study of changing traditions, calls "historical interdependency." Thus, the kantele may, as it is claimed, be an ancient instrument, but its significance as such is a contemporary construct and its repertoire can be either old or new. New compositions and the reinterpretation of existing ones conform to present-day aesthetic sensibilities, but at the same time present-day perceptions of the past mean that today's kantele repertoire seems to follow an established tradition, one which permits and even expects change.

By incorporating influences from American folk, folk-rock, bluegrass, and string band music in his interpretations of Finnish folk music, Hannu Saha was able to forge other points of contact with the Finnish-American musician Eric Peltoniemi. The Peltoniemi-Saha collaboration was thus a meeting of general aesthetic, symbolic, and musical sensibilities in which both musicians drew upon familiar repertoire and shared an interest in using the traditional material creatively. Their performance of "Velisurmaaja" contributed to the festival celebration of Finnish identity, but it was an interpretation of the ballad that also revealed interdependent relations between past and present and between local and nonlocal. The festival theme, "Roots in Finland," with its evocations of longevity, roots in the past, the Finnish landscape, and the transplanting of tradition, is called into question. Peltoniemi and Saha's performance may have been one readily identified as Finnish new folk music (a novel treatment of a familiar folk ballad), but it was a performance which did not fall neatly onto either side of the musical boundary between "ours" and "theirs" which so broadly demarcates differences between music represented as "folk" and as "world."

SEVEN

A Family of Folk Musicians

THE JÄRVELÄS

In Kaustinen there is a saying: People do say that here there are only musicians or horsemen, or some say that here there are only musicians or fools (Arto Järvelä, personal communication).[1] Histories of local music making in rural contexts contribute to musicians' sense of folk musical continuity. In Kaustinen, these histories center on musical biographies and on the repertoires of Ostrobothnian fiddling traditions in particular.[2] While fiddlers are found throughout Finland, gathering in a variety of rural and urban contexts to form (usually) amateur pelimanni groups, the folk fiddler from Kaustinen, Konsta Jylhä (1910–84), played a central role in drawing attention to fiddle practice in Ostrobothnia during the folk revival movement of the 1960s onward.

In this chapter, intertwining musical biographies, historical narratives, and images of locality are explored in relation to the new folk music group JPP (an abbreviation of Järvelän Pikkupelimannit, "Järvelä's Little Fiddlers"). The discussion on JPP explores new folk music treatments of Ostrobothnian fiddle traditions. In turning to the repertoire, compositions, and performances of this ensemble, considered in relation to pelimanni practice from the seventeenth century onward, the ways in which JPP adheres to and departs from traditional models will be highlighted. The discussion addresses questions about the traditional social contexts of Finnish fiddle performance, the ways in which fiddlers learned their repertoires, the major stylistic trends, and the content of fiddle repertoires. This chapter looks at the ways in which Finnish folk fiddlers have always engaged with and drawn on musical models from a variety of sources, thus further probing the shifting intersections of local and global spaces. Before turning to JPP, a historical perspective on fiddling in Finland is outlined to provide a contextual framework within which the ensemble's practice may be analyzed.

THE FIDDLE IN FINLAND: A HISTORICAL PERSPECTIVE

Narratives on Finnish folk music history usually point to three major trends (for examples see Asplund and Hako 1981; Folk Music Institute 1988 [video]). The first period is categorized as "ancient." This was the period of epic, kalevalaic song, as well as kantele, jouhikko, mouth harp, and shepherds' aerophone instruments. Following the Reformation, "newer folk music" styles appeared and became prominent from the seventeenth to the twentieth centuries. This was the period of songs in rhyming verses, including lullabies, ballads, and dancing songs, and of pelimanni instrumental music played on fiddles, bigger kanteles, accordions, harmoniums, and clarinets. The third major division is the revival from the late 1960s onward, the "period of transnational popular culture" (Austerlitz 2000, 185) and the incorporation of instruments such as bass, drums, and saxophone. The three major divisions in the history of Finnish folk music present us with a neat abstraction; but these are "overlapping periods" (Austerlitz 2000, 185). Folk traditions in the past as in the present have coexisted and intermingled. When folk songs in rhyming verses and instrumental dance music were the dominant forms in western Finland, songs in *Kalevala* meter were collected in eastern regions. Similarly, while instrumentally based new folk music groups like Ottopasuuna arrange their materials experimenting with a variety of instrumental textures and timbres, pelimanni groups based on Konsta Jylhä's model of fiddles, harmonium, and double bass remain prevalent throughout Finland.

Instruments most often associated with pelimanni musicians (from the Swedish *spelman,* "folk musician") are the fiddle, clarinet, and accordion. The earliest documented fiddle performances in Finland date back to the 1550s at the court of Duke Johan in South Finland, in Turku (Talve 1997, 256). As elsewhere in European contexts, the fiddle has been one of the most important instruments in Finnish folk music performances. The fiddle spread through Finland via Sweden, becoming a popular instrument at weddings and dances during the eighteenth and nineteenth centuries. Fiddle repertoires consisted of wedding marches, polskas, and minuets (a dance in binary form with eight 3/4 bars in each section). The polska (from the Polish polonaise) was played in Sweden as a couple dance structured in two parts (1590–1630). The first part was in duple time (2/4), the second in triple time (3/4). The second part became more important (1630–1730), eventually with stresses on the first and third beats in the bar (1730–1830). Polskas and minuets were played in Finland from the beginning of the eighteenth century, although dances in even meters were also categorized as polskas. From the nineteenth century new dances were introduced into fiddle repertoires, like the *katrilli* (a quadrille, mostly 2/4 meter but also 3/8 or 6/8), *sottiisi* (schottische, from Germany, also called *jenkka* in Finland), mazurkas (from Poland), and waltzes (Asplund 1981c). The main contexts of performance were dances, weddings, and *kruunuhäät* (literally "crown weddings"). *Kruunuhäät* were big wedding occasions of peasant landowning families following the dress and hospitality codes of the gentry, which are now staged performances at festivals like the one at Kaustinen.

In western and southern Finland (Ostrobothnia, Satakunta, and Swedish-speaking coastal areas) fiddlers also played the clarinet at weddings, and ensembles of one or two fiddlers and a clarinetist playing in unison were sometimes hired for these occasions. The clarinet had been introduced into Finnish military bands by the 1770s, and its heyday as a folk instrument was between 1850 and 1910. Its repertoire was the same as the fiddle's (Helistö 1989).

Toward the end of the nineteenth century, in the wake of religious movements, the fiddle, which was often used to provide music for dancing (regarded as a sinful activity), was perceived as being the instrument of the devil and was denounced by preachers. In Finland, as in other European contexts, including Sweden, Norway, and Scotland, many fiddlers put aside their instruments. Some even destroyed their fiddles. By the beginning of the twentieth century another challenge to fiddle performances was presented in the shape of the accordion, which began to establish itself as the most popular instrument for dance music. The accordion reached Finland via both Russia and Sweden (the most successful Swedish company to manufacture accordions was based in Älvdalen, and the Magdeburg accordion, a one-row instrument manufactured around the turn of the century in the German city Magdeburg, was also popular). One- and two-row instruments reached Karelia via St. Petersburg around the mid–nineteenth century and from Sweden spread to the western parts of Finland during the 1870s. Many accordion players in both Finland and in Sweden transferred tunes from the fiddle repertoire to their instruments. Fiddle playing techniques also seem to have shaped accordionists' performance styles. In fact, fiddlers could be accordionists too, just as they were sometimes also clarinetists.

From the late 1920s, pelimanni musicians were exploring popular music trends from the States, including foxtrots and jazz-influenced arrangements. Austerlitz (2000) relates the story of an American luxury cruiser arriving in Finland in 1926 with around six hundred Finnish-Americans on board visiting the homeland. Several travelers formed a jazz band during the journey and went on to perform in Finland to popular acclaim. Finnish dance bands were formed incorporating the saxophone, banjo, and drum set. Exchange between these kinds of dance bands and pelimanni musicians was bidirectional: "while dance bands incorporated the older Finnish repertory, pelimanni musicians were influenced by the new sounds" (Austerlitz 2000, 192). Fiddlers may also have become members of such bands. Between the pages of a 1984 issue of the folk music magazine *Kansanmusiikki,* I came across a poster of a photograph taken around 1930 of the Finnish Jambo-Jazz band. Four seated musicians playing banjo, mandolin, fiddle, and a drum set painted with the image of an African-American and the band's name perform in the Finnish countryside, in front of wooden houses, a music stand before them. While pelimanni musicians traditionally learned their repertoires by ear, these musicians are playing from notated scores. One further point about the influences of these dance trends, which has a bearing on analysis of JPP's style, being a standard feature of the group's arrangements, is Leisiö's observation that the pizzicato (plucked) double bass playing style of pelimanni bands from the 1950s on also signals the African-American impact on Finnish musical tastes (Leisiö cited in Austerlitz 2000, 193).

Besides dances and weddings, other traditional social contexts for fiddle performance from the mid–nineteenth century onward were work-related festivities and public spaces such as markets. Fiddling families in central Finland reminisced about harvesting occasions (called *talkoot*) from the late nineteenth to the mid–twentieth centuries. *Talkoot* involved neighboring families' helping to harvest rye or barley, or to undertake other tasks such as repairing houses, for example. These were one-day events that concluded with evening entertainment of food, beverages, and a pelimanni fiddler or accordionist playing for dancing (Manninen, fiddling family, personal communications). Between 1940 and 1960 there were also more formal performance contexts through folk music competitions in Ostrobothnia, central Finland, Häme, and Satakunta (Talve 1997, 259).

Musicians' multi-instrumental abilities and the social contexts of performance reveal some versatility in pelimanni musicianship, which is a legacy for today's players. Pelimanni musicians were sometimes self-taught players who adopted a variety of playing techniques. While some fiddlers played with the instrument under the chin, for example, others held the fiddle nearer to the elbow. Players were also instrument makers who used what materials were available. A folk clarinet made from wood and dating to the 1850s is displayed in the Finnish National Museum (Helistö 1989). Fiddlers often played on homemade instruments. Despite the iconic status of the fiddle as a folk instrument, players take a pragmatic approach to their instruments. The Ostrobothnian fiddler Otto Hotakainen (1908–90) received his first fiddle from his brother ("an unlucky, terribly bad model") and ordered his third via fax (Otto Hotakainen cited in Helistö 1992, 21; my translation).

Evident from the above survey is that pelimanni fiddle practices and repertoires have long been shaped in interaction with other folk instruments and with musicians, musical ideas, and trends elsewhere. It does not necessarily follow, however, that pelimanni repertoires and playing styles are subject to rapid or constant change. Comparison of archive and contemporary recorded materials can in fact point to preservation in traditional practices. In this respect, one can usefully compare the early-twentieth-century recorded rendition given by the Swedish fiddler Evert Åhs (1908–70) of a polska by Gyris Anders Andersson (1822–1909; recorded on Musica Sveciae 1995, track 37) with a more contemporary one recorded by the Swedish fiddler Sven Ahlbäck in collaboration with the Finnish new folk accordionist Maria Kalaniemi (Kalaniemi 1992, track 7). The tune is the same. The similarity in performance styles is striking.[3] The same is true of Maria Kalaniemi's renditions of "Yxi Kaunis Papillinen Polska" ("One Beautiful Priestly Polska," Kalaniemi 1992, track 6; see example 7.1) and "Samuell Dikströmin Polska" ("Samuel Dikström's Polska," Kalaniemi's variation on the original title; Kalaniemi 1992, track 4; see example 7.2), which are notated in a book of tunes dating back to 1809 and attributed to Samuel Rinta-Nikkola (see below; tunes 27 and 84 in Krohn [1897] 1975). While Finnish-American travelers introduced new dance styles to Finnish pelimanni musicians in the 1920s, Finnish researchers are now looking at

Example 7.1: "Yxi Kaunis Papillinen Polska"

Example 7.2: "Klockar Samuell Dikström"

Finnish-American recorded repertoires from 1907 to the 1950s as examples of Finnish folk playing styles prevalent in the early years of the twentieth century and as reminders of songs now forgotten in Finland (Westerholm 1992).

BIOGRAPHY, LOCALITY, "AUTHENTICITY"

In the book *Kyläsoitto*, written by Toivonen in collaboration with the fiddler Mauno Järvelä, an attachment to place and histories of local families of musicians are emphasized in representations of music making in Kaustinen. The musical history of Kaustinen is traced and illustrated with archival photo-graphs, together with documentation of the present musical activities of this particular village. Features of the village—the river, houses and streets, music, and particular families (Järvelä, Varila, Virkkala)—are linked in the book's introduction.[4]

In *Kyläsoitto,* Mauno Järvelä delves into his own musical heritage and relates the story of the Järveläs as musicians. Kaustinen was an acclaimed center for music in the 1850s owing to the performances of the kantele player and singer Kreeta Haapasalo (1812–93), who was born into the Järvilä (Järvelä) family. She has been described as the first professional Finnish folk performer, and she gave concerts in Helsinki, St. Petersburg, and Stockholm (Jalkanen 1992, 25). By fo-cusing on the biography of this famous performer and in tracing the family's involvement with folk music, the Järveläs are established as having been central players, and their village, Kaustinen, as a principal locality, since this period. The family also boasted other well-known kantele players. The Järveläs, to-gether with the Ojala and Virkkala families, also achieved acclaim as fid-dlers. Today's fiddlers from these families are following a tradition that has ex-tended into the seventh generation. Some of the musicians, like Aaro Kentala (1920–91)—who was a descendant of the Virkkala family through his maternal line, were trained as professionals. Kentala taught in Finland's first *kansanopisto* (folk high school) and established the Kaustinen wedding choir, which contin-ues to perform at the Kaustinen Festival. The most famous fiddler from Kausti-nen, Konsta Jylhä, was also related to the Järvelä family, being the son of Viljami Jylhä and Marjaana, the widow of Jaakko Järvelä. Fiddlers from all of these families, along with some other players from Kaustinen, formed music groups, which continue to play together today. JPP is one of these groups (Toivonen and Järvelä 1991).

JPP comprises five fiddles (played by Mauno Järvelä, Arto Järvelä, Jouni Järvelä, Jarmo Varila, and Juha Varila), a harmonium (Timo Alakotila), and a double bass (Janne Virkkala) and is one of the most successful new folk music groups. Several of the fiddlers have had a classical training in addition to learn-ing folk fiddling from their familial environment. Mauno Järvelä, for example, used to play with the Finnish National Opera and Finnish Radio Symphony Orchestra, and when he moved back to Kaustinen he joined the Kokkola Or-chestra before he abandoned orchestral playing to concentrate on teaching (Mauno Järvelä, personal communication). Arto Järvelä studied with his uncle, Mauno, and now uses classical violin playing techniques in his own teaching practice (see chap. 4). Classical violin playing techniques have long informed folk performers in Scandinavian contexts. Ling notes, for example, that the violin methods of Francesco Geminiani and Leopold Mozart were familiar to fiddlers in southern Sweden in the first half of the eighteenth century (Ling 1997, 154). The harmonium player, Timo Alakotila, is also a jazz pianist, and he is responsible, together with Arto, for many of the group's arrangements and original compositions (see examples 7.3–7.6, below).

As in Norway (Goertzen 1997) and in Sweden (Arnberg and Mattsson 1995), fiddlers in Finland participate in competitions. In 1982, JPP took part in and won first place at the Finnish Championship Competition for Folk Music Groups in Mäntsälä, leading to performances all over Finland. The group financed and released its first record of eight traditional tunes from Kaustinen in the following year. JPP continued to perform, appearing at the Kaustinen Festival, where it was voted "Band of the Year" in 1986, and releasing another recording, *Laitisen Mankeliska* (JPP 1986, issued as LP and cassette). A double album released in 1988, *JPP*, half of traditional melodies and half of original compositions, won the Tunnustus (Recognition) Prize awarded by the Finnish Radio Corporation and the "Album of the Year" award from the national newspaper *Helsingin Sanomat*. As well as representing local music traditions every year at the Kaustinen Festival, JPP has represented Finnish folk music elsewhere—for example, at festivals in Switzerland, Germany, Norway, and Sweden, and more recently in the United States, Thailand, and Pakistan (plate 16).

Most of the members of JPP are also involved with other music groups. Arto works (or has worked) and has made recordings with Koinurit, Salamakannel, Pinnin Pojat, Niekku, Tallari, and Maria Kalaniemi. Mauno teaches in Kaustinen and leads the group Näppäripelimannit. Both Mauno and Timo play with Hot Club de Karelia. Jouni is a member of Kulkuripojat and Kantavaras, and Janne plays with Nikulanpelimannit and Krannin Laki. Juha and Jarmo maintain their occupations as full-time farmers. In doing so they continue in the traditional pelimanni role that involved taking on multiple activities (musical and subsistence-directed) in village life.

Mauno Järvelä's narrative (*Kyläsoitto*) interlinks place, history, and local performance traditions and contributes ideas about musical continuity and change to discourses about the new folk music group JPP and the wider folk music scene in Kaustinen today. If much of Kaustinen's folk musical scene has changed, there is also much that continues to signify the distinctive musical character of the village. Local traditions provided the basis for the Kaustinen

Festival project and feature prominently in formal transmission contexts at the Folk Music Institute.

Like *Kyläsoitto,* images on the covers of JPP recordings reveal much about notions of musical continuity and provide visual representations of the musical markers of identity.[5] These images contain clues about the musical style and direct audience expectations. They make reference to biographies and localities provoking multilayered readings of the group's recorded performances in relation to issues of musical authenticity and innovation. On the cover of the first recording (JPP 1983), ideas about the music as part of a family tradition are evoked. The border of the LP cover looks like an old-time photograph frame. The image is of the musicians with their instruments: fiddles, harmonium, and bass. There are obvious visual references to Konsta Jylhä (with whom such an ensemble is associated) and to the wedding folk music traditions of their region (Ostrobothnia). The dress of the musicians—hats and suits—and the bell and floral designs in the background also testify to the music as part of a festive regional expression and draw attention to the social context of the wedding, at which pelimanni music would often have been performed. The theme of the performer and his instrument, the fiddle, recurs in the second LP cover (JPP 1986). The musician shown is Mauno Järvelä (who joined the group from the second recording venture), acknowledging the reception of an audience. The viewer can thus interpret this recorded performance in relation to a live one. The context of "authentic performance" (live and with an audience present) is evoked as if suggesting that the recording captures those performance conditions. Alongside the main image, two smaller ones juxtapose past and present. The photograph at the bottom of the cover shows an elderly traditional player in the background from whom the principal player, Mauno Järvelä, is walking away. Tradition is in the background. There is an emphasis on a new departure, reinforced by the photograph at the top of the cover. This shows the next generation of musicians: the young players in the Järvelä family. The third cover (JPP 1988) presents a new departure of another kind. The group have adopted a somewhat less cumbersome name, JPP, and the subtitle, *New Finnish Folk Fiddling,* is in English. Instead of images of musicians, this cover shows two violin scrolls against a background of the sun rising. These are gestures toward a wider audience, for whom the family history of folk music activity may have less importance. While the first two images pay homage to the past, the third one looks to the future. The black-and-white photographic imagery in the earlier record covers, which itself is a reminder of an older technology, is now replaced with color images. While the audience seems to be more specified in the first two images (participants in the wedding context, a "local" audience), in the third one it is generalized: birds come to rest on the fiddle's pegs. Any passer-by might stop to listen. The dominant image is the violin scroll. This is, as it turns out, to be a repeated visual motif. With the fourth recording (JPP 1990), the group is seen as having moved even further from its original context. *I've Found a New Tango* is the title. Yet we return to familiar images of the performers and their instruments, and for those who know, the tango dance venue depicted on the cover is typical of those in the local context (it is the Kalliopaviljonki Kaustisen Nuorisoseura, the Rock Pavilion of Kaustinen's Youth Center). This is, after all, a Finnish tango. In the images of the fifth (JPP 1992) and sixth (JPP 1994) covers the focus is once again on the fiddle. The fiddle is washed ashore on the fifth CD cover, and the title is in Finnish: *Pirun Polska* (*The Devil's Polska*). The return to Finnish is significant, for during the early 1990s, part of Värttinä's success could be attributed to their evocations of "Finnishness." Just as Värttinä were seen as being bold and straight talking (chap. 5), the fiddle as used by JPP emerges as resilient, resistant even to the turn-of-the-century fiddle burnings. The photograph on the reverse side of *Pirun Polska* shows the group playing on the back of a tractor as it winds its way through the Ostrobothnian countryside. This recording contained many old favorites in the group's repertoire. In the sixth recording, the fiddle scroll motif is presented in an abstract form.

These kinds of visual representations are paralleled by those used by other new folk musicians and new folk music groups. We find a focus on performers, instruments, landscapes, and traditional designs. But here I come to my central points in discussing visual representations on these new folk music recordings. Studies of representation as a signifying practice have tended to focus on the production of meaning through language, discourse, and image (see Hall 1997). This discussion of the visual imagery that features on the recorded canon of a Finnish new folk music group seems to reproduce a familiar line of inquiry. Images are read for the meanings and messages contained therein. But many of the images discussed above can be interpreted as significant within musical parameters. Musical instruments such as the fiddle, the harmonium, and the double bass are not just material objects. They are sound-producing objects with textural properties (offering distinctive and recognizable timbres) that are important in new folk music performances. These are the musical markers of identity, identified as much by their sonic properties as by their form. Visual images on JPP's record covers reflect the musical dimensions of the group's practices that link it to the past. As I shall point out in the following discussion, timbre has in fact become one of the musical properties that links JPP's contemporary treatment to traditional parameters of folk fiddling.

If any folk musical "authenticity" need be claimed for the group JPP, it is asserted in *Kyläsoitto* and in recording cover imageries, by drawing on notions of historical, biographical, genealogical, and musical continuity in Kaustinen. The group can be situated within conventional parameters of folk music expression such as rural location, generational transmission, and pelimanni musicianship embedded in the broader social context of village life. Any changes in the group's approach to folk fiddling (writing new compositions, undertaking musical tours around the world, experimenting with and recording a variety of repertoires) are expressed as conscious strategies in terms of the musicians' abilities to ensure that their traditions achieve contemporary musical relevance. This approach, too, can be viewed as following a family tradition. Jalkanen (1992) notes that the kantele musician Kreeta Haapasalo had to adapt to the musical tastes of the gentry and thus added her own new arrangements of folk songs from songbooks to her concert repertoire.

COMPOSING NEW FOLK MUSIC:
THE OSTROBOTHNIAN EXAMPLE

As folk music composers, Arto Järvelä and Timo Alakotila are following an Ostrobothnian tradition. Yet the emphasis on the concept of "folk composer" is another indication of the shifts in perceptions of folk music. The dual role of composer and performer is significant in new folk music, for folk composers often perform their own compositions. In this respect, new folk musicians can be seen as following established traditions. Well-known folk revival musicians set a precedent for the role of performer-composer and are regarded as important models for contemporary folk practitioners. Arto Järvelä, for example, identified the violinist and composer Konsta Jylhä as having changed public perceptions of the folk performer and composer as well as being an influential figure in the transmission of Ostrobothnian fiddle traditions. Such was his profile that other musicians added song texts to Jylhä's compositions and were inspired to compose too (Arto Järvelä, personal interview, June 10, 92). While Konsta Jylhä has been regarded as having been a "natural" composer, his compositional processes reveal the careful thought and skill put into his works. He notated his compositions in the process of polishing them, later also using cassette tapes to do so. He worked out his compositions on the fiddle or the harmonium and tried different arrangements of his materials—for example, moving from major to minor tonalities (Helistö 1991, 25).

Konsta Jylhä overshadowed other folk performer-composers because he achieved national renown and became an icon for folk music during the revival period, but he was not an isolated example. Otto Hotakainen, too, was an Ostrobothnian folk performer and composer. He described his compositional process in the following terms: "Certainly I believe that music men who are proper (learned) note men [able to write music] can also compose. But I must have it from inside; it just starts sounding in my head. . . . Those first pieces almost always came while working on the farm, in the cow house. It was what happened when I was walking, it depends just on the pace of walking: as I'm a small man, I had to take more steps and then a polkka came. If it was something less rapid, then it was a waltz" (Otto Hotakainen cited in Westerholm 1991b, 5; my translation).[6] Otto Hotakainen locates his compositional processes within the social context of everyday farming life. As well as shaping his musical expressions, these activities sometimes inhibited his music practice. Farming and family commitments left Otto Hotakainen little time to practice the fiddle during the late 1930s. Reflecting ideas at the time that fiddling was somehow sinful, he was also reluctant to play a repertoire of dance music when there were children around ("It might have been because of a religious influence from my mother. I felt that I couldn't play dance music when there were children"; cited in Helistö 1992, 21).[7]

Otto's son, Risto, estimates that Otto composed about eighty pieces. While Otto's testimony points to the model of oral composition which is inspired by the rural environment, many of his compositions, particularly from the latter half of the 1960s onward, were recorded (on audiovisual tape as well as sound recordings) and have been transcribed and presented in written form. A recording (Hotakainen 1989), produced by the company Olarin Musiikki in 1989, presents the eighty-one-year-old Otto Hotakainen playing his composition "Ylikuun polkka" ("Over the Moon Polkka") with Matti Ojala on harmonium. Other tracks are interpretations of his compositions by now-familiar new folk musicians such as the group Tallari (of which Risto is a member) and the accordionist Maria Kalaniemi, as well as the kantele player Tytti-Leena Laasanen and the group Kaustisen Hääpelimmanit (Kaustinen's Wedding Folk Musicians).

Risto has transcribed forty-six of his father's compositions, scrupulously notated, and they have been published by the Folk Music Institute as *Otto Hotakainen's Notebook* (Westerholm 1991b). This notebook contributes to an already extensive body of transcribed examples of earlier folk compositions, providing materials and models for reinterpretation by new folk musicians, as well as "new tunes" for pelimanni players upon their "rediscovery." Transcribed examples include the compositions of the Ostrobothnian folk violinist Matti Haudanmaa (1858–1936), who was recorded by the Finnish composer Toivo Kuula, by the farmer Antti Sauna-aho, by the teacher Ernst Järvi, and by the folk music researcher Armas Otto Väisänen (also published in a Finnish Literature Society compilation: Asplund, Kangas, and Valo 1990); the notebook of the group Leikarit (Tarkkanen 1985), who mainly drew on the unpublished repertoire of the folk violinist Martin "Macko" Hellström, born in Espoo in 1898; and Ilmari Krohn's (1893–97) collection, *Vanhoja Pelimannisävelmiä* (*Old Folk Compositions*, published in a compilation by the Finnish Literature Society in 1975 [Krohn 1975]). In his editorial comments, Krohn mentions an "excellent and old" collection containing ninety-four dance compositions (incomplete, since the last pages are missing) that had been found in Oulu by Spjuti in 1891. The collection appears with the name Samuel Rinta-Nikkola (in the original, Rinda Nickola) and is dated 1809. Krohn's manuscript analysis revealed that most of the collection had been written by the same hand (text, comments, and notation), although some details (rhythmic and key signatures) were missing (Krohn 1975, 111–12). Another manuscript collection from Oulu is *Vepsa Kirja* (*The Vepsa Book*), also believed to date from the early nineteenth century. A farmer, Lauri Kokko, rediscovered the manuscript in his attic in the 1940s. It bore an inscription, "Abraham Brunni." Kokko therefore gave the manuscript to another farmer—Arvid Brunni—who he thought would be related. It was stored in a shed until the 1960s, when Brunni donated it to a village association, from which it was eventually sent to the Regional Museum of North Ostrobothnia (Karinen 2001). Erkki Ala-Könni, the folk music scholar, undertook an initial reading of the manuscript, which consists of nineteen pages presenting sixty-one tunes (polskas, waltzes, and marches). In this source, too, there are some notational errors: incorrect or missing key signatures and accidentals (Karinen 2001, 19–21). Karinen points out that this collection has become one of the most important sources in contemporary constructions of "local tradition" and that some of the tunes are reproduced in more recent publications (Karinen 2001, 21).

JPP (Alakotila and Järvelä 1988, 1990) follow the tradition of providing musical scores (called *nuottivihkot* or *nuottikirjat*, "notebooks") that, in this case, specifically accompany their sound recordings (JPP 1986, 1988; see examples 7.3–7.6). Arto Järvelä and Timo Alakotila annotate their compositions

Example 7.3: "Ellun Sottiisi," by Arto Järvelä. (Source: Alakotila and Järvelä 1988, 8. Reproduced with permission, all rights reserved by Arto Järvelä.)

Example 7.4: "Häämarssi," by Arto Järvelä. (Source: Alakotila and Järvelä 1990, 4. Reproduced with permission, all rights reserved by Arto Järvelä.)

Example 7.5: "Kruunupyyn Katrilli," by Timo Alakotila. (Source: Alakotila and Järvelä 1988, 6. Reproduced with permission, all rights reserved by Timo Alakotila.)

Example 7.6: "Ruotsalaispolska," by Timo Alakotila. (Source: Alakotila and Järvelä 1988, 7. Reproduced with permission, all rights reserved by Timo Alakotila.)

themselves to assist players who want to have access to JPP's repertoire through notated scores (in the forewords to the notebooks, they advise players to listen to the recordings as well as read from the scores). JPP's scores indicate important departures from the earlier transcribed examples of folk compositions. A focus on the violin's melodic line, which dominates earlier transcriptions, is retained, but JPP's scores usually present two-part violin writing to which a harmonic outline and some bass notes have been indicated by chord symbols. While the realization of the bass line is omitted from the score (although the double bass generally plays the root of the given chords), these folk compositions are nevertheless distinguished from the earlier examples by their richer, thicker texture and by a more clearly prescribed accompaniment. These differences are in part a result of following the model set by Konsta Jylhä, to which Timo Alakotila, like Arto Järvelä, drew attention in describing his compositional concerns (Timo Alakotila, personal interview, July 1992).

Common to Otto Hotakainen's and JPP's folk compositions, as well as examples in transcribed collections, is the structural and contextual format of dances: polskas, minuets, mazurkas, schottishes, and wedding and drinking marches.[8] Ling notes that the violin spread all over Europe and that it was particularly successful as an instrument to accompany dancing: "with its beautiful, piercing sound and its infinite technical potential, it stood out as a brilliant competitor to traditional instruments" (Ling 1997, 160). Otto Hotakainen specified that his walking pace determined compositional structure in terms of dance form and tempo. New folk compositions have incorporated a new dance: the tango. JPP, for example, seems to be drawing upon musical traditions far removed from its local context with its third commercial recording, the compilation entitled *I've Found a New Tango* (JPP 1990). Although the tango is more often associated with Argentina, JPP's presentation can be interpreted as following a Finnish tradition, albeit one whose origins can be traced to another place.

The Argentine Angel Villoldo gave the first performance of the tango in Europe (in Paris in 1907). He was followed by several other tango musicians from Argentina. Tango was first performed in Finland in 1913. Throughout the 1930s and 1940s the tango was popular throughout Europe, but in Finland it "gained a national character" during the Second World War. In the 1960s, the tango was adopted as music "which would sound truly Finnish" (Gronow 1987, 28) and provide an alternative to listening to the music of, for example, the Beatles. Tangos were played in restaurants and dance halls. The tango band of the 1960s consisted of an accordion, guitar, double bass, and drums, to which violins, piano, and woodwinds were sometimes added. The ambivalent status of the tango as "Finnish" is emphasized, however, by JPP's arrangements of non-Finnish tango compositions on its recording.[9] Although Timo Alakotila composes tangos and considers the genre to suit pelimanni traditions, he does not regard them as "folk music" (Timo Alakotila, personal interview, July 1992).

Gronow (1987) states that the Finnish tango is always a song, and that the lyrics (often about unrequited love) are very important to the listener, expressing deep emotions and experiences that one cannot speak about and that are easier to communicate through song. Nowadays, however, JPP play instrumental tangos with no vocal line. Another change in the instrumentation is that whereas the accordion was essential to the tango band of the 1960s, the essential instrument in the tango music of JPP is the violin. In the 1960s the tango was categorized, along with other dances like the waltz and the foxtrot, as "popular music." The only domestic records that featured in the top three of record charts were those of tango music. Tango in Finland is still part of popular culture, but it has also become a part of folk culture through its incorporation in the new folk music repertoire.

LOCAL MUSICIANS, GLOBAL STAGES

There are obvious similarities between new folk composers turning to a dance structure that is both Finnish and non-Finnish and the Peltoniemi-Saha collaboration (chap. 6). Both cases probe the question of how musicians draw on musical ideas from diverse traditions yet retain specific ideas about Finnish new folk music. Adopting historical perspectives and examining new folk music in terms of changes in the transmission, representation, and performance of music constructed as "folk" offer insights into the ability of these musicians to reconcile musical borrowings with their sense of music as a marker of specific identities and as contributing to a continuing musical tradition. Contemporary folk music is imagined and represented as local musical expression by drawing on familial, genealogical, and musical biographies and histories even as methods of transmission change, as it conforms to global trends and as it finds a place on the world music stage.

Both the Kaustinen Festival and the local group JPP have moved from local to international arenas. Although the Kaustinen Festival was intended to be "international" from its inception, its performing stage has expanded over the years to include more musicians from around the world. Likewise, with the release of recordings and performances in various venues, JPP have achieved a wider public acclaim, which has launched them from the regional stage to the international one, where they represent Finland as a nation. Their repertoire reflects this progression. Beginning with folk melodies from Kaustinen, they soon added folk melodies from all over Finland, were influenced by Swedish folk music, and in the recording of 1990 performed arrangements of compositions like Malando's "Noche de Estrellas" (track 1) and Williams and Palmer's jazz melody "I've Found a New Baby" (track 2).

This is not, however, equivalent to a simple progression from local to global. Rather, it involves the incorporation of more identities as the stage has expanded or shifted. Larger, more widespread audiences perceive the group in increasingly diverse ways. In Kaustinen, JPP represents local tradition; elsewhere in Finland the group is taken to represent a style of fiddle playing associated with the Western part of the country, while abroad it presents a generalized image of contemporary Finnish folk music.[10] JPP, like the Kaustinen Festival itself, is an amalgamation of the local, national, and international.

The further the group is detached from the local context, the greater the emphasis placed on elements specific to the local region. When JPP play a jazz melody or one of their tango compositions, the element of the "exotic" (the melodic line) serves to emphasize the familiar: the stylistic traditions of their region. The textural, timbral quality (the combination of fiddles, bass, and harmonium), is the same as that of their other compositions and arrangements. The combination of the familiar and the new, of tradition and innovation, can prove to be successful.[11] It is a combination for which new folk musicians strive: to present the familiar in new ways or to incorporate new elements within recognized traditions. These aims were already apparent in the revival movement of the late 1960s. But the boundaries between these categories are indistinct. In focusing on the "Roots in Finland" theme (chap. 6) and on new folk music compositions following Ostrobothnian models, areas of ambiguity in the delineation of music as "ours" and "theirs" are apparent. I discuss this boundary in part 3, in which I consider further the relationship between "folk" and "world" music.

Folk Music, World Music

When a jazz musician quotes Beethoven,
when a Latino singer mixes English phrases into his Spanish,
when an ultra-Orthodox Jewish songwriter sets Hebrew texts to a rock tune,
we can hardly imagine that they do so accidentally.

Mark Slobin

EIGHT

Musical and Social Identities

BORROWING FROM THE
TRADITIONS OF "OTHERS"

For new folk musicians, Finnish contemporary folk music is deeply rooted. It is historically and culturally situated. Even as transmission and performance contexts have changed, it continues to operate as a marker of specific identities and gives people a sense of belonging to particular places: a village, a region, or a nation. Another performance context is the world music stage. The Kaustinen Festival is an international celebration of folk music. In this kind of global arena folk music belongs to everybody. Indeed, Finnish new folk music "borrows" from the traditions of "others," from everybody and from anybody. Looking, therefore, at what seems to be "localized" musical expression leads to pondering the workings of global networks of musical exchange. The questions which surface in current thinking about local and global processes are variations of those concerning the migration and borrowing of tradition which have occupied folklore scholars since the publication of Lönnrot's epic text in the nineteenth century. Schade-Poulsen offers the pertinent observation that music is one of the first topics to be raised in discussions about the local and the global, for it is "seemingly one of those 'things' in the world that most easily 'flows,' becomes 'creolized,' 'syncretized,' 'heterogenized' etc." (1997, 59). Kimmo Pohjonen adds a thumb piano from Tanzania to the musical texture of a traditional Finnish composition found in the notebooks of Rinta-Nikkola, "Yxi Kaunis Papillinen Polska" ("One Beautiful Priestly Polska"). JPP perform the "Texas Blues," which they introduced into their repertoire when they collaborated with

Erik Hokkanen, a Finnish-American musician who visited Kaustinen in 1989. Värttinä sing "Ruskoi Reggae" (Värttinä 1989, track 12). These are the kinds of musical borrowings that characterize contemporary Finnish folk music. We have already seen that Finnish new folk music encompasses diverse traditions. So far we have encountered pelimanni repertoires—Ostrobothnian fiddle traditions, the kantele repertoire, which is transmitted on a nationwide scale, experiments with electric kanteles, vocal music from the eastern regions, especially from Karelia (which featured prominently in the construction of the national epic, the *Kalevala*), folk revival experiments presented by jazz and rock musicians and by folklorists, ballads, Finnish-American popular songs, and the tango. In observing transmission strategies at the Department of Folk Music at the Sibelius Academy, I participated in Cuban drumming, Senegalese drumming, and Estonian singing classes. At the Finnish folk music courses in Kaustinen I participated in mandolin classes in which we learned Greek bouzouki pieces. Musicians spoke repeatedly of their interests in learning about "other" musics and their use of such knowledge to reinvigorate and reinterpret "Finnish" traditions. In borrowing musical elements, Finnish new folk musicians can be thought of as being "net importers of culture" (Hannerz 1989, 214). What is imported, however, is exported under different guises. The reinterpreted composition "Yxi Kaunis Papillinen Polska" is recorded by a Finnish company (Kalaniemi 1992, track 6) and marketed as Finnish folk music under world music categories in record shops outside Finland. So too is the *Texas Blues,* with the acknowledged composers being Helen G. Phillips, Erik Hokkanen, and Arto Järvelä (JPP 1994, track 5). These kinds of musical treatments and representations of a national folk music do not fit easily in local-global frameworks. Neither viewing the world in terms of bounded local (or national) cultures in which the local is a domain resistant to global influence nor looking at processes of transnational cultural flow as "an intercontinental traffic in meaning" (Hannerz 1987, 547) account for the reconciliation of musical multiplicity within new folk music, with its status as a marker of identity. Finnish new folk music contains evident borrowings, which both counter notions of coherent, fixed musical and/or social identities and seem to provide evidence of a "traffic in meaning." Yet it remains a symbol of a nation, and musical meaning depends on the contexts in which interpretations are offered.

"Borrowing" is a term that needs some examination. In relation to processes of creative composition and in contexts of musical collaborations, it is somewhat disparaging in implying that one takes what is not one's own. This is particularly true when the origin of the "loan" is eventually forgotten. The external element can then operate as an active agent of musical change. The problems raised and the possibilities for creative innovation afforded by musical borrowings are discussed in this chapter by looking at the interactions of Finnish new folk music with various disparate musical examples (Karelian, Saami, Senegalese, Argentine, and Irish). These examples are not entirely capricious personal choices. They were the musics to which Finnish new folk musicians were turning when I was doing my fieldwork. Although musicians certainly have a wide sphere of available musics from which to draw, the musical eclecticism of new folk music is determined by processes of selection (see Slobin 1993, 55). How are these musical choices made? In the last chapter I discussed how new folk musicians have opportunities to make musical choices from a global sphere but continue to imagine and represent their music as local expression because of specific music histories and genealogies. Robertson (1990), Hannerz (1996), and Smith (1990) provide insights for interpreting the ethnographic material considered here in exploring the question of selectivity. Robertson suggests that the "distinction between global and local is becoming very complex and problematic—to such an extent that we should now speak in such terms as the . . . localization of globality" (1990, 19). Hannerz uses a wonderfully evocative image in writing with reference to particular cities that they are centers "not because they are the origins of all things, but rather because they are places of exchange, the switchboards of culture" (1996, 149). Although the exchange of cultural elements has been viewed according to center-periphery relations (Hannerz 1989), these "switchboards" can in fact be located anywhere. The global ecumene turns out to be the "creation of a turning and twisting history, and derives some of its enduring polycentricity from this fact" (Hannerz 1996, 145). Polycentricity stresses distinctive histories rather than a single grand narrative of a global history. A homogenous global culture is therefore distant, for as Smith notes, "a world of competing cultures, seeking to improve their comparative status rankings and enlarge their cultural resources, affords little basis for global projects, despite the technical and linguistic infrastructural possibilities"(1990, 188). In different ways the following examples of musical borrowings and exchanges attest to Hannerz's view of a polycentric global ecumene, to Smith's notion of cultural competition, and to Robertson's suggestion that globality is localized. The exchanges investigated occur over an East-West frontier, within the nation-state, by looking to the exotic "other," and by searching for affinities with those who seem to share musical and social characteristics. As it turns out, these kinds of exchanges are fundamental to the perception of new folk music as contemporary and modern and are a defining feature in according a place to Finnish new folk music in global spaces.

It was the Christmas party at the Folk Music Department (Sibelius Academy). "That's Santtu Karhu. You should interview him too," suggested Hannu Tolvanen, pointing to a musician I did not recognize.

"Why? Who is he?" I asked.

"He is the only singer singing in Liivi" was Hannu's response.

Santtu Karhu is from Petrozavodsk (Petroskoi in Finnish), a town with nearly three hundred thousand inhabitants near Lake Onega in Russian Karelia. He was in Finland only for a brief visit. He had come to buy a *keikkabussi* (a van for traveling to gigs), and he was visiting the Department of Folk Music to meet his contacts in the folk music world and to perform at the party. We arranged to meet for an interview two days later in Café Socis, opposite the main railway station. His ideas about his musical activities, the aims of his band, and his experiences in Finland offer an interesting view of musical and social interactions between particular individuals over the East-West frontier.

Santtu Karhu usually sings in Liivi (a Finno-Ugric language closely related to Finnish and also known as Livonian or Karelian). In discussing the language of his song texts, Karhu spoke of the significance of Liivi in terms reminiscent of the nineteenth-century concern with the status of Finnish. In Petroskoi, people usually speak Russian, although both Russian and Finnish are official languages in Karelia. Karhu told me that people rarely speak either Finnish or Liivi. Liivi is known as the *kotikieli* (home language) and is not used in writing. Few people speak the language now, although it was the language of some songs in *Kalevala* meter. Karhu drew a comparison between the preservation of Karelian culture and language, and of the cultures of other related peoples who were drawn into the Soviet Union. He believes that Karelian culture has not been preserved and that young people nowadays are not familiar with their cultural history and their language. This is in contrast to the situation in Estonia, where young people are more aware of their culture and where the Estonian language continues to be spoken in everyday life. Karhu stressed the importance of speaking Liivi, asserting that it is a beautiful language, and expressing his hopes that one day it will be in general use again. It is for these reasons that he sings in Liivi and is, in fact, the only recorded artist in the world to do so. The aims of his band,

Talvisovat, are to attract an audience of young people and to help revive Liivi language and culture. His own familiarity with the Liivi language and folk music extends back to his childhood (Santtu Karhu, personal interview, December 12, 1991).

The band's name, Talvisovat ("winter clothes"), is a pun on the Finnish word *talvisodat*, meaning "winter wars." In the Winter War of 1939–40 the Soviet Union attempted unsuccessfully to conquer Finland following Finland's resistance to Soviet demands for territorial concessions in the autumn of 1939. The war has assumed the significance of an epic episode in Finnish history. It "represents the single most important collective experience in the history of the Finnish people" (Häikiö 1992, 25). Despite the losses of people and land, Finland, unlike other Baltic countries, resisted incorporation into the Soviet Union. Old hostilities among the Finns themselves, remaining from the 1918 civil war, were tempered, and patriotic feelings were strengthened, as Finns fought their Soviet neighbors.

There are five musicians in the band, who have been playing together since 1988. The musicians and some of the instruments they play (for example, on their first record) are Santtu Karhu (acoustic guitar, voice), Leo Sevets (flute, jouhikko, violin), Arto Rinne (accordion, harmonica), Feodor Astashoff (electric guitar), Andrei Bronnikoff (bass guitar), and Pekka Vasiljeff (percussion). Karhu described the music that the band performs as folk-rock. While the band has chosen a musical style which is both folk (drawing on notions of ancient origin) and modern in reaching for an audience of young listeners, Karhu noted that in Finland, the people who are most interested in listening to this band are musicians at the Department of Folk Music, "because they are specialists," and old Karelians "because they relive their past" (Santtu Karhu, personal interview, December 14, 1991). The band performs in Finland in venues found for it by an informal arrangement with one of the main managers in Finland for recording artists, Tapio Korjus. These venues are summer festivals or *kapakat* (from the Russian word *kabak*—pubs). At a festival performance in Joensuu, a town in Finnish northern Karelia, many old Karelians were part of the audience. For many of them, the performance brought back memories of Karelia, and they were in tears as they listened to Talvisovat's songs.

Talvisovat's recordings (Santtu Karhu and Talisovat 1990, 1991) were produced by Eino, a small company involving about twenty people (see chap. 9). By 1991, the band had made three records. Talvisovat's links to the new folk music circles in Finland are based on a shared wish to promote folk music in a modern idiom. The emphasis on modern idiom has a bearing on the concern of preserving Liivi through the song texts. Liivi is promoted to an audience interested in the sounds of the latest folk music and is thereby represented as a language of contemporary relevance. The links established between Karhu and musicians in the Department of Folk Music, a recording company, and a manager for recording artists are indications of a positive reaction to his music and on the success of the band in performing in a modern folk idiom. On the other hand, Karhu mentioned some of the negative reactions he has encountered, which arise because of the political and economic disparity between Finland and Russia: "In one performance in Joensuu, an old man shouted out 'we used to shoot you in the last war' and I was very upset about that" (personal interview with Santtu Karhu, December 14, 1991; my translation).

Sociopolitical conflicts are explored in Talvisovat's recorded repertoire. Their second record (1991) includes the song "Aunuksen Anja" ("Anja, the Pearl of Aunus"), originally recorded during World War II, in 1942, by Matti Jurva. It is a humorous wartime song in which a Finn is depicted as triumphing over the Russian characters. At that time, the towns Aunus and Petroskoi in Soviet Karelia were occupied by Finnish troops. The song text describes how a girl from Aunus, famous for her beauty, is courted by the Russians Vasili and Vanja but is rescued by a Finn, the "gallant son of the North."

AUNUKSEN ANJA

Kaukana kasvoi neiti
kuin kukka tummainen
oli kauneudesta kuulu
tuo helmi Aunuksen.

Chorus:
Anja, Anja
sua kosiskeli Vaseli ja Vanja,
oli tuttu koti saari
mutta rukkaset ne sulta sai.
Anja, Anja,
sai rukkaset Vaseli ja Vanja,
olithan sä kauneudestas kuulu
sinä tumma tyttö
olit helmi Aunuksen.

Pohjan poika uljas
kun joutui Aunukseen
hän kaunoisen Anjan
pelasti armaakseen.

Chorus

ANJA, THE PEARL OF AUNUS

Far away a maiden grew
Like a dark flower,
She was noted for her beauty,
She was the pearl of Aunus.

Chorus:
Anja, Anja,
You were courted by Vaseli and Vanja,
It was in a familiar home island
But they were brushed off by you.
Anja, Anja,
Turned down were Vaseli and Vanja,
You were famous for your beauty,
You dark girl,
You were the pearl of Aunus.

The gallant son of the north,
When he landed in Aunus,
The beautiful Anja
He rescued to be his sweetheart.

Chorus

This kind of propaganda is evident in many of the wartime popular songs, and because of the anti-Soviet sentiments expressed, they were not played on the radio after the war in the politically sensitive climate. Today, new editions of wartime popular music material are available (for example, the compilation edited by Ilpo Hakasalo [1992], *Sininen ja Valkoinen: Suomalaisten rakkaimmat sävelmät 1917–1992* [*Blue and White: The Most Well Loved Finnish Compositions 1917–1992*]). Karhu said that his band presents this song in a humorous form; it is a joke for them. Two reasons for this have been suggested to me: first, from a musical point of view this is not the kind of repertoire and musical material that Talvisovat usually perform; and second, the song is an interesting historical relic from the days when Soviet Karelia was occupied by Finns (Hannu Saha, personal communication). In terms of personal narrative, this area is interesting for the group's members. Karhu's parents were from Aunus (Santtu Karhu, personal interview, December 12, 1991). Whereas Karhu normally sings in Liivi, this song was recorded in its original Finnish version.

The inclusion of the song "Aunuksen Anja" in the repertoire of Talvisovat can be read as an ironic reflection on the experiences of the musicians in the band, and as an expression of the ambiguous relationship between neighboring peoples. A Finnish wartime song, an anti-Soviet text in which the narrative is situated in the hometowns of the former Soviet musicians who have recorded it and who have links with both Finns and Russians, is interpreted parodically and has been produced by a Finnish record company. In the song, the character Anja is taken from Soviet Karelia by the Finn, but in this particular recording, this action is reciprocated by the Soviet Karelians' appropriation of the Finnish song.

Karhu noted that he is perceived by Finns as being Russian even though he speaks Finnish. It seems that Karelians, Estonians, and Ingrians are perceived as having a closer affinity to Russians despite linguistic and cultural connections to Finns. They come from the "other side." The generalization of the "other side" overlooks the differences between these "others," positing a view of Finland as distinct from neighboring Finno-Ugric peoples who are more closely related to each other by virtue of their ties to Russia. Karhu's experiences and his band's recorded repertory nevertheless highlight some of the contradictions and ambiguities in the relations between Finno-Ugric peoples over the East-West frontier. Santtu is an example of an individual who moves back and forth over the frontier and who is identified differently by others according to the context in which he is operating. When he performed in Moscow, he was identified with Finns and Karelians. In Finland, his interactions with Finns, and the ways in which he is identified, exist on two different levels, marked, respectively, by a sense of similarity and a sense of difference. On the first level, in his role as a musician, Karhu is identified as a Russian Karelian, whose musical activity is significant because he is the only musician who sings in Liivi on the public stage. Yet this is a construction of musical difference that is compromised. The musical boundary that separates Finnish and Karelian turns out to be indistinct.

Karelian music has exerted such a strong influence in Finland that it is hardly considered separate from Finnish music. During the period of nineteenth-century nationalism, the interest shown in Karelian culture, the Karelianism movement, extended to all artistic genres—music, painting, and literature. Folklorists and artists who traveled to Karelia to collect material considered this to be the region where "ancient Finnish" culture still survived. There are parallels in the ways that Finns adopted Karelian music during the nationalist period and have adopted it today. In the nineteenth century, songs in *Kalevala* meter collected from Karelia were compiled into the *Kalevala,* which became the national epic of Finland. Nowadays, Karhu aims to promote Karelian music and the Liivi language, but in doing so, his music has become incorporated into Finnish new folk music. His music, like much of the repertoire of Värttinä, is Karelian, but it is also a part of Finnish musical culture. Karhu considers that Karelian culture has not been preserved, but "Karelianism" ironically has been a major strand in the construction of Finnish identity and culture. Karhu is a musician who is not well known among the Finnish population as a whole, but this point about the incorporation of Karelian music, which can be extended to Finno-Ugric music in general, was also evident in the group Värttinä, a dominant "folk voice" of Finland on national and world music stages for nearly a decade now. Thus, a thriving Finnish musical identity has been—and continues to be—built from fragments of the traditions of neighboring Finno-Ugric peoples, traditions which are themselves seen to be fading away.

On one level of interaction, then, the focus is on similarity and on the sense of being related peoples who have a common culture. Karhu's interactions with Finnish musicians represent an area of collaboration between individuals over the frontier. The only significant difference in terms of musical style identified above lies in Karhu's song texts sung in Liivi. Otherwise he shares with Finnish new folk musicians an interest in contemporary treatments of folk material. On another level of interaction, the focus is on difference, and here, Karhu is seen as an example of an individual who comes from the "other side." This is a level of conflict and contestation. Karhu is perceived as a Russian. As he was reminded by a member of the audience at one of his performances, "we used to shoot you in the last war."

SAAMI MUSIC IN HELSINKI

Collaboration in the midst of contestation was also found in a performance of Saami music in Helsinki. Musical exchange over an East-West frontier (in

Santtu Karhu's case) is an example of the role of music in border politics where musical differences become an important part of defining distinct identities. In the absence of a politically demarcated border, the assertion of musical difference in the case of the Saami compromises images of a united nation-state. In June 1992, Saami representatives arrived in Helsinki to discuss their position in a changing Europe with delegates from Finland, Sweden, Norway, and Russia. These discussions included negotiations for Saami independence. A Saami Festival—an evening of musical performances in Vanha (the Helsinki University student union building) marked the end of the proceedings. The performers included a Saami group, Angelin Tytöt, and Pohjantahti (the Finnish group with whom the folk revivalist musician Ilpo Saastamoinen plays), who were joined by a joik singer. They all sang Saami joik melodies. In the audience were many Saami people in Saami dress and many Finnish musicians interested in Saami music. These performances were intended as a way of asserting and reinforcing a distinctive Saami identity and thereby lending substance to the political objectives pursued in the meetings.

To joik is "to sing someone or something" (Leisiö 1986, 49) rather than to sing *about* someone or something, and awareness of the timbres of vowel sounds and voiced consonants is crucial to the aesthetic appreciation of joik singing. In the past, Saami shamanic beliefs were drawn into the leather skins of shamanic drums, and joiks were sung to make contact with spiritual agencies. Shamanism and joiks were subsequently prohibited in Christian Finland, and at least ten people have been recorded as having been executed for singing joiks. As recently as the 1970s, the Saami language and the joik were "forbidden in some schools in Finland because they were the Devil's language" (Leisiö 1986, 50).

Angelin Tytöt sang joiks to the accompaniment of a guitar and a shamanic drum, linking ideas of Saami past and present. In joiking in the city center, singers revived themes about the origins and distinctiveness of the Saami people, and about Saami relationships to nature and to the supernatural. They asserted their right to sing joiks and to claim and present these sounds as integral to their sense of being. In so doing within this specific performance framework, they reinforced their own Saami identity. Gathering in Helsinki for the purpose of discussing their political status, Saami musicians used their voices and instruments in performance to highlight those elements—language, song and shamanistic belief—which had once been suppressed (plate 17).

Saami music has also found its way into the repertoire of Finnish new folk music. Collaborative projects undertaken by Finnish "revival" musicians and by Saami musicians reveal these musical exchanges. In 1980, the joik singer Nils-Aslak Valkeapää ("Ailu") was listening to Dvořák's Ninth Symphony (*From the New World*, in which the composer is often said to have drawn upon the spirituals of African-Americans). He asked Seppo Paakkunainen if he would compose something similar on the basis of Saami joiks. The result was the composition Symphony no.1, *Juoigansinfoniija*, scored for a symphony orchestra, improvising instrumental group, two solo joik singers, and solo saxophone. In the program notes to the recording of this work, Paakkunainen writes: "This is the way the luodit I have learned by ear from Ailu have been reshaped in my soul."[1]

Paakkunainen composed this symphony for the performers who recorded it. On this recording, Valkeapää and Johan Anders Baer, another joik singer, sing the solo vocal parts. Paakkunainen plays the solo saxophone, and his group, Karelia, play the improvising instrumental parts. He has learned much about Saami music from Valkeapää, but Paakkunainen does not reproduce these sounds precisely. Valkeapää similarly recognizes that the joiks are sung in new idioms. In commissioning the *Juoigansinfoniija* Valkeapää himself was responsible for a particular kind of reinterpretation and performance of joiks. Joiks performed in the "hills"[2] are re-presented on the concert stage and in the recording studio.

To express interest in Saami music, even though it is incorporated in new idioms, is to express interest in Saami people and in their concerns. This is directly related to Saami political aims and objectives. Most contemporary joik song texts deal explicitly with the subjects of "Saaminess," Saami self-esteem, nature and childhood, environmental issues, pollution, the destruction of nature, and infringement on Saami land. The performance of Saami music in Helsinki, in the aftermath of the political meetings, thus carried a message of contestation regarding the values and ideologies of the state, as well as celebrating a distinctive Saami identity.

Saami assert their right to sing joiks, but, like other indigenous peoples, they do so from a position of little power within the nation-state. Performances do, however, bring their concerns into the public arena. They are members of these nation-states, but they will no longer accept being recognized as anything less than "distinctive members with special rights" (Dyck 1985, 22). But these performances continue to present us with the paradox that on one hand distinct identity is claimed through one's musical expression, yet on the other, that same music absorbs musical influences from various corners. The paradox is captured in a story related by Leisiö about a poem dealing with the disappearance of Saami culture: "The poem [written by Paulus Otsi] received a musical treatment in the early 1970s. The music was written by a young man then working in a gas station, Lars Svonni, who had in his mind the sound of a joiku and at the same time that of the slow, tight-reined bouzouki accompaniment of a Greek szardas. Svonni made the melody accompanying himself on the guitar, and in this way created a new kind of song, which the entire Saami population has now adopted almost as a national anthem" (Leisiö 1986, 53).

New folk Finnish and Saami musical exchanges feature in the recorded canon. The members of Angelin Tytöt were taught to play the guitar by a musician at the Department of Folk Music at the Sibelius Academy, as they wished to use this instrument to accompany their songs. This group's first recording was issued by the Mipu label, a company that was established in 1992 by Sari Kaasinen (the leader of the group Värttinä) and Heikki Kemppainen to promote the music of young Finnish folk musicians. In terms of vocal performance style and instrumental accompaniment, Värttinä's two recorded versions of the song "Kylä Vuotti Uutta Kuuta" ("The Village Waited for the New Moon") differ considerably. The first recording was produced in 1989 (Värttinä 1989, track 9), the second in 1992 (Värttinä 1992). The instrumental texture of the first version is generally thinner than the second, although the instrumentation is broad and includes a bell, drum, accordion, fiddle, kanteles, and birchbark aerophones. The second version includes percussion, string bass, accordion, fiddle, banjo, kantele, and keyboards. In terms of vocal performance style the most distinctive difference between the two versions is the rising pitch at the ends of some phrases, which is characteristic of a joik singing style. But maybe that is just the way I hear it, knowing that Värttinä's leader had just produced a CD of joik singers when she was working on this performance.[3]

LEARNING FROM SENEGALESE MUSICIANS

Malang Cissokho, born in Thies, near Dakar, the capital of Senegal, is the son of Jali Soundioulu Cissokho, a renowned *kora* performer, and Maimouna Kony, a singer who was born in Guinea. He has been a member of some of the most well known groups in Senegal, for example, Youssou N'Dour's Super Étoile de Dakar, and Ismael Lo Pro. He also worked with Hasse Walli and his band Asamaan (set up in the early 1990s), moving to and settling in Helsinki in 1989.

The following year, in 1990, Eino produced a recording (Cissokho 1990) of Malang Cissokho singing and playing the *kora* on nine tracks. On two tracks, the folklorist Hannu Saha once again collaborates with a musician by adding the five-string kantele. The *kora* is played by *jalis* (musicians and storytellers of the West African Mandinka people) in Senegal, Gambia, Guinea, and Mali. The role of *jali* passes from father to son. Many *jalis* were formerly attached to royal courts, where they sang praise songs and historical epics. Now they perform at social occasions, for rites of passage—births, marriages, deaths, and so on—and for radio and club nights. The *kora* is a twenty-one-stringed harp-lute. In the combination of *kora* and kantele, images of two distinct pasts, a Mandinka and a Finnish past, are brought together. It is a combination that epitomizes Cissokho's position, which unites his Mandinka heritage and his present, as well as his future, in Finland.

Saha had some prior knowledge of the *kora*. He had performed, as a member of the group Primo, with another *jali*, N'yana Suso, at the Kaustinen International Festival of Folk Music in 1985. When Jali N'yana Suso left Finland, he left his *kora* with Saha. Saha found some similarities between *kora* and kantele music. These were repetition and variation of short musical ideas—what he called "minimalist tendencies" (Hannu Saha, personal communication). His interest in twentieth-century minimalism shaped his view of music for the *kora*. For both N'yana Suso and Cissokho, the role of musician has been inherited from their forefathers. For Saha, in contrast, the *kora* is an instrument he plays only occasionally, having come across it through brief encounters with two of its exponents.

If Saha's collaboration with *jalis* has been fleeting, other Finnish musicians, notably Hasse Walli and Sakari Kukko, have had more extensive and long-term contacts with Senegalese musicians. Walli has been studying *mbalax*. *Mbalax* is a Wolof word that means "rhythm," specifically the rhythm of a drum called *mbung mbung*. Based on the rhythmic patterns played on these drums, *mbalax* has become known worldwide through the performances of Youssou N'Dour and his Super Étoile de Dakar. Walli's aim in studying Senegalese music is to build a bridge leading to a "new style" in which rock, jazz, and Senegalese rhythms are combined. He believes that his most challenging and important work with Senegalese music still lies ahead, but it is his intention to use this knowledge in his "own way" (Hasse Walli, personal interview, December 12, 1991).

Walli believes that his musical thinking has changed as a result of becoming more familiar with Senegalese music. These changes are especially apparent

with regard to rhythmic structures. He talked about some of the rhythmic difficulties he faced initially in collaborating with Senegalese musicians and revealed a surprising solution which enabled him to play at jam sessions on his
first visit to Senegal. His account reveals the extent to which his musical conceptualizations (particularly with regard to assessment of rhythmic figurations)
informed his encounter with a Senegalese musician. I quote at length:

> In 1982, I was jamming with Youssou [N'Dour] and I found that the hardest
> thing to do was to find where the first beat came. A song may be in 4/4 time
> but they might be playing in 6/8 time with 4/4 on top. Also the chords may
> change on odd beats of the bar. We are used to chord changes on the first
> beat [of the bar], but in Senegalese music it may change before or after—on
> the second, third, or fourth beat—and also in syncopation. One has to lis-
> ten to the drummer to find the beat, but this can also be off the beat and not
> what you expect to hear. When the *sabar* line is transferred to a drum set,
> the first beat might not be played on the bass drum as I would imagine, but
> on the snare drum. So this also gives it an upside-down sound. In addition
> to that the harmonies can change either in a simple or a complex manner.
> The first thing you have to learn is how to hear the music correctly. Sene-
> galese musicians and the audience hear immediately if you are lost. I even-
> tually managed to locate the first beat through various means. I watched
> people dancing and I listened to the long drum patterns, which culminate
> on the first beat. These drum solos can be from eight to sixteen bars in
> length, or even more.
>
> On my first visit to Senegal, when I met Sakari [Kukko] there, we
> found that one way of locating the first beat was through our familiarity with
> the Finnish tango. In the 1950s the tango was especially popular in the Fin-
> nish countryside. Of course the tango was associated with Argentina, and
> there were links in Cuba with the habanera rhythm. These were also inside
> Senegalese music, because Cuban music was so popular there. We used this
> tango aspect to play with Senegalese musicians. If we didn't know where we
> were in the metric structure we just played the tango rhythm and it some-
> how fitted in [example 8.1]. Can you imagine how surprised I was? I had
> traveled six thousand kilometers to find the same beat that I knew in Fin-
> land. (Personal interview with Hasse Walli, December 12, 1991)

This kind of musical interaction is based on a prior knowledge of music from
diverse sources. Finding common elements which resonate with one's musical

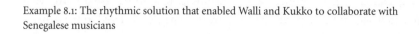

Example 8.1: The rhythmic solution that enabled Walli and Kukko to collaborate with
Senegalese musicians

thoughts, and using them in new contexts, leads to the mobility of musical material and flexibility in musical conceptualizations.

Nearly all of the musicians in Walli's band, Asamaan, relocated from Senegal to work with him on Helsinki-based projects. Walli described the rehearsal process and the structural format that the band follows in putting together a new piece. First of all the rhythm guitarist plays triads, to which Walli will often add suspended minor sevenths "to widen the chord" and "to put a little jazz inside the music." The rock guitarist and the vocalist, using a wailing technique, begin a dialogue and improvise as the music progresses. They follow a basic musical structure, which Walli believes the musicians have not used in Senegal before. To an A-B format they add two further sections, resulting in an A-B-C-D structure which is adhered to strictly in working out and rehearsing new pieces. A piece is typically put together as shown in figure 8.1. Meter can be changed, so that a riff might first appear in 6/8 and then reappear in 4/4 time. The band members play together for hours and repeat a song over and over. After many repetitions it should still "swing." Once all the players have composed and learned their parts, the songs are recorded as part of the rehearsal process. The recording acts as a memory aid.

FIGURE 8.1: STRUCTURAL PRINCIPLES GUIDING THE
REHEARSAL OF A NEW ASAMAAN COMPOSITION

Introduction | A: Two versions of the vocal theme | B: "Bridge," which
could be a repetition of the introduction | Instrumental solo | C: New
thematic material | Vocal solo with percussion or talking drum; traditional
Senegalese rhythmic patterns can be changed here | D: New material |
Last theme and coda (repetition of the introductory material) |

Two members of Asamaan, Yamar and Papp Sarr, played an active role in Finnish new folk music circles, particularly when they broke away from the group and attempted to establish a musical niche for themselves elsewhere. I first encountered them when I attended an exhibition on African art in the center of Helsinki. They were running a workshop. Sitting in the audience, a drummer from the Department of Folk Music at the Sibelius Academy listened attentively to the explanations and transcribed the rhythmic patterns. This was going to be an ongoing project, for opportunities to absorb these patterns were presented later at the department. Such workshops were offered to the department's students, and Yamar and Papp Sarr were also invited to perform at the Christmas party.

THE FINNISH TANGO

If the tango was the common element which Walli and Kukko found while collaborating with Senegalese musicians, the circumstances under which the tango was itself introduced to Finland reveal similar processes whereby Finnish and Senegalese music are linked. The tango, as in the repertoire of the Ostrobothnian group JPP, has been transformed, recontextualized, and re-represented as a Finnish form of expression.

The ethos of melancholy that Taylor (1987) describes as a feature of the Argentine tango reappears in the Finnish interpretation. From this perspective it is hardly surprising that Finns should have so intensely embraced this form of expression: what is noteworthy is their understanding of this ethos as an indigenous attribute, as their own imprint on the tango. Despite sharing the interpretation of the tango as "melancholy," in taking it, refashioning, and representing it as a Finnish form of expression, important differences emerge. Argentines regard Carlos Gardel, who died in a plane crash in 1935, as the greatest tango singer ever. Few people in Finland have heard of him. They have their own tango kings and queens, and the hero of Finnish tango music is Olavi Virta. The Finnish tango to which people dance is usually a song, whereas Argentines traditionally will not dance to a tango that is sung. Argentine tango song texts narrate the experience of exile and longing for one's homeland, and they describe life in Buenos Aires. Themes of identity and introspection are explored. Finnish tango song texts differ from Argentine ones, in that they seem to be escapist, or expressions of sentimental and melodramatic emotion. One of the most popular Finnish tango songs (example 8.2) deals with the longing for another land, a land which may only exist in the imagination or in one's dreams:

SATUMAA

Aavan meren tuolla puolen jossakin on maa,
missä onnen kaukorantaan laine liplattaa.
Missä kukat kauneimmat luo aina loistettaan,

Example 8.2: "Satumaa," by Unto Mononen

siellä huolet huomisen voi jäädä unholaan.
Oi jospa kerran sinne satumaahan käydä vois,
niin sieltä koskaan lähtisi en linnun lailla pois,
siivetönnä en voi lentää, vanki olen maan.
Vain aatoksin, mi kauas entää, sinne käydä saan . . .

WONDERLAND

Somewhere beyond the vast ocean there is a land
Where a wave laps at fortune's distant shore.
Where the most beautiful flowers bloom

And tomorrow's worries can be left forgotten.
Oh if once to that wonderland I could go,
I would never leave, never fly away,
But without wings I cannot fly,
On this land I am a prisoner.
I can reach there only in my thoughts . . .

(My translation)

In Finland the tango has become a part of national identity because of its vital role in popular culture (captured so vividly in Aki Kaurismäki's films). Via popular culture, the tango has been established as a "Finnish" genre that new folk musicians can develop according to their own individual aesthetic wishes. In addition to JPP, the accordionist Maria Kalaniemi (one of the initial class at the Department of Folk Music and now a teacher there) performs tango extensively. Her first "solo" album includes a track which pays tribute (acknowledged in the sleeve notes) to the Argentine influences in a piece which grew from particular enthusiasm for a Rom song, "Olin Sairas Kun Luokseni Saavuit" ("I Was Ill When You Came to Me"; Kalaniemi 1992, track 5).

IRISH MUSIC IN HELSINKI

Sometimes similarity (based on stereotyped ideas of shared characteristics) is stressed rather than exotic otherness. This is the case with Irish music in Finland. Olli-Pellikka, chairperson of the Finnish-Irish Society, summed up some views of similarity and difference in the following statement: "Our history is similar. Finland has been under Sweden and Russia, Ireland under England. Our heavy drinking habits are similar, although the Irish drink in pubs any day and the Finns drink at home during the weekend. In country dances you can see the same sort of behavior. The girls stand in a row and the boys rush to get a partner because if they are not quick they may not get one. Of course the differences are many too. Religion for example. Finns are mostly Lutheran and do not go to church. The Irish Catholics are always going to church" (personal interview with Olli-Pellikka, February 19, 1992).

Some of the bands playing "Irish" music in Helsinki are Korkkijalka, Boolabus, and Shindig. They play in the pubs and restaurants "O'Malley's," "Wanha Eerik," and "Kappeli" and for private parties and receptions. The type of membership, the repertory, and the musical and marketing aims of the band Boolabus are illustrative of the Irish-Finnish musical scene. There are six members of the band. Three of them are Irish, one is English, one French, and one Finnish. Apart from the Frenchman, none of the musicians in the band had been involved with Irish music before they came to live in Finland. They realized, however, that there was a market for performances of Irish music and with an authentic membership they felt well placed to offer them. Their repertoire includes Irish songs, which everyone in the audience recognizes, like "Whiskey in the Jar." It also includes some reggae and pop material (Bob Marley's "I Shot the Sheriff" and Elvis Presley's "Heartbreak Hotel").

For most of the musicians, playing in the band is just a hobby, and to me they emphasized that they are not "professional" musicians and that they do not play "real Irish music." Theirs is a generalized image of Irish music, and due to their conceptual models of what constitutes authentic performance they regard themselves neither as professionals nor as authentic players. Their assessments of authenticity are in contrast to those of their audiences. Many members of their audience who regularly attend performances insist that the band does play real Irish music.

One member of the audience at one of Korkkijalka's performances in O'Malley's commented: "I like this place because I can drink Guinness, hear Irish music, and talk to people. We can be more lively than we are normally and really feel that we are in Ireland." The performers contribute to this feeling and to the ambience of the pub: "The audience especially like it when the lead singer swears even if they don't understand everything he says . . . but they know he is swearing and they associate that with being Irish" (personal interview with Francis Weaver, a member of Boolabus, October 20, 1991). The sense of "Irishness," the "lively" behavior, is constructed in particular performance settings. As well as music, perceived behavioral characteristics may be appropriated and transformed. The ethos of liveliness, of talking even to strangers, contrasts with the sense of melancholy at tango venues. In nonperformance contexts, the musicians' links and interactions with Finnish society are emphasized. All of them, like the West African musicians, have established links, mainly through family and work, with Finland. There are also links between Irish and Finnish new folk music circles—the kantele player Minna Raskinen, for example, used to play the fiddle with Boolabus, the Finnish fiddler Kari Reiman plays with both Korkkijalka and Värttinä, and Harry Bent, the Irish singer with Korkkijalka, teaches Irish song at the Department of Folk Music at the Sibelius Academy.

These musicians acknowledge that their musical activities bring them opportunities to participate in commercially orientated markets as well as to represent specific identities. All of these Finnish-Irish bands have appeared in the
annual Irish Festival held in Helsinki, Tampere, and Turku. Bands from Ireland
are invited to perform at the festival, and they are the main attractions. There is
a state and commercial involvement in the promotion of Irish music in Finland.
The festival attracts financial support from both Finnish and Irish bodies, highlighting institutional and commercial awareness of music as a medium for political and cultural activism. In 1991, for example, the Irish Ministry of Foreign
Affairs awarded £2,000 and the Guinness firm £3,000 to the festival. Finnish
sources were the Ministry of Education (120,000 FM), a Parliament special
grant (70,000 FM), and the Finnish Performing Music Promotion Center (un-
specified amount; information from Olli-Pellikka, chairperson of the Finnish-
Irish Society).

APPROPRIATION, ORIGINALITY, REPRESENTATION

Most of the preceding examples indicate musical interactions between individuals. Karhu visits the Folk Music Department at the Sibelius Academy. So, too,
do Yamar and Papp Sarr. Pakkunainen and Valkeapää are long-standing friends
and musical collaborators. Walli travels to Senegal and develops an enthusiasm
for *mbalax*. How do musicians perceive these collaborations? How can musical
performances based on notions of exchange actually fix ideas of musical difference? What one learns from these exchanges can be used later in "original"
compositions. Walli plans to use *mbalax* music to create something new. For
Senegalese musicians, however, who have played with Asamaan, the music of
this group is already removed from their experience of *mbalax*. Yamar[4] and
Papp Sarr told me that their own style changed a lot while playing with
Asamaan, and they have returned to more "traditional" practices.

Papp Sarr plays the *sabar*, which he is learning from Yamar: "Yamar leads our
practice and teaches me. He has taught me everything I know about the *sabar*.
The rhythms I know already. As children we use all kinds of surfaces, like pots,
to tap these rhythms. But you know there are "secrets"—how to get the best
sound from the *sabar*. This is what the *jalis* teach. Yamar cannot remember
when he first started playing because it was in his family and he was so young.
If we make a mistake in a performance here in Finland, nobody notices because
they are not familiar with the rhythms. But if we make a mistake in Senegal,

everybody knows. Even if they are dancing, they would still hear the mistake" (personal interview with Papp Sarr, December 3, 1991).

Yamar and Papp Sarr are acutely aware of changes in *mbalax* music as performed in Finland. They also spoke about changes in the performance contexts and the differences between audiences in Senegal and in Finland: "In Finland, people come to hear some music, meet friends, and talk. In Senegal, they listen to music and dance. I would like it if people here would dance or clap in accompaniment even from the first song. Sometimes I can see that people want to dance but they are too shy to get up—they wait for other people to dance first, or they wait until they have been drinking enough. Dance is very important, however, and it gives a good feeling to the musicians. At first I did not know that people were shy to dance, now I know that if I wait long enough, they will start" (personal interview with Papp Sarr, December 3, 1991).

One of the first Senegalese musicians to go to Finland in the 1980s was Badu N'diay. He played with the group Piirpauke for seven years before leaving to set up his own band. He uses musical material that he played in Senegal ten to twenty years ago, but he wants to combine it with rock music. I asked him whether he felt that he was maintaining links with Senegal by using this same musical material. His response was that he was not: "It is not to link myself to Senegal. Being an African in Europe, I am constantly reminded that I am Senegalese" (Badu N'diay, personal communication).

N'diay finds that because of his work with Finnish musicians he has had to change rhythmic patterns, simplifying them and using them repetitively. He sometimes plays the *tama* in Finland, which he never does in Senegal: "I do not play these drums, I am a guitarist." The majority of N'diay's audiences do not recognize that he is not a *tama* player (plate 18).

The discourse of several Helsinki-based West African musicians pointed to the ways in which "domains of difference" (Bhabha 1994) marked their everyday movements around the city. Feelings of frustration, hostilities encountered, and the constant imposition of the status of outsider within Finnish society arose beyond the context of collaborative musical projects. Racism became an issue when embarking on Finnish-based projects, exacerbated in the early 1990s with the Finnish acceptance of refugees from Somalia, with whom these musicians were sometimes associated. Despite the small numbers of musicians involved, the kinds of musical exchanges that characterize the case of Hasse Walli and Asamaan must also be viewed in relation to the "politics of multiculturalism in the New Europe" (Modood and Werbner 1997). These exchanges are contributions to the musical hybridity of the "multicultural society." They are interesting in the Finnish example because they cannot be easily explained in multiculturalist terms despite Finland's place in the New Europe. Finnish-Senegalese collaborations cannot be explained in the ways that, for example, reggae in Britain or rai in France often are—as products of postcoloniality in places populated by immigrants and their descendants (Werbner 1997, 261).

Here are some of the statements of other West African musicians in Helsinki that reveal their experiences of difference:

When I first came to Finland, being Black was a novelty. People were friendly. They asked me to come for coffee. Now people just think I am another Somalian refugee.

The first two questions Finnish men ask me are "Where are you from?" and "How long are you going to stay in Finland?" I used to say that I did not know how long I would be here, and I would be hassled. Now I say that I am going to Africa tomorrow and then the men become a bit more friendly and might even chat for a while.

Some people say to me: "I do not like Black people but you are all right." Since 1990 there have been more incidents.

I asked Finnish musicians what they know about the impressions and experiences in Finland of the African musicians with whom they work. Although they have formed close bonds, the Finnish musicians knew little about the sentiments outlined here. Compare the above statements to those I heard from Finnish musicians:

I want to go to Africa to learn African music. . . . ["Why not learn from African musicians in Finland?" I asked.] I do not want to meet Africans here, I want to see the real Africa.

I think that Finnish girls in particular react positively to African musicians. It is still quite new to see Africans here and they have an exotic image. I think that problems are nonexistent. At first I wondered whether I should discuss possible racism, but I did not want to alarm unnecessarily. Of course I advise them to mingle with "nice people" so potential trouble is avoided.

I have not asked African musicians what they think about Finnish society. Sometimes African and Cuban musicians ask me to go to bars with them, but maybe that is because they think they might have language difficulties. Sure there may be problems with racism, but I have not witnessed any incidents. The musicians do not discuss these things with me, and I have not asked.

One of the most striking examples of music as a product detachable from the person was the use of the *tama* at the private viewing of an exhibition at the Amos Anderson Art Museum in the center of Helsinki (February 15, 1991). The designer, Stefan Lindfors, set up an exhibition on the theme *Reges Insectorum (Rulers of the Insect World)*. Sculptures made from steel, brass plate, and fiberglass represented grasshoppers and caterpillars. Lindfors asked N'diay to play the *tama* at the preview, which was attended by some of the elite of Finnish society. He wanted to evoke, as interpreted by N'diay, an atmosphere of the exotic, of the unknown, of the jungle. The viewers circulated around the exhibition with champagne glasses in hand, often casting a seemingly perfunctory glance at the sculptures, and in their attention to the art of mingling, hardly noticed the exotic touch. The drummer only seemed to be there to provide background sounds.

It represented not only separation of music as product from person, then, but also difference in meanings. For Lindfors, the drum was in the background to add an exotic element to his sculptures and to form some kind of frame for their interpretation. The viewers, however, seemed to be barely aware of the drummer's presence. For N'diay himself it was just a way of earning some money, and in any case the *tama* is an instrument on which he does not feel competent. He is a guitarist whose musical idol is Mick Jagger (Badu N'diay, personal communication).[5] There is no evidence here, then, of an "intercontinental traffic in meaning" (Hannerz 1987, 547). N'diay interpreted the event as one that played on stereotypes of "others" on display with their markers (such as the *tama*) of "otherness."

Lindfors adding timbral affects with the *tama* to his exhibition, Walli turning to *mbalax* for musical inspiration, and the incorporation of tango in Finnish popular culture are obvious cases of "borrowing." But musical traditions from specific regions within the nation-state—for example, from Karelia, or from Ostrobothnia—have themselves been appropriated, transformed, and re-represented as parts of a "national" culture. The processes are the same whether the musical material comes from different regions or neighbors (Saami joiks, Karelian song, Swedish instrumental dance music) or from further afield (Argentina, Cuba, Senegal). These kinds of musical processes within musical practices labeled "national," which involve musical multiplicity and turning to traditions beyond national boundaries, emphasize the point that the nation is not a site of musical homogeneity.

These processes of appropriation are an aspect of creative transformations that are based on musical choices. At the beginning of this chapter I posed the question of how musical choices are made. This is a topic that has occupied the attention of several commentators. For some, musical choices are made because of the inherent value of particular musics (Dahlhaus [1970] 1983, 3). For others, musical choices are socially determined (Bourdieu 1984; Shepherd 1991). This is a view which contrasts with Finnegan's suggestion that what makes people embark on certain musical "pathways" "is all a bit of a mystery, as, perhaps, basic life choices usually are" (1989, 307). While these writers offer very different perspectives on the question of musical choice, in various ways they provide insights into the borrowing of traditions found in the case of Finnish new folk music. New folk musicians certainly turn to those musics that they find interesting and aesthetically pleasing. I watched Arto Järvelä as he listened to Hungarian folk fiddlers at the 1992 Kaustinen Festival. He was engrossed in their performance. Two years later, the first (and title) track on JPP's recording *Kaustinen Rhapsody* (JPP 1994) reveals the influence of the Hungarian group's performing style. As for the second view of how one can account for musical choices, a refined notion of social determination is suggested by Meyer, who writes about composition as a process involving the making of musical choices: "Every composition . . . is an actualization of possibilities latent in the constraints of a style. And in this sense, every composition is the solution of a problem: that of choosing musical materials and discerning how their implications might be realized, given the alternatives possible in the style" (1989, 110). For Meyer, musical choices are constrained by internal and external factors. It is external constraints (political, economic, social, intellectual, technological) which "always impinge upon and sometimes influence both the invention of novelty and its selection" (1989, 106). But because of the contingent nature of musical choices, which prevents them from being predicted, they can appear, as Finnegan suggests, "mysterious."

Slobin, too, probes the issue of musical choice in looking at musical processes particularly relevant to the Finnish new folk music example. He writes that although it is difficult to account for musical choice, "when a jazz musician quotes Beethoven, when a Latino singer mixes English phrases into his Spanish, when an ultra-Orthodox Jewish songwriter sets Hebrew texts to a rock tune, *we can hardly imagine that they do so accidentally"* (Slobin 1993, 86; emphasis mine). He suggests that we think of this process as one of "reevaluation": "over time, new perspectives cause a reordering of group priorities, a changed understanding of what is 'authentic,' what represents 'us' best to outsiders, what sells best to a new generation of listeners, or what is now 'ours' that once was 'theirs'" (95). New folk musicians in Finland, working within the framework of "tradition," are guided in their choices by aesthetic sensibilities that seem to embrace musical change. The process of reevaluation over the period of about a decade (from the late 1980s through the 1990s) can be charted through the recorded repertoires of groups like JPP and Värttinä, which demonstrate an expanding view in terms of incorporating musical elements and even performance styles from increasingly diverse sources. Sari Kaasinen (of Värttinä) was pleased when a techno-mix recording of two of the group's songs, "Miinan Laulu" ("Miina's Song") and "Kiiriminna," was made by the group Local Off (Local Off 1992) and featured Värttinä's vocal lines (Sari Kaasinen, personal interview, August 5, 1992). In 1996, Värttinä used similar kinds of electronically manipulated vocal sounds (on the album *Kokko* [1996]). This is a philosophy of experimentation, looking to external models and composing and arranging folk music that has been encouraged by the institutionalization process of folk music in Finland and entry into competitive commercial musical markets.

Musical choices and borrowings are important in the global sphere. Musical ideas travel to all parts of the world through the movements of people and processes of global communication and musical commodification. Trends such as world music give rise to the fear that increased musical interaction and wider communication systems will be the standardization of music and cultural "grey-out" (Nettl 1983, chapter 27). If all musics sound the same, it seems logical to suppose that "folk" music will lose its representational role and its status as a marker of identity. A more optimistic view of creative processes is that these conditions of contemporary musical life will allow a multitude of music cultures to continue to emerge and to thrive (Wallis and Malm 1984, chap. 10). Hannerz offers a similar perspective in observing that the "contemporary globalization of culture cannot . . . be easily summarized in some single formula, and there is no easy assessment of its impact in evaluative terms" (1989, 214). The difficulties that arise in attempting to categorize music as either world or folk lie in the mobility of musical material and in the possibility of attributing diverse meanings to music. The geographic, historical and cultural contexts of any particular music are open to reformulation.

World music seems to occupy a global performance space and is often represented as the result of a Western hegemony, but it is composed of a host of musical traditions, including Finnish new folk music, that show local responses to global trends. Those traditions themselves, in turn, may be made up of various borrowed elements. The tango is just one of the many recontextualized musical elements which contribute to the formulation of Finnish new folk music. Participation in workshops on Senegalese music offers Finnish new folk musicians musical ideas that they may also incorporate in their own music performances. The labels "world" and "folk" are an aspect of competition between performers, promoters, and audiences. The idea of difference is sometimes maintained even if there seems to be no analytical basis for the making of musical distinctions. Conversely, perceivable musical differences do not prevent musical elements or performances as being categorized as, for instance, "Finnish" or "folk," and "world."

To end this chapter, I return to one example of a musical collaboration discussed above to pose further questions about national identities, musical identities, and their representations. The recording of Cissokho and Saha was made by a small, rather obscure, local company. It was financially supported by the Finnish Performing Music Promotion Center (see chap. 9). This is an organization which aims to influence the "professional capacities of Finnish artists, the quality and quantity of Finnish phonogram production, and the international competitive position of Finnish performing music" (as stated in its information leaflet). Cissokho, playing the *kora* in collaboration with Saha playing the kantele, is at least perceived as having the potential to influence the "international competitive position of *Finnish* performing music." In another context he is known as the son of one of Senegal's most famous *kora* players and as a musician who has played and recorded with one of the "stars" of the world music circuit, who presents us with Senegalese traditions, Youssou N'Dour. Is Cissokho a "world" musician in Helsinki or a musician who draws on Senegalese musical traditions which admittedly may be a little "exotic" but which contribute nevertheless to the advancement of the local (Finnish) phonogram industry?

Perhaps the "very act of labelling" (Frith 1989, 102) plays its part in determinations of musical meaning and representation. Labels evoke sets of associations. Musics in differentiated cultural arenas, as being one thing or another, depend on them. Why is tango Finnish, but *mbalax* not (yet) Finnish? One difference lies in the presence of the exotic Senegalese performers who inhabit

Helsinki's urban landscape. Their otherness is visible and affects all of their interactions in Finnish society. By contrast, tango performers in Finland are no longer usually Argentine. Viewing musical material separate from specific performers assists in processes of recontextualization. So the Finnish musician Walli wants to use *mbalax* in his own way. Maybe *mbalax*, or something bearing a resemblance to it, will one day be as Finnish as Karelian songs, Saami joiks, or the tango.

NINE

Global Commodities

THE NEW FOLK MUSIC RECORDING
IN WORLD MUSIC MARKETS

"Of course it's folk music—it's world music and world music *is* folk music!" exclaimed Hannu Tolvanen in response to another of my questions (Hannu Tolvanen, personal interview, March 24, 1992).

Finnish new folk music, like many other folk musics, has become increasingly interconnected with the world and popular music market through the efforts of its practitioners. Finnish new folk musicians reach out to audiences wherever they find them. In this respect the record industry plays a vital role, and this chapter focuses on the recording as a representation of Finnish new folk music and identity in the global market.

We have seen that at the same time that new folk musicians borrow from "others," conform to global trends, and establish a place for themselves on world music stages through performances and recordings, they continue to imagine and represent their music as localized expression. The recording as a global commodity contributes to the shifting spaces in which Finnish new folk music is performed and to the different labels by which it is known: "Finnish new folk" or "world" music. If location in a village, regional, or national context is an important marker of folk musical authenticity, world music, by contrast is not tied to a particular place. It offers "the specter of a global ecuneme" (Erlmann 1993, 7). It exists in transnational spaces. Commercial interests assume an increasing importance as world music is marketed and sold as a musical product. As one of the products in a global market it is produced and disseminated through mass media systems and shaped by technological advances. Yet world music, as Hannu Tolvanen observes, "feeds" from folk musics around the world. These do not necessarily meet with each other (although they often do) but are shaped by popular aesthetics. It is precisely because "world music" is seen as the meeting of electronic Western popular and traditional musics that it gives rise to fears of musical homogenization marked by asymmetric exchanges (Baumann 1992).

If promoters of world music emphasize difference to conceal a fundamental "sameness," as Erlmann (1993, 8) suggests, folk music is a medium through which ideas about unity and difference are emphatically expressed. The "otherness" of world music in Finland is apparent in considering how music journalists have used the term. "World music" began to be used extensively by Finnish music journalists in 1989. In the same year, the Finnish Society for Ethnomusicology published an issue of the journal *Musiikin Suunta* (*Trends in Music*; 1989, no. 2) focusing on world music. Four different concepts of world music, based on the writings of music journalists, were outlined in this issue. World music could be (1) "A commercial and exotic fad, . . . a superficial show of ethnic music"; (2) "Modern or authentic music from all over the world—an alternative to industrial standard entertainment and rock"; (3) "Music of unknown and forgotten peoples, which in its authenticity will conquer the world . . . [a view held by] those concerned over the future of peripheral music cultures"; (4) "Modern pop music . . . that has developed from an ethnic basis" (Kurkela and Laakkonen 1989a).

Authors contributing to this journal issue examined world music in Finland, including the operation of Digelius as a world music retailer (Iltanen 1989), world music journalism (Kurkela 1989a), the reception of Finnish rock audiences to world music (Kurkela and Laakkonen 1989b), and Finnish bands playing "ethnic" music (Heikkilä and Penttilä 1989). In the same year, a later issue of the journal (*Musiikin Suunta* 1989, no. 4) focused on the questions, Folk music—which folk and which music? (These are Tolvanen's questions; 1989, 1.) All the contributions discussed developments in Finnish folk music. These publications indicate the interest of Finnish commentators in analyzing trends in folk music and world music.

The local-global debate seems an appropriate forum for theorizing the relationship between folk and world, but it has proved elusive.[1] If world music "does away with time and place" as Erlmann puts it (1993, 12), the folk musics from which it emerges are seen as being clearly situated in identified historical and geographic contexts: symbols of nations, of regions, of villages. In fact, it is in this very tension between notions of a total system and localized cultural practices that Erlmann identifies a space for musical ethnography. Musical ethnographies, he suggests, "will increasingly have to examine the choices performers worldwide make in moving about the spaces between system and its multiple environments" (1993, 6). This draws us close to Robertson's view of local-global questions. He frames the debate in terms of universalism (the trend toward a homogenous world system) and particularism (in which local differences are emphasized) and tries to draw these two opposing tendencies together in claiming that "we are in the late twentieth century, witnesses to—and participants in—a massive, twofold process involving the interpenetration of the universalization of particularism and the particularization of universalism" (1991, 73).

My central questions concerning how Finnish new folk music continues to be a marker of national identity (where nationalist ideology stresses an internal coherence) at the same time that new folk musicians are obviously involved with processes of musical borrowings from a global sphere stem from the tensions between universalistic (world music as an "encompassing system") and particularistic (the construction of musical difference) tendencies highlighted by both Erlmann and Robertson. Some attempt at a resolution is made by Robertson when he claims: "our commitment to the idea of the culturally cohesive national society has blinded us to the various ways in which the world as a whole has been increasingly 'organized' around sets of shifting definitions of the global circumstance. . . . the idea of global culture is just as meaningful as the idea of national-societal, or local, culture" (1991, 89–90). World music and the new folk music recording in global markets throw us the challenge to conceptualize music in wide-ranging systems, yet the shadow of the particular is never far behind. World musicians often see themselves as individual representatives of a local culture. New folk musicians in Finland are committed to the idea that they perform "Finnish" folk traditions. As a child, Minna Raskinen would have liked the opportunity to play other instruments. As a kantele player, however, she now has many opportunities to travel and perform around the world, representing Finnish music and Finnish culture (Minna Raskinen, personal communication). These opportunities are often provided by the kind of state ideology expressed in a report produced and published by the Arts Council of Finland: "Finnish artists need, in order to survive, grant systems and strong professional organisations to bargain with cultural policy makers;

and the nation needs artists for the maintenance of a national cultural identity" (Mitchell and Karttunen 1991, 12; emphasis mine).

The four Nordic countries (Finland, Denmark, Norway, and Sweden) established well-structured public sector systems after the Second World War to finance the arts and cultural services (Mitchell 1989). In Finland, the notion that culture is a route to international recognition had its antecedent, however, in the views propagated in the national romantic movement by figures like Snellman, who believed that the development of a nation's cultural strength was a prerequisite to combating overpowering, external forces. During the nineteenth century such strength was located in folk culture, but this is an ideology that informs all kinds of music making in Finland.[2] Current policies formed with regard to music as a marker of national identity are also shaped in relation to thinking about the role of the Nordic Fringe (Tuomioja 1991) in a changing Europe (Koivisto and Paasio 1990, major speeches; Lander 1991). Internal scrutiny as well as affirmation of nationalist stances has been well documented. The Arts Council of Finland, for example, has produced working papers dealing with patterns of cultural participation and consumption (Mitchell 1991), surveys of the economic situation and social status of the Finnish artist (Mitchell and Ristimäki 1992), and the training of cultural administrators and arts managers (Mitchell and Fisher 1992). Ethnomusicological contributions to the evaluation of music policy have also been solicited in reflexive consideration of state policy-making processes (Lahtinen 1991).

Minna Raskinen's views on her kantele performances around the world and state funding and policy formulation processes provide evidence in support of Robertson's charge of the commitment to the "idea of a cohesive national society." The new folk music recording in the global marketplace, by contrast, encourages us to explore the "global circumstance." As Finnish music is taken into the world through recordings, it becomes, as does West African music in Finland (see chap. 8), a product that can be detached from particular (national) contexts and persons. This is a point that Wallis and Malm (1984) illustrate at length in a study resulting from a three-year research project entitled "The Music Industry in Small Countries." They focus on the music industry—the relationships forged with the local music scene and the effects on it of large transnational record companies (e.g., CBS, RCA, EMI, Polygram), with their electronic technology and mass-produced popular music. Individual musicians interacting with a music industry weave a contrapuntal tapestry between the particular and the universal. Individuals in the public eye—the soloist, composer, or conductor in the classical music world, or Konsta Jylhä in the 1960s and Värttinä and JPP in the 1990s in the Finnish folk music world—reach their public status through the marketing of music as a product. A huge trans-national music industry involved with production, mass reproduction, mar-keting, distribution, copyright, complex ownership and financial relationships (Wallis and Malm 1984), and mass media (Lehtiranta and Saalonen 1993; Manuel 1993) plays its part in representations of music. It has links to govern-ment bodies, cultural policy-making processes, and organizations with differ-ent vested interests. The following discussion will highlight the production and promotion processes of new folk music recordings and consider the recorded new folk canon as a sonic representation of "Finnishness."

While individual musicians as representatives of Finnish culture perform around the world, their recordings provide another kind of representation of Finnish music in which musical sounds are detached from the players who pro-duce them. Thomas Edison's invention, the phonograph (1877), was to play a central role in shaping ideas about the widespread availability of music and provide a medium for the representation of musical sound (for the recording is not totally faithful to the acoustics of live performance).[3] Just as the perception of what music is changed around 1800 with the notion of the "masterpiece" as a work preserved (in the form of the musical score) in the permanent repertory of Western art music, whether or not it is actually performed (see Goehr 1992), so too, around 1900 with the invention of the phonograph, musics as sound (in the form of recordings) could be perceived as objects separate from ourselves, existing independently of our active, contemplative, or interpretative stance to-ward them.

Wallis and Malm's (1984) comments on the removal of music from its tradi-tional context and on changing attitudes to music have a bearing on our chang-ing concepts of "folk music," music in place, and the folk recording as a repre-sentation of folk music sound which is circulated as a commodity in global markets. They observe that in attaining independent status and in being re-garded as part of a nation's "culture," music is used more and more as a symbol of identity: "With specialisation, professionalism and mediaization (adaptation to modern media), music becomes an independent phenomenon, a sound structure which can be performed outside its original context. At the same time other art forms (drama, dance, sculpture etc.) also attain independent status, and together with music become known as 'art' or 'culture' " (Wallis and Malm 1984, 15). This is applicable to new folk music, which is a potent symbol of national identity because it is part of a "national culture." The new folk music recording in a global market further exemplifies music achieving independent status in a new performance arena. As Manuel notes, recording technology presents a "fixed rendition of a performance as a tangible, salable entity" and as the recording acquires commodity status "it takes on a social life of its own" (Manuel 1993, 7).

In Finland, the emphasis on the recording of new folk music highlights the reformulation of local self-images in response to representations of national culture in the international marketplace (see Guilbault 1993). In representing Finnish identity and culture it is increasingly contemporary developments in folk music rather than notions of the traditional that attract attention. This is partly due to commercial success, for it is new folk music that sells. New folk musicians have become the representatives of Finnish folk music around the world because they interpret Finnish traditions in ways that reach out to diverse audiences. For those who take a purist view, new folk music recordings are decontextualized products in a transnational industry. Nevertheless, as sonic representations of new folk music they effectively contribute to ongoing hopes for the acknowledgement of "Finnish identity." In furthering the aim of marking a Finnish identity and reinforcing the place of Finnish music in the world, new folk musicians are supported by institutional, state, and commercial bodies with overlapping interests, such as local recording companies and music promotion centers.

SMALL RECORD COMPANIES IN FINLAND

Small record companies in Finland have played a vital role in the promotion of new folk music through recordings. One could even argue that without the interest and recording projects of small, local companies, Finnish new folk music would not have established a presence in the world music market as rapidly as it has done. Such an argument accords with the results of Wallis and Malm's study of the spread of the music industry around the globe, which highlights the role played by small companies in determining what kinds of music people listen to. They address the issue of musical homogenization as a result of a transnational industry in asking whether people are consequently listening to

the same sounds: "The answer . . . is yes and no, for two reasons. One is the rela-
tive availability of low-cost phonogram technology. The other is the complex
relationship between the big and the small in the phonogram industry. The big
get bigger by swallowing up the small. But the small keep cropping up" (Wallis
and Malm 1984, 73).

Three small recording companies have played a central role in producing the
recorded canon of Finnish new folk music. Olarin Musiikki has been one of
the most active companies in producing Finnish new folk music recordings.
Other small companies, Eino and the Folk Music Institute's recording departments, have also contributed to the transmission of contemporary folk music
performances.

OLARIN MUSIIKKI: Timo Närväinen, a label manager[4] for Polygram when
I interviewed him, also has his own record company (which was set up as
a "hobby")—Olarin Musiikki. By early 1992, this company had released, with
financial support from ESEK (see below), about forty recordings, most of
which were of Finnish new folk music. The company was established in the
early 1970s and used to import blues recordings from the States. Närväinen described how he turned his attention to new folk music:

> I used to hate folk music; I could not stand it. In the midseventies I some-
> how got curious to find out about folk music and to check some music
> festivals. I realized it was very human music, so that is how my taste just
> changed. When I noticed that the seventies folk boom was over and that
> there was hardly anybody who released folk music records, I thought that I
> could give it a chance and see if something would happen. In the beginning
> it was planned just to release one album and to see what kind of response
> there would be. The first record was successful, especially mediawise, so
> I just could not stop. In the beginning it was only one or two albums a
> year. . . . basically it started to grow and I noticed that I was almost the only
> one who produced folk music records. There was only the Folk Music In-
> stitute, who had a couple of old recordings, but no one was recording any
> new artists, so that is why I continued. In the last three years we have been
> the busiest: we have released over twenty albums. (Timo Närväinen, per-
> sonal interview, March 10, 1992)

Since the time of my fieldwork, Närväinen's company has continued to flourish
and is still one of the main producers of Finnish new folk music recordings.

OY EINO LEVY: It was the idea of three people in particular—Vesa Kaartinen, Hannu Saha (the Director of the Folk Music Institute) and Heikki Laitinen (the first Director of the Folk Music Department at the Sibelius Academy)—to set up the record company Oy Eino Levy. They wanted to produce recordings of music that had a "crazy" element (although it proved to be difficult to give a clear definition of what this entailed), and of music which would not otherwise be recorded (Vesa Kaartinen, personal interview, June 23, 1992). This was the company that recorded Eric Peltoniemi's version of the ballad "Velisurmaaja" (see chap. 5) and Santtu Karhu's "Aunuksen Anja" (see chap. 8). By mid-1992, there were eleven recordings on the Eino catalogue. The records were mostly sent to radio stations and to journalists for publicity, rather than sold for commercial purposes. As Olarin Musiikki was for Timo Närväinen, Eino was regarded as being a "hobby" for Kaartinen, the director of the company. Most of the company's financial returns came from copyright revenue.

An examination of the list of shareholders in this record company shows that the promotion of music through recordings is another way in which people involved with new folk music circles collaborate. Some of the shareholders (who have appeared in these pages in other capacities) were Vesa Kaartinen, Hannu Saha, and Jari Sikander who were childhood friends and used to play together in the band Mummi Kutoo (Granny is Knitting); and Heikki Laitinen, Arto Järvelä, Hannu Tolvanen, and Hannu Lehtoranta (from the folk revivalist band Tuulenkantajat), among others.

FOLK MUSIC INSTITUTE: The recordings produced at this institute can be regarded in the same way as folk music recordings produced by other small companies, but there is an important difference. The institute also releases recordings of folk performances that are unlikely to find a niche in commercial markets. These recordings are made because of the ethos of preserving folk traditions, and they function as historic sound documents.

THE FINNISH PERFORMING MUSIC PROMOTION CENTER (ESEK)

The Finnish Performing Music Promotion Center (Esittävän Säveltaiteen Edistämiskeskus, hereafter, ESEK) is predisposed to providing support for recordings of music such as "folk," "jazz," and "experimental" music. This is one agency that has financially supported the folk music recording projects of small, local companies that have contributed to establishing Finnish new folk music in global performance spaces. It is the most important organization for the promotion of music in Finland. The center was established (on paper in 1982 and as a functional office in 1983) as a separate unit in connection with Gramex (see below). The aims of this organization are to influence "the professional capacities of Finnish artists, the quality and quantity of Finnish phonogram production, and the international competitive position of Finnish performing music." It does so by supporting phonogram and audiovisual music program production, performance, the provision of training courses and master classes, and publishing. These activities are financed by funds received from copyright legislation (Rome convention) and the blank tape levy introduced in 1984 to compensate performers and producers for home taping (information from Leena Hirvonen, secretary general of ESEK; and an ESEK leaflet). The center was also asked by the Ministry of Culture to support Finnish artists performing abroad and to take care of projects involving the export of performing music (for which the Ministry of Culture gave subsidies).[5] The aims and activities of this center indicate some ways in which government bodies have become involved with, and have reacted to, global processes and markets. Supporting local phonogram production, for instance, is a way of maintaining a local music industry faced with the competition of large transnational companies. Supporting performing music projects abroad allows Finnish music to be heard on a worldwide scale.

Applications for financial support are mostly received for the production of rock and pop phonograms. In an interview, Leena Hirvonen commented on the increasing international reputation of folk music and elaborated on the way in which ESEK's funding is distributed between light music (almost 80 percent, including folk music at about 5 percent per annum) and art music (Leena Hirvonen, personal interview July 2, 1992).[6]

MUSIC AS PRODUCT: QUESTIONS OF OWNERSHIP

Folk music, world music—whose music? It seems easy to think about music as a product that can be bought and sold when we focus on the "object"—for example, the CD recording in a commercial transaction. On the other hand, musical borrowings—exchanges as part of a creative process—raise difficult questions about "ownership," "creative identity," and the ways in which the work of creative agents can be evaluated. These are questions addressed explicitly in, and complicated by, copyright conventions that deal with notions of both the "creator" and the creative work as a "product." The basic principle of copyright conventions, such as the Berne Convention of 1886, is that "the creator of a work of music or a text is entitled to some kind of remuneration when the work is performed in any country that has ratified the convention" (Wallis and Malm 1984, 47). This principle joins the recognition of the individual, on the one hand, with recognition of the individual's music (the "work"), as a product on the other. With the growth of the phonogram industry, international copyright agreements have been supplemented by the Rome Convention of 1961 and the Geneva Convention of 1971. These agreements stipulate that performers and phonogram producers are also given the rights to remuneration when a phonogram is played on the radio or television. The involvement of remuneration complicates the relationship between "ownership" and "creative process." The commercial transaction that occurs in the implementation of copyright procedures relies on attributing music to identified sources. In the productization of music (in the case of the recording, for example) attribution is further complicated, for, as Goldstein observes in his discussion of the impact of technology on British folk song, "the primary result of the technological breakthroughs . . . has been to supply new media for the presentation and communication of ideas and information" (1982, 7). The issue of how music is represented in contexts of communicating ideas and information is linked to the relations of power between musicians (cf. the Graceland debate, described in Meintjes 1990; Feld 1994b).

The conditions for the ratification of the Rome Convention in Finland provide an example of the interaction between global and local demands, aims, and concerns. Under the Finnish copyright act of 1961, performers and phonogram producers were granted the rights to remuneration for certain public usages of phonograms.[7] Gramex, the Copyright Society of Performing Artists and Producers of Phonograms in Finland, was established during the latter half of the 1960s. It was an organization that collected remuneration for the playing of phonograms from Finnish Broadcasting companies. All money from copyright revenues was distributed on an individual basis in the ratio of 50 percent to the performer and 50 percent to the producer. During the latter half of the 1970s, discussions took place about whether some part of the money, which amounted to significant sums, should, in addition to its distribution to individual Finnish right holders, be used collectively—for example, to train musicians and to promote the production of recordings which could not be produced on a commercial basis. At the same time, attempts were being made to get the Rome Convention ratified in Finland. There was a struggle between musicians and producers against the agents of broadcasting organizations. The latter argued that the ratification of the convention would cause a unilateral flow of money out of Finland. Musicians and producers in contact with their foreign counterparts obtained written assurances that they would be able to use internally the money gained from copyright revenues for "foreign" music broadcast in Finland. The proposal that Gramex would use copyright money to promote music in Finland was presented to the government. It was under this provision, the nondistribution agreement, that the convention was ratified in 1983 (Jukka Liedes, special government adviser to the Ministry of Education, personal communication).[8] The Finnish Performing Music Promotion Center (ESEK) was established in order to carry out these promotional activities.

Such international agreements emphasize developments in the local rather than the global arena. They reveal ideas about having rights to claim music as one's own. Copyright principles operate by attributing music products to specified "creators," and disagreements arise from contested ownership of particular music materials. They would seem to preclude "borrowings." How then do Finnish new folk musicians play the "Texas Blues" or Swedish polskas under categories of representation that identify them as "Finnish folk"? How do they incorporate songs from Ingrian, Setu, and Mordva peoples, which are similarly represented as "Finnish folk"? These questions do not seem so far from Julius Krohn's deliberations (see chap. 2). For him, borrowed cells were reinterpreted and imbued with qualities expressing the national spirit. Viewing music as a product, which is sold in forms that will generate commercial interest, or as transformable, movable, and exchangeable material offers particular perspectives on questions of ownership. Together with perceptions of creative process in which borrowed materials are seen as transformed, they reinforce notions of bounded musics. Music is also bounded in being attributable to identified creators. Here we return to the musical choices made by musicians as they reinterpret traditional material and enter a world music arena. Borrowed materials result from making musical choices, which revolve around notions of how best to express the musicians' "creativity" as they reach out to global audiences as well as maintain an adherence to "tradition." In the sleeve note to Värttinä's (1992) reissued 1987 recording, the leader of the group, Sari Kaasinen, observes that in later albums the kantele and jouhikko parts have been replaced by electric guitar and saxophone. Her observations are pertinent, for in the case of this group, changes in instrumental texture are obvious. The choices that lead to perceived musical changes in their repertoire center around timbral effect. The kantele is still used in the group's 1996 recording, but it is no longer as prominent as in the earlier albums. The accompaniment is a familiar texture of another kind: bass, percussion, and electric guitars. By contrast, instrumental texture in the performances of JPP is an indication of musical continuity, as they expand their repertoire by looking at fiddle traditions around the world.

Erlmann's comments about choice are illuminating. It is the musical choices that new folk musicians make that enable them to move "about the spaces between system and its multiple environments" (1993, 6). By focusing on the practices of individual musicians or groups and on the dissemination of their performances through recordings, I have sought to trace the movements of new folk music and new folk musicians in local and in global spheres. The rhetoric of the "new" is vital in this respect. We have seen how, in an ongoing process of redefinition that was aided by the revival movement of the 1960s and 1970s and subsequent state implementation of folk music education programs, the idea of a "new" folk music stresses individual innovation and originality. It encourages looking to diverse sources for "inspiration." The discourse of the new legitimizes musical change. It also legitimizes musical borrowings, for what is borrowed becomes an agent for change. The world music scene has been entered enthusiastically by Finnish new folk musicians, because it offers opportunities to redefine folk music, to gather musical ideas that seem to contribute to "reinterpreting" local traditions, and to assert a "Finnish" identity in the world. Yet entry into the world music scene has both highlighted a commitment to, and reinforced the challenge offered to ideas about, Finnish folk music as a "national" musical expression.

TEN

Epilogue

In the final pages of the *Kalevala,* Väinämöinen departs, leaving his kantele and "mighty songs" to the people of Suomi (Finland). These lines resonate with the model of folk music as collective, inherited musical expression, bounded within a national arena—the kantele and the songs are for "Finnish children":

Siitä vanha Väinämöinen
laskea karehtelevi
venehellä vaskisella,
kuutilla kuparisella
yläisihin maaemihin,
alaisihin taivosihin.

Sinne puuttui pursinensa,
Venehinensä väsähtyi.
Jätti kantelon jälille,
Soiton Suomelle sorean,
Kansalle ilon ikuisen,
Laulut suuret lapsillensa.

Then the aged Väinämöinen
Went upon his journey singing,

Sailing in his boat of copper,
In his vessel made of copper
Sailed away to loftier regions,
To the sky beneath the heavens.

There he rested with his vessel,
Rested weary, with his vessel,
But his kantele he left us,
Left his charming harp in Suomi,
For his people's lasting pleasure
Mighty songs for Finnish children."

(*Kalevala*, rune L, lines 501-512)

Finnish new folk music departs from the traditional paradigms of folk music research in terms of the composition process (individual, not just collective), transmission strategies, and performance arenas (including the world stage). "I do not want to be classified as a 'pure' folk musician," Seppo Paakkunainen told me. "It is not a band for 'purists,'" explained Hannu Saha. "I want to use the music in my own way," Hasse Walli asserted. "Before it was like that and now it is like this" was Arto Järvelä's pragmatic response to questions about folk music change. These comments from practitioners, cited in earlier chapters, point to musicians making creative choices. Whether they appropriate, transform, and represent as "new folk" music material from Finnish archives, or whether they choose material from, for example, Argentina, Senegal, or Ireland, their concepts of contemporary folk music allow for the processes of adaptation, reinterpretation, and re-representation. These are conscious and deliberate processes.[1] Inspired by, and engaged with, a world of musical sounds available to them, musicians create, compose, and arrange "new folk music."

The relation between the "new" and the "old" is nevertheless significant in representations of new folk music as being both "Finnish" and "folk." New folk music is still a marker of national identity. Within the national arena, the traditions from which it is made up are also markers of other kinds of identities: of the "other," the region, the village, the family, and the individual creative musician who develops a personal musical style. Contemporary folk music is distinguished from folk music of the past by the supplementary adjective "new," by the musicians who claim to produce this music, and by media agencies. But notions of the historical-musical past continue to inform the reconstructions and reinterpretations of folk music, and even the composition of completely new material, and to demarcate the traditions as "Finnish." The notions of both change and continuity are essential to the construction of new folk music. In this study, the relation between the past and the present has been explored with particular reference to learning processes. Contemporary Finnish folk musicians are not expected to assimilate skills through the environment of the family or the community or to be self-taught practitioners. The training and specialization of folk musicians takes place through education programs extending from school to university level. These programs have been implemented, and are supported, by the state. They are the result both of general notions of the importance of national culture, and of networks formed by individuals with specific interests in promoting folk music. With such specialized training, folk musicians are now recognized as "professionals," and they come into contact with various forms of aesthetic expression that influence their musical conceptualizations as they travel around the globe. The element of change is vital, for this is what makes folk music a "living tradition" even if these kinds of departures compromise a folk music's authenticity. Folk music finds new methods of transmission (organized education programs and projects, notated sources, and commercial recordings), new performance contexts (festivals, streets, concert halls, schools, and music academies), and new interpretations, in order to remain relevant to people. The historical perspectives that have informed this ethnographic account of new folk music show that some of these practices turn out not to be so "new" after all. Kreeta Haapasalo, Larin Paraske, Teppo Repo, for example, were also touring professionals, arranging materials in their own ways, composing, or using notated sources.

MUSICAL SPACES

Finnish new folk music appears in various musical spaces: in villages, cities, music academies, and festivals, in the national arena, in the global music marketplace, in the places where new folk musicians perform.

Mitsuo Iguchi, chairperson of the Hokaido-Finnish Association, contacted the Sibelius Academy to ask if a kantele player could go to Japan to teach and perform for a short while. So Minna Raskinen set off in February 1991 with forty-five five-string kanteles that she ordered from the Folk Music Institute for the project. For four weeks in Hokaido and one week in Tokyo, she taught beginner kantele classes to interested Japanese participants and gave some concerts on the five-string, ten-string, and fifteen-string kantele. Minna thought it would be too expensive to arrange these kinds of courses on an annual basis. She advised her students to continue practicing what they had learned from her and to use that knowledge to create their own style. They could, for example, make kantele arrangements from the repertoire of Japanese songs (Minna Raskinen, personal interview, November 18, 1991).[2]

The aesthetics of synthesis and change that Minna encouraged during her visit to Japan are the striking features of the kinds of music often encountered by ethnomusicologists in complex musical contexts marked by interaction and exchange across cultural and class boundaries (Blum 1993), and they are highlighted in the global culture. In Finland, folklorists have long been concerned with charting the migration of tradition (the geographic-historical method of the Finnish school). My reflections on the changes in new folk music and the borrowing of tradition can be seen as a variation on this theme and have followed persistent lines of inquiry that revolve around geography and chronology. Some elements are represented as coming from "outside" the nation. Such borrowings can be viewed as contributing to musical changes. Yet the variation in the approach pursued in this study has been fundamental to shifting the focus from "migration of tradition" to musical changes as part of creative processes. Through exploring new folk music practices and interactions with musics and musicians in a global forum, I have tried to indicate the limits of conceiving of both folk music as "national" expression and ethnomusicology as the study of "music in place."

Posing the question of how Finnish folk music continues to operate as a marker of identity highlights problems raised by associating music with specific places even as it travels beyond those boundaries. It is a particular problem in considering folk music, which has become so closely linked with the nation. Finnish new folk musicians "borrow" from "other" musical traditions because they view those musical elements as belonging to other national arenas, just as their folk music belongs to them. Finnish new folk music is certainly an example of music providing the "means by which people recognise identities and places, and the boundaries which separate them" (Stokes 1994, 5). Yet the availability of diverse musics in any soundscape highlights difficulties in mapping musical practices onto geographic entities (see Bohlman 1992).[3]

The problems raised by the view that cultures and societies are mapped onto geographical territories have been addressed in relation to issues of asserting cultural differences (Ferguson and Gupta 1992) and nationalism in a trans-national world (Gupta 1992). Feld (1994a) emphasizes "acoustic dislocations" in reflecting on world music,[4] and Kun writes about music as a spatial practice: "music does not respect places precisely because it is capable of inhabiting a particular place while at the same time moving across several places—of arriving while leaving" (Kun 1997, 288). Music in place is only in a transient state. New folk musicians represent their music as "Finnish." They borrow from various musical traditions at the same time as they take "Finnish" music to several places in a global market. Finnish new folk music, then, is a "shifting ethno-musicological object" (see Olwig and Hastrup 1997).

The testimonies of new folk musicians in Finland seem to exemplify Robertson's suggestion that "the form of globalization is currently being reflexively reshaped in such a way as to increasingly make projects of glocalization the constitutive features of contemporary globalization" (1995, 41). Adopting the notion of glocalization, however, still reveals a concern with place. The narrative of the global destroying the local is replaced by the argument that "the global has involved the reconstruction of locality" (Robertson 1995, 30).

Our view of "culture" as a mosaic "of separate pieces with hard, well-defined edges" (Hannerz 1989, 201) is challenged by processes of cultural flow (Hannerz 1987), such as musical borrowings. When a musician responds to music by borrowing some of its elements and using them in a different way, previous affiliations and images of the "other" that are evoked may become subsumed as the musical material is recontextualized. Such creative processes make us question notions of a shared, and by implication homogeneous, culture. But this kind of borrowing is not necessarily, as Hannerz suggests, an "intercontinental traffic in meaning" (Hannerz 1987, 547), for meanings can be diverse even in the context of the collaboration between two musicians (as in the Peltoniemi-Saha and Cissokho-Saha examples).

How do Finnish new folk musicians retain specific ideas regarding the identity of their musical practice in the face of musical "hybridity" and collaboration? Since "culture" in the national imagination is increasingly perceived as a detachable, separable package (Wallis and Malm 1984)—something that people own—despite the processes of cultural flow, Finnish new folk musicians, by drawing from the cultures of others, add to their own. It is the quality of separability that allows the use and incorporation of, for example, the *mbira,* the *tama,* or the *kora* in recordings and performances of music that are represented as Finnish.[5] Musical (cultural) material, regarded as being detachable, can be

borrowed and appropriated from others, and through processes of incorporation, transformation, and re-representation, it is recontextualized as Finnish.
Finnish new folk music draws on forms from around the world: the tango,
Swedish and Irish fiddle music, West African *tama* and *sabar* drumming; it also
draws from diverse local traditions within the nation-state: songs in *Kalevala*
meter, ballads, Saami joiks, Rom music, and Ostrobothnian instrumental traditions. As the musical expression of the nation, folk music consists of "decontextualized" local traditions. Parts of the cultures and identities of others (from
other regions or other nations) are extracted and become a part of one's own
national culture and identity. In focusing on musicians' ideas about collaboration and exchange, within and beyond national borders, I have stressed the importance of musical encounters between individuals, as well as borrowing from
a global arena, which contribute to the ways in which musicians make musical
choices. The willingness of musicians to listen to, experiment with, and incorporate diverse cultural influences might be seen, as Hannerz suggests, as providing them with "access to technological and symbolic resources for dealing
with their own ideas, managing their own culture, in new ways" (Hannerz
1987, 555).

Hannerz's notion of managing one's own culture in new ways is paralleled in
the discourses of new folk musicians for whom the creative transformations of
juxtaposed traditions allow for the emergence of a "new" music. Even collaborative projects, then, reveal ideas about musical difference. Transformed and re-
represented as "Finnish new folk music," what is borrowed is returned to the
global arena through, for example, recordings and performances. As an inde-
terminate local musical expression, Finnish new folk music illustrates Robertson's view that the local is "best seen as an aspect of globalization" (1995, 30).

One of the main points that I have tried to emphasize in this book is that new
folk music as a form of "national" expression challenges ideas about nationness.
Finnish new folk music practices simultaneously reinscribe notions of musical
boundedness and expose the fragilities of both the fictions and frictions of difference. Minna Raskinen's teaching practice in Japan takes us beyond ideas of
musical locality and potential placelessness. It takes us beyond ideas of borrowings in pursuit of individual creative transformations that are disguised by
the rhetoric of the "new" and that come to represent Finnish new folk music in
the international arena. That musicians describe themselves as Finnish new folk
practitioners marks their claims to a distinct musical identity tying them to a
specific nation. They perceive their borrowings as the musical choices they

make which accord with new folk music practice. What I have tried to show is the extent to which these choices are often determined by individual encounters between musicians, whether in, for example, an institutional context like the Sibelius Academy or on musical tours. Since the choices (or borrowings) of new folk musicians are often based on musical collaborations, they have a sense of engaging in shared musical experiences. These shared experiences are open to subsequent interpretation in various and multiple ways by each participant. Raskinen's suggestion for a continuing kantele practice among her Japanese students illuminates the ways in which new folk musicians perceive shared musical encounters as offering material for creative reflection and reformulation so that the music can become "one's own." Raskinen's pedagogical approach furthermore demonstrates that musical giving is as important to a creative new folk aesthetic as musical taking. She urges her students to use the kantele, a symbol of Finnishness, in their own ways—to use the instrument to perform other kinds of repertoires. Her vision is that "Japanese" songs would be played on a "Finnish" instrument. Thus, she both dissolves and maintains musical (and national) boundaries. The shared musical experience, which is nevertheless open to plural interpretations, means that new folk musicians simultaneously experience their musical practice as both taking them beyond the boundaries of the nation and reinforcing their sense of national, regional and familial affiliations.

WRITING HISTORY

As I was preparing to leave "the field" at the end of 1992, I asked students in the Department of Folk Music at the Sibelius Academy how they thought folk music would develop in the future. Their predictions revealed, yet again, the importance attached to the present. Folk music of the present was seen as the music that matters, and notions of the directions it would take in the future were grounded in what they already saw happening around them. Some thought that folk music would become more "commercial," that it would continue to "take influences from other music," that there would be "more groups," that the "level of technical proficiency would increase," that there would be "more amateur and professional" folk musicians, and that "more electric instruments" would be used. One person commented, "hopefully no one knows how folk music will develop." In putting together these final pages at the end of this decade, I am conscious that I have been writing a historical account. Many of the predictions above have been realized and there have been other kinds of changes in the new folk music world revolving around, for example, changing memberships of groups and new recording ventures. Sari Kaasinen left Värttinä. Koinurit's members have stopped playing together as a group. A Saami musician, Wimme, has begun to promote a new joiking.

When Minna Raskinen was a child, she had an electric harmonium at home (a farm near Koivula). Her grandmother also had a harmonium. It was about one hundred years old and had foot pedals. Minna played these instruments by ear. When she was ten years old she started going to summer kantele courses. Later on she joined a local kantele group that had been set up in the late 1960s by an elderly villager, Mauri Saikko. He was the leader of the group Pärhä and wrote arrangements for it. As they became more proficient, the younger players also started providing arrangements. This initially caused some conflict, but Saikko accepted that coplayers wanted to develop their own ideas and eventually stopped playing with the group, although he remained the leader in name (Minna Raskinen, personal interview, November 18, 1991). Today, Minna takes her kantele far away from that village setting: to Japan, to the United States, to Ireland. The last news I heard about her came from one of my own former students, who reported that he had come across her on a study tour looking at Karnatak music in south India[6]. Minna's story resonates with the final words of the *Kalevala* (in which a new generation offers to overturn preceding representations of folk singers as a tradition-bearing collective). Both testimonies attest to the shifting interspaces between local practice and the musical global network, to the inevitability of musical change as part of the creative process, and to folk performers as innovative and creative agents who forge their own musical pathways:

Elkätte, hyvät imeiset,
tuota ouoksi otelko,
jos ma, lapsi, liioin lauloin,
pieni, pilpatin pahasti!
En ole opissa ollut,
Käynyt mailla mahtimiesten,
Saannut ulkoa sanoja,
Loitompata lausehia.

Vaan kuitenki kaikitenki
La'un hiihin laulajoille,
La'un hiihin, latvan taitoin,

Oksat karsin, tien osoitin.
Siitäpä nyt tie menevi,
Ura uusi urkenevi
Laajemmille laulajoille,
Runsahammille runoille
Nuorisossa nousevassa,
Kansassa kasuavassa.

May you not, O friendly people,
As a wondrous thing regard it
That I sang so much in childhood,
And when small, I sang so loudly!
I received no store of learning,
Never traveled to the learned.
Foreign words were never taught me,
Neither songs from distant countries . . .

But let this be as it may be,
I have shown the way to singers,
Showed the way, and left the markers,
Cut the branches, shown the pathways.
This way therefore leads the pathway,
Here the course lies newly opened,
Open for the greater singers,
For the bards and ballad singers,
For the young, who now are growing,
For the rising generation.

(*Kalevala,* rune L, lines 593–600 and 611–620)

Notes

1. The term *nykykansanmusiikki*, which can be translated as "contemporary folk music," is also used.

2. These issues were brought into focus by doing "ethnomusicology at home"— looking at a part of that "tribe called Europe" (Phillips 1987; De Chiara 1996) and learning from "unfamiliar compatriots" (Jarvenpa 1989). I adapt the term "anthropology at home" to emphasize a reflexive shift to looking at music that is familiar. In the context of an anthropology of Europe, such a shift has encouraged consideration of processes of globalization as well as of local community practices. Phillips (1987) writes about his sense of otherness and his search for an identity in the European contexts he inhabits. De Chiara (1996) explores Philips's work to discuss the blurring of boundaries between self and other and ambiguities in discerning the narrative voice that shifts from one position to another. Jarvenpa (1989) focuses on the problems and advantages of carrying out field research in culturally familiar yet unfamiliar settings and on what kinds of knowledge can be generated when the anthropologist's possession of knowledge is assumed by his or her informants. The notion of "ethnomusicology at home" is relevant too in the context of Finnish ethnomusicological research. Contributions to Moisala (1994) introduce this research to the English-speaking reader and explore the study of Finnish folk music as central to ethnomusicological inquiry in Finnish scholarship.

3. Examples of such studies include Leisiö's research on early Finnish and Karelian aerophones (1983), the Folk Music Institute's exhibition and catalog on "ancient Finnish instruments" (1985), compilations of early ethnomusicological work such as Väisänen's essays (Pekkilä 1990), and biographies of performers which include transcriptions of their repertoires, such as the biography of the fiddler Matti Haudanmaa (Asplund, Kangas, and Valo 1990).

4. Bibliographic sources on new folk music at the time of my field research were not extensive but included Hannu Saha, who had explored the use of the kantele in contemporary contexts in the article "Kantele: New Life for Finland's National Instrument"

(Saha 1988); and Hannu Tolvanen (1991), who had reported on the "new wave of Finnish folk music." An issue of the Finnish music journal *Musiikin Suunta* (1989, no. 4, "Trends in Music") focused on developments in Finnish folk music. Muikku (1989) explored the revival movement by looking at the involvement of jazz and rock musicians with folk music. Pietilä (1992) wrote about the new folk music group Värttinä.

CHAPTER 1

1. Bartók defined urban folk music as follows: "We may connote urban folk music, that is, popular art music, as melodies of simple structure that are composed by dilettante authors from the upper class and propagated by that class. These melodies are either unknown to the peasant class or arrive there at a comparatively late time by way of the gentry. They are well known to us under the designation 'Hungarian popular tune'" (Bartók 1976, 5).

The second type of material encompassed by the term "folk" music he defined in these terms: "[peasant music] connotes all the melodies which endure within the peasant class of any nation, in a more or less wide area and for a more or less long period, and which constitute a spontaneous expression of the musical feeling of that class" (Bartók 1976, 6).

2. Finnish musicologists continue to debate the "Finnishness" of Finnish music. Kalevi Aho (1985) examines the Finnish art composer turning to the *Kalevala*. Mikko Heiniö (1992) critiques the notion of "Finnishness" as an inherent musical property and argues that, "the 'national character' is ultimately no more than a metaphor for the constellation of different cultural-historical properties" (1992, 11). A symposium meeting was organized in London (1992) to examine nationalism and internationalism in twentieth-century Finnish and British music as features that "keep irritating aesthetic and analytic minds" (Tomi Mäkelä, roundtable comment, 1992).

3. See, for example, Rosenberg 1993; *World of Music* 38 (1996), no. 3, a thematic issue on revivals; and Livingston 1999.

4. See his comments in the essays "Folk Song Research and Nationalism" (1937) and "Race Purity in Music" (1942), both in Bartók 1976.

5. The chorus sings mostly in unison. Features that reveal (or at least resonate with) folk singing practices include melodic inflection (falling at the ends of phrases), rhythmic structure (based on the *Kalevala* meter), choice of language (Finnish), and textual repetition (phrases such as "Kullervo, Kalervon poika" [Kullervo the son of Kalervo]).

6. Yleisradio recorded this in 1952.

CHAPTER 2

1. I have used an edition of Lönnrot's *Kalevala* published in 1984, and I use translations of the *Kalevala* into English by Wlliam Forsell Kirby in an edition published in 1985.

2. These poems were popular all over Europe and were translated into several European languages. The poems inspired other artistic endeavors: Mendelssohn composed the overture *Fingal's Cave* after visiting the Hebrides; and Herder, who maintained a life-long fascination with Ossian (Gaskill 1996), collected folk songs in Riga. Ossian was described by Blair, a friend of Macpherson, as the Celtic Homer (Burke 1978, 10).

3. The main proponents were A. I. Arwidsson (1791–1858), A. J. Sjögren (1794–1855), A. Poppius (17931866), and C. A. Gottlund (1796–1875). Arwidsson and Gottlund collected and published folklore material. Gottlund's researches into folk music and the historical context in which he carried out his work are explored by Pekkilä (1990).

4. There was some continuity in his work, however, for he wrote his dissertation for the degree of doctor of medicine on the topic of Finnish folk medicine.

5. The *sampo* has been variously interpreted as a symbol of, for example, the sun, a shaman's drum, or even culture.

6. Hasse Walli, for example, referred to this kantele melody in describing his early involvement with the group Piirpauke; see chap. 3.

7. Two-part singing was performed by men sitting down, each with one hand clasping that of his partner and holding a drink in the other hand. Group singing was primarily performed by women and involved movement either in free processions or in organized circles, chains, or single files. The performance contexts included wedding and religious and secular festivals.

8. Walking through the forest toward Ainola, we continued our discussion about music, landscape, and "Finnish" musical elements. We pondered the questions, Can music be identified as "Finnish" and if so, what is it that makes music identifiable? We did not dwell on analysis of musical sound, on melodic, rhythmic, and textural features. We considered the forest setting that we were walking through as a source of creative inspiration. I am grateful to Paakkunainen for highlighting musical evocations of landscape. These comments have contributed to my thinking about music, place, and identity. In fixing "Finnishness" within a national landscape, Paakkunainen revealed the ongoing ideological importance of the links between music, territory, and national sensibility.

CHAPTER 3

1. Sebo relates his "discovery" of Hungarian folk music as follows: "I was commissioned by the Twenty-fifth Theatre to compose incidental music for the text of an old Chinese opera for a one-person ensemble. To achieve an exotic quality, I had chosen a real folk instrument, the *citera,* and used it together with drums and gongs. I tried to use these instruments in as many different ways as possible; for instance, I hit the strings with a stick. When the ethnomusicologist Laszlo Vikar heard this, he asked whether I knew of the instrument *gardon* [a cello-like instrument] from Gyimes [East Transylvania] whose playing technique was very similar. When he saw my surprised expression as

I answered 'no,' he said that it was a waste of time to discover things that have existed already for centuries. I realised that he was right and began to find a way to know 'real' folk music" (Sagi, cited in Frigyesi 1996, 61).

2. The practice and use of folk music from the 1920s to the 1950s has been studied by Vesa Kurkela, who focuses on the fusion of nationalist concepts with working-class ideology (see Kurkela 1989b).

3. 1968 Kaustisella oli ensimmäiset kansanmusiikki juhlat ja ne oli sellainen käännekohta . . . Kun Kaustisen kansanmusiikki juhlat pidettiin, maaseudulla oli kulttuurijuhlia ehkä kymmenen tai kaksikymmentä koko maassa. Viisi vuotta myöhemmin niitä oli seitsemän sataa, että siitä alkoi sellainen uusi maaseutukulttuuri elämän vilkastumisen aika, ja Kaustinen oli tässä tullut keskeiseksi juuri sen takia että se oli ensimmäinen.

4. This text includes chapters on *Kalevala* songs, laments, folk dances, Swedish-Finnish folk music, Saami music, Finnish-Roma music, and folk music in contemporary Finland (which focuses on the Kaustinen Festival and on competitions).

5. Nelipolviset syntyi myöskin sitä kautta esittämään tälläistä. Sehän ei ole muusiikkojen yhtye vaan tutkijoiden yhtye, ja oli itse asiassa aika sattuma että se syntyi, mutta se syntyi enemmänkin tutkijoiden halusta kertoa ihmisille että on tälläistäkin laulua ollut olemassa.

6. The source for these examples is Asplund and Laitinen 1979, 13.

7. Hyvin harva soitti seitsemänkymentä-luvun lopulla viisikielistä kanteletta, juuri kukaan ei soittanut jouhikkoa, kukaan ei soittanut paimen soittimia. Halusimme luoda yhtyeen joka tekee työtä nimenomaan tämän kalevalaisen perinteen parissa, se oli se alku idea miksi perustimme Primo yhtyeen. Vocal sounds, such as cattle calls, also feature prominently in this recording (1984, OMLP 8).

8. The opposition between "light" and "art" music is not tenable in the context of the individual's musical experience, as is evident from the biographies outlined in this chapter. In what context does the opposition surface? The main context in which it does so is in the formulation of music policy and in the system of awarding grants and state support to musical activities. A research project of the Arts Council in Finland has shown that the organizations concerned with music policy—the Parliament, the State Council, the Ministry of Education, the Arts Council, and the Music Council—have accorded greater importance to art music, as reflected in the amount of state subsidies that art musicians receive. One of the Arts Council's reports concludes: "It is supposed that cultural (or arts) policy is a fruitful symbiosis of two different systems within a culture [art and politics]. The politics should, ideally, facilitate creative and performing artists and their audiences in developing the quality of musical culture. . . . However, it can be seen that some areas of music are taken almost totally under the auspices of the society, nationalised, one might say. Art music takes the major part of all public support, while others may use the ways they can to finance their activities, usually through commercial

means" (Lahtinen 1991, 7). The opposition, then, is one of competition for economic resources, the perception of the need for state funding for one kind of music, and the availability of commercial returns for another. A further discussion on the differences between the categories "light" and "art" music in terms of institutional rather than musical factors is given by Heiniö 1990.

9. Seppo Paakkunainen has received a number of accolades as a jazz musician and is one of the most prominent in the Finnish jazz world. He was a member of Soulset, an ensemble that won the gold medal at a student youth festival in 1968. With the ensemble Tuohi he won the Montreux competition for European jazz bands in 1971. He was winner of the Yrjö award in 1973 for the most outstanding Finnish jazz musician of the year. He has worked with jazz musicians like Charlie Mariano, Palle Mikkelborg, and Mal Waldron and was a member of the George Gruntz Concert Jazz Band. As a composer he has been awarded the Helsinki Festival Jazz Composer of the Year title (1981) and the Prix Futura by the West Berlin radio and TV festival (1989).

CHAPTER 4

1. Students who wish to pursue their interest in folk music can take courses offered by higher educational institutions throughout Finland: in Helsinki, Turku, Tampere, Jyväskylä, Joensuu, and Kokkola, as well as at the Sibelius Academy. Elsewhere, I have highlighted the self-conscious way in which folk music is presented and formally transmitted through comparing it to a contrasting situation in England (see Ramnarine 1996, 136–38).

2. Notions held by Finnish practitioners of the relation between tradition and innovation are paralleled in other ethnographic contexts and seem to be a particular feature of thinking about "traditional" music in the modern world as subject to processes of commercialization, globalization, and technological developments (Bohlman 1988; Turino 1993; Rice 1994). Since the 1980s there has been a rise in European contexts of "new" musics (described, for example, in Slobin 1996). The distinction between "old" and "new," between "tradition" and "innovation," highlights the use of music as an agent of social and political change and the connections of folk music with issues of nationalism and political self-definitions.

3. The *nyckelharpa* is mainly associated with Sweden. There is limited evidence, however, pointing to its dissemination in Finland before the 1990s and Arto's practice. An instrument found in 1909 in Ähtävä is thought to date from 1615–1745. Åland judgment books of the late seventeenth and early eighteenth centuries also mention the instrument (Talve 1997, 256).

4. In the process of specialization, the students devote a substantial part of their daily lives to the study and performance of folk music, and they work in an environment in

which folk music activity is the focus of attention and of their social interactions with each other. To an extent, social life for these individuals revolves around the department and other folk music circles. That the social and musical identities of members of the Department of Folk Music are bound up with their involvement with, and in particular their study of, folk music is in contrast to Herzfeld's observation of nineteenth-century Greek folklore scholarship (noted in chap. 2) that the ability to think in terms of "studying folklore" marks the separation between folk and folklorist (Herzfeld 1982, 8). The identity of the new folk musician is constructed through studying the tradition in formal, just as much as in informal, contexts. The paradox of contemporary practice, then, is that an intense engagement with folk music can be accompanied by a certain detachment from the past contexts of folk music activity. This is a paradox of which contemporary practitioners and educationalists are well aware. It contributes to the distinctions made between "old" and "new" folk music.

5. Gilroy writes that his study exploring discourses in Britain linking "race" and nation, *There Ain't No Black in the Union Jack* (1987), grew from challenging the ethnocentric dimensions of his discipline, cultural studies. He notes, "I have grown gradually more and more weary of having to deal with the effects of striving to analyse culture within neat, homogeneous national units reflecting the 'lived relations' involved; with the invisibility of 'race' within the field and, most importantly, with the forms of nationalism endorsed by a discipline which, in spite of itself, tends toward a morbid celebration of England and Englishness from which blacks are systematically excluded" (1987, 12). There is an obvious parallel between Gilroy's analysis of national discourses and the politics of exclusion with this study of folk music in Finland represented as a "national" form of musical expression while nevertheless containing diverse musical elements "borrowed" from far beyond national borders. Both instances issue a challenge to representations of the nation as a tidy, homogeneous category for analysis. Studying music from this perspective also challenges models of music "in" place, which has been one of the basic paradigms of ethnomusicological research.

CHAPTER 5

1. I use both the ethnographic present and the past tense in this chapter to demonstrate historical specificities (my analysis is largely based on the late 1980s to the early 1990s) and the continuing importance of this group in Finnish folk musical life.

2. Mä oon kotoisin maatalosta, eli meillä on karjaa, lehmiä ja mä oon elänny ninku niitten kanssa. Eli se on ollut sellaista maaseutu elämää johon kaikki nää perinteiset asiat on liittyny kauheen voimakkaasti, ja on ollu olennainen osa sitä elämää. Siitä ei ikinä tehty niinku sillätavalla perinnettä et sitä ois tiedostanu, vaan se kaikki oli siinä, koko siinä elämässä niinku ihan normaalina asioina. Eikä niin että nyt kun leivotaan näitä piirakoita, niin ne on karjalan piirakoita, ne on perinteisiä asioita: vaan ne oli niinku

ne opittiin ihan luonnollisella tavalla. Sitten mun äiti on oikeastaan sysänny miut ja mun siskon Marin—Mari on myös Värttinässä mukana—laulamaan ja soittamaan. Hyö anto—meijän vanhemmat, meille mahdollisuuden opiskella soittamista, eli myö käytiin soittotunneilla viidenkymmenen tai kuudenkymmenen kilometrin päässä Rääkkylästä, Joensuussa. Äiti ja isä kuljetti meitä joka viikko kuus vuotta siellä Joensuussa edestakaisin. Mä soitin kannelta, ja soitan vieläkin, ja minun sisko Mari soitti harmonikkaa. Siitä läksi niinku musiikinharrastus. Ja sitten mun äiti johti tällaista lausunta ryhmää, luento ryhmiä jotka teki -lausu, laulo, leikki—niinku mä oon lapsesta pitäin esiintynyt just näissä äitin ryhmissä. Ja sitten äiti keksi et no, soitapa kanteleella, säestä tää laulu kanteleelle. Minä en tieny mite sitä säestetään, koska ei kukaan ole opettanu mulle ikinä kuinka jotakin asiaa säestetään, mä oon vain soittanut kappaleita. Sit mä rupesin vähitellen niinku ite opskelemaan, ja ite soittamaan, ite koettamaan. Sitten äiti sanoo että teeppä tähän lauluun toinenkin ääni. Mikä toinen ääni? Et en mä ikinä o kuullukaan mistään sellaisista asioista. Sit mä tein toisen äänen, et mikä minun korvaan kuullosti hyvältä. Siitä se kaikki ninku läks. Oikeastaan niinku itse opiskeltuja asioita ennenku menin Sibelius Akatemiaan, niin kaikki tää alku mitä Värttinään liitty, ja mikä liittyy niinku lapsuuteen, nuoruuteen, kaikki ne asiat on niinku löydetty, koettu ite ja opittu sen myötä.

3. Oikeastaan Suomessahan ei harrastettu muuta kuin pelimanni musiikkia joka tulee taas läntiseltä puolelta, ja Länsi-Suomesta. Mäkin soitin myös viulua, mä koitin soittaa mut se ei ollu hyvä, mä en niinku tuntenu sitä omakseni ollenkaan. Jotenkin se laulaminen, ja se laulujen kautta lähteminen liikkeelle, ni se tuntu heti omalta. Johtuen myös siitä että kun Karjalassahan on se nimenomaan lauluperinne joka siellä on elänny, Länsi-Suomessa on taas soitto perinne enemmänkin—meil on laulettu, niin se on niinku luonnollista.

4. Aina on ajateltu että suomalainen kansanmusiikki on tylsää, se on ihmisille tullu semmoinen mielikuva koska sitä on soitellu vaan vanhat ihmiset—vanhat miehet. Ja välttämättä kun me on aina ihannoitu ameriikkalaisuutta ja mikä tulee muualta, ja se on oikeastaan tylsää ku välillä se on ollu epävireistä niinku meijän korvaan, ja kaikki tämmöiset asiat—nii sitä ei o osattu tehä sillätavalla että se ois kiinnostanu ihmisiä. Aina on vaan niinku ajateltu että se on nyt sitä kansanmusiikkia eikä kukaan o kiinnostunu. Ja nimenomaan se että kun sitä ei tehty nuorille. Kun me ollaa ite nuoria, me tehää sitä samanikäisille ihmisille, niin se on sitten varmasti sitten sysäys että nyt on innostuttu Suomessa uuvella tavalla kansanmusiikista koska kansamusiikkihan täytyy elää nimenomaan ihmisten mukana. Nyt eletään vuotta 1992, niin se kansanmusiikkikin täytyy elää vuotta '92, se ei voi olla viiskymmentä vuotta meistä jälessä. Että näin Suomessa on ajateltu, kansanmusiikki täytyy olla jotain arvokasta, vanhaa, pölyyttynyttä, ja just semmoinen et se ei sais muuttua ensinkään. Nimenomaan, niinhän se kansanmusiikki elää, se muuttuu, se menee eteenpäin ihmisten mukana, silloin se elää.

CHAPTER 6

1. It is interesting to note that Tallari is the state-supported folk music group, the "official" representative of Finnish folk music, and that it can be categorized as a "new folk music" ensemble. The only official folk music group is thus one that keeps up to date with contemporary developments.

2. The emigrants left, according to Häikiö, only to seek a better life in the New World (Martti Häikiö, Suomi Seura [Finland Society], personal interview, March 12, 1992).

3. Hiski Salomaa was born in Finland and migrated to the United States of America in 1909. He first recorded for Columbia in 1927. The song, "Lännen Lokari" in "Finnenglish" was recorded in 1930 and was played on Finnish radio. It had become a very well known song by the 1960s. Further information on Salomaa is given in an article marking one hundred years since his birth (Westerholm 1991a).

4. Progelaulu on Koinureitten oma biisi (vähän tradilta varastettu tosin). Se pohjautuu vanhaan Kauhavalaiseen rekilauluun: "onko sinun paperisi kastunu. . . ." Rekilauluissa on aina ollut tapana yhdistellä vanhoja ja keksiä uusia säkeistöjä. Teksti on laulusoloisti Rantasen kokoama. Suurin osa teksteistä varmaan löytyykin Kauhavan laulukirjasta. Progelaulusta (Koinurit-versio) ei ole nuottia koska sovitukset ovat syntyneet soittamalla.

CHAPTER 7

1. Ihmiset sanookin että ei täällä o muita kun muusikkoja tai hevosmiehiä, tai jotku sanoo että täällä on vaan muusikkoja tai hulluja.

2. In fact, Finnish fiddlers also perceive their traditions as part of a generalized pan-Scandinavian repertoire. Fiddle traditions came from the West. The Kaustinen Festival organizers established links with folk music festivals in Sweden and in Norway to highlight shared musical traditions. Fiddlers from Finland, Sweden, and Norway perform at festivals in all three places. Goertzen notes in his study of Norwegian fiddling (1997) that additional items to traditional repertoires are important in the transformation of "folk music" because their status as regional or as national is under debate. Another layer to this kind of debate is added in the Finnish case, for Ostrobothnian fiddle traditions are also "Scandinavian."

3. The Älvdalen fiddlers—Evert Åhs, Lars Orre, Gereon Fält, and Elg Emanuel Andersson—inherited elements, in terms of style, technique, and repertoire, from two of their predecessors, Gyris Anders Andersson and Anders Södersten. The importance of these musical genealogies is highlighted by the emphasis placed in the liner notes to *Folk Music in Sweden: Låtar från Orsa och Älvdalen* (Musica Sveciae 1995) on the preservation of particular ways of ornamenting a tune. Matts Arnberg writes in the liner notes, for example, that "as far as we are able to judge from sound recordings made in the early

years of this century and from tunes taken down in the 1920s, Gössa Anders has conscientiously preserved both tunes and the manner of playing them" (Arnberg 1995, 12).

4. I am grateful to Arto Järvelä for telling me about this book and giving me a copy. The main part of the book is the *kuvakaappi* (the photographic materials).

5. The front covers of JPP's recordings are presented on the web pages of the record shop Digelius. Digelius Music Store is a small retail outlet. It was established in 1971 in the center of Helsinki. In the early 1990s it was one of the few commercial establishments to stock recordings of Finnish folk music produced by small companies. Digelius has played an important role, particularly since 1987, when Phillip Page from the United States was employed, in importing and distributing music under the label "world music," as well as in promoting the sale of Finnish folk music, especially new folk music, in Finland and abroad. In fact, Digelius is self-described on its web home page as "northern Europe's largest supplier of folk/ethnic/trad/world, jazz and O Zone recordings . . . with an inventory of over 30000 titles" (www.digelius.com). The rise of Finnish new folk and world music from the late 1980s is linked to the expanding business and sales promotion of this commercial enterprise. Phillip Page is conscious of the role he plays in drawing upon his contacts in music promotion to find new markets for Finnish new folk music. He said that hearing a live performance of JPP had sparked his enthusiasm for Finnish new folk music and that this had inspired him to undertake his current marketing and sales project (Phillip Page, personal communication).

6. Kyllä minä uskon, että musiikkimiehet, jotka on täysiä nuottimiehiä voi tehäkkin sävellyksiä. Kyllä minun täytyy se sisältä, se vain rupiaa soihan pääsä. . . . Noita ensimmäisiä kappaleita silloin aikanaan melekhen tuli tuola tilluuhommissa, navetassa. Se oli miten sattuu kävelehän, se riippu siitä aivan jos käveli tihiään, ko minä oon pieni mies, tihiäkäyntinen, niin silloin tuli polkka. Jos on jotenkin harthaammalla päällä niin sitte valssi.

7. Olisko se ollu vähän niinku uskonnollisen äidin perua. Tuntu että ei voinu soittaa tanssimusiikkia, kun oli lapsia.

8. Fiddle music was essentially dance music and this function is retained and shapes JPP's repertoire, although audiences now do not always dance at performances, but sit and listen.

9. Also by some of the statements about the tango in Finland heard on the BBC television program *Rhythms of the World:* "There is no tango elsewhere. Argentina has a copy of the Finnish tango. . . . it is quite OK for Argentines but not in general. It was born here, the tango. It was imported to [sic] the United States and then it went south to Argentina and then they brought it to Europe" (Aki Kaurismäki, film director); "The Finnish tango is something special, it is a way of life. It is something that has always been and always will be in Finnish musical culture" (Topi Sorsakoski and Agents, a tango band). Other people considered that there was a mixture of influences in the Finnish

tango, including German and Russian, and some even detected in them hints of Russian folk melodies from the 1930s. This mixture was nevertheless something entirely "Finnish": "An extremely typical Finnish mixture: can't be imitated, can't probably be understood elsewhere" (Peter von Bagh, film director).

10. In some contexts all these identities appear concurrently, with shifting emphases, as in the performances of JPP as a group with regional interests, from the nation Finland, on the WOMAD (World of Music and Dance) stage.

11. Cf. Turino 1993, chap. 3, pp. 92–93. Turino writes about the reception to one of his own compositions to discuss how musicians balance creativity and tradition. Tracing Peruvian Conimeno musical traditions in an urban (Lima) and a rural (Conima) setting, he describes how he composed a piece for a festival using "stock resources, formulas, and style of repetition . . . to create a piece that would sound as if it were from Conima" (Turino 1993, 92). The group with whom he played accepted the composition and it went on to become a festival hit. Turino was initially satisfied that he had composed a "Conimeno" piece, but it was described a few months later as "weird" by Conimeno commentators in Lima. It was a combination of the novel and the accessible that seemed to make the piece successful. Turino suggests that while the "balancing of new ideas with stock resources" is universal in musical composition, different cultural situations determine the nature of this balance. A lack of specialization leads to the introduction of innovative elements that do not stray too far from the traditions. At the same time, competitive musical life places an emphasis on "originality." In examples from specialists, the evidence from JPP and Värttinä points to musicians making choices about which musical parameters can be treated in an innovative manner and which parameters should adhere to "tradition." These choices depend on which musical resources are regarded as essential to the tradition—for instance, the voice and the song text or instrumental texture.

CHAPTER 8

1. Here is Paakkunainen's line in context: "In my heart there is joy, happiness, and gratitude for the twenty-year-long migration with Aillohas: thanks, Ailu. During those years I have traveled as a kindred soul in different regions of Saamiland. Many a time I had a fire together with Ailu by Adja when Golle (sun) made it hard on us. . . . There is an infinite number of golden brooches in Saami nature. Lights/shadows, days/nights, and the different seasons make them vary and alter them. In the same way, the joiks live and change in the interpretations of different performers. This is the way the luodit I have learned by ear from Ailu have been reshaped in my soul."

The sentiments expressed by Paakkunainen about his relations with the Saami people are reciprocated by Valkeapää, evidenced in his commissioning this symphony and in one of Valkeapää's poems about his colleague and this work, which is included in the sleeve note to the CD recording (Paakkunainen 1992; the poem is in the Saami language):

BARON, SAMI LUONDU JA GOLLERISKU (extract, verse 2)

Luohtegoallus ja juoigansinfoniija.
Nu no, dein cudjet badjel guoktelogi luodi.
Dego duottarmearra; algguhaga, loahpahaga,
balddalaga, buohtalaga.
Ja go coru nala goardnju,
sahtta deid oaidnit vaikko man eatnat.
Nu guhkas go calbmi guodda.
Duoddarat. Juoigame.
Beaivi.
Ja Baronnai.

BARON, SAAMI NATURE, AND THE GOLDEN BROOCH

The Joik Train and the Joik Symphony.
Well, there are over twenty joiks resounding in them.
Like a sea of hills: no beginning, no end,
Side by side, opposite to each other.
And when you climb to a ridge,
You can see them to the infinity.
As far as your eye can reach.
Hills. Joiking.
The Sun.
And Baron, too.

Paakkunainen's extensive involvement with Saami music, and Valkeapää's appreciation of his interest, is evident in their writings, cited above. These writings reveal a mutual acknowledgement and appreciation of each other's different musical activities and interpretations.

2. This is a reference to the poem cited in n. 1.

3. This is perhaps an example of license taken with the ethnographic ear, and I do not wish to overemphasize the similarity to a joik singing style that I hear.

4. Yamar was described as "the best *tama* player in Senegal, in the world—his twin brother, Assane plays in Youssou's band, and Yamar and Assane have created the band

Tama Cha" (Papp Sarr, personal interview, December 3, 1991). In my interviews with these musicians, Papp Sarr translated and acted as spokesperson for Yamar, who spoke in Wolof.

5. N'diay incorporates his own impressions of Finnish society in his song lyrics. This is one he wrote on a table napkin as we spoke several months later. It is about drinkers in a well-known bar: "Not so far—jimbei, in Vanha Bar—jimbei, are same people—jimbei, at the same table—jimbei, taking same drinks—jimbei, telling same things—jimbei, getting more down—jimbei, in the down town—jimbei."

CHAPTER 9

1. As Monson (1999) concludes, "In our continuing attempts to make sense of what culture can possibly mean in a thoroughly globalized system of musical production and distribution, perhaps we can use all the help we can get" (61). In her discussion, musical organizations provide insights into problems of relationality and the intercultural relationships operating among diasporic musics. Riffs, repetition, and grooves highlight "the fragmenting and totalizing approaches in thinking about globalization" (1999, 60).

2. It was, for example, clearly expressed in the building of the new opera house in Helsinki. The influence of this ideology—Snellman's belief that through cultural strength a small nation survives and its identity remains intact—led a state reeling from the economic difficulties following the post-Soviet era to invest in such a "cultural" enterprise in the hope that it would provide an international platform for the representation of Finnish culture, thereby building "cultural strength." The story of the Finnish opera house has an interesting relevance to new folk music in the global arena. In representations of Finnish music, opera has played a significant role, since Finnish operas (especially those by Sallinen and by Kokkonen) and opera singers have achieved acclaim on the world stage. It was the fame of Martti Talvela, the bass, that convinced the state that the opera house must be built, and he was to be the artistic director. As a result of an interview with Sallinen (whose opera based on a *Kalevala* story, *Kullervo,* was intended originally to inaugurate the new opera house but, because of delays, was premiered in Los Angeles instead), representatives from a radio station in Santa Monica arrived in Kaustinen to find out more about Finnish folk music. They wanted to find out more about "authentic" *Kalevala* sources. Following the premiere of the opera, Värttinä's *Oi Dai* record (1991) was played on the radio and reached the top twenty (Chris Douridas, music director, Santa Monica's National Public Radio, personal communication).

3. For the first time, as Curt Sachs noted, "sound, with its characteristic inflections and individual timbres, could be recorded, reproduced, and preserved for future generations" (Sachs 1962, 13). Sachs related that he "witnessed for many years how, with the

Berlin *Phonogramm-Archiv* as their headquarters, Carl Stumpf and his disciple Erich M. von Hornbostel persuaded explorers to take an Edison along, to record songs they might hear in native villages, and to bring them back for conserving treatment, dubbing, storage, transcription and analysis" (Sachs 1962, 14). Moreover, studying recorded material was preferable to inviting musicians from afar to give live performances. Sachs continued: "It will not do bringing the 'natives' to our cities and record their music in commercial studios or academic laboratories. They are as a rule very ill at ease in an alien environment and rarely yield the qualities available at home in familiar surroundings in the midst of their fellow tribesmen and on the very occasions for which their songs are intended. . . . A song is an essential, inseparable element in primitive life and cannot be isolated from the conditions that are its cause, its sense, and its reason of being" (16). What was, hitherto, musical expression linked with specific social processes ("inseparable from its reason of being") in one context became matter for contemplation in another. Musical sounds were now detachable from the musicians who produced them. The musicians' physical presences were no longer required.

4. Also known as an A & R (artist and repertoire) man, whose job involves seeking out artists and signing contracts with them. This is a job that involves being aware of market trends. Timo Närväinen saw the market potential of Värttinä and transferred them to the Sonet label [Sonet is the local Finnish branch of Polygram], a bigger record company. Närväinen's involvement with Sonet and with Olarin is itself an illustration of the relationship between large and small record companies. Yet I heard in January 1994 that Timo Närväinen had left Sonet in order to work solely with the Olarin label. This move gives some indication of the growth of interest in Finnish new folk music. His plans for Olarin were that more recordings would be released in 1994 than in any other previous year.

5. One of these projects was the Barbican Scandinavian Festival in London (1992). As part of the cultural exchange programs assigned to the direction of ESEK by the Ministry of Education, ESEK awarded 100,000 FM to the festival. The state also supports the publication of the *Finnish Music Quarterly,* a journal written in English in order to reach a wider audience.

6. Other organizations provide support for Finnish music. The Foundation for the Promotion of Finnish Music deals with copyright for composers, arrangers, lyricists, and so on. Another source of support for classical music is the Ministry of Culture, and the Ministry of Foreign Affairs has on occasion taken part in supporting the export of Finnish music.

7. This was a provision corresponding to article 12 of the Rome Convention.

8. Jukka Liedes (who was chairperson of Gramex during the 1970s) played an important role in getting the Rome Convention ratified in Finland and also in the establishment of ESEK.

1. Although new folk music is widely accepted as the contemporary expression of Finnish folk musicians, in contrast to other ethnographic contexts, its "authenticity" as a folk practice has nevertheless been questioned by some researchers. As recently as 2000, Järviluoma, for example, suggested that new folk practitioners are "avant-garde traditionalists" whose practices have not received scrutiny because they share academic, urban lifeways with researchers. In Harkerian mode (Harker 1985), Järviluoma contrasts new folk musical practice with (a more authentic and hence more valuable) "working class, rural based pelimanni groups" expression. I hope that this study has scrutinized new folk music, but I do not question the "authenticity" of this musical practice. Surely one value of the ethnomusicological enterprise is its recognition of the worth of all musical expressions. The term "avant-garde traditionalism" cannot in any case be understood as a critique of new folk music. Combinations of the new and the old are precisely what new folk practitioners strive to achieve. Yet the ongoing debates about folk music practices and changes reveal the extent to which they have been implicated in political projects. When commentators debate folk music, they are also addressing questions about identities and belongings; this is why the debates can be so heated.

2. An account of this project is given in *Uusi Kansanmusiikki* (Raskinen 1991).

3. Questions about music and geography have occupied Bohlman's attention in considering the creation of "European music" in contradistinction to other categories of music. He describes the variety of musical sounds heard in strolling through the streets of modern Vienna (street musicians singing in Hungarian, others playing Slovenian folk music instruments, an Andean panpipe ensemble performing songs of political protest in Spanish, organ music by Bach in a cathedral, and notices for opera productions and for performances of Viennese waltzes at a festival). Would, he asks, "the Andean panpipe ensemble we heard in Vienna be European music? And would the music of Islamic Spain in the Middle Ages be European music?" (Bohlman 1992, 202). Whichever way we respond, we are left with even more questions: "If we answer 'no' . . . we seem to argue that Europe is more a shared culture than a unified geographic entity. If we answer 'yes,' we place greater importance on what happens within the geography, allowing even that the geography shapes the culture" (202).

4. Looking at the discourses and practices of "world music," Feld turns to Murray Schafer's term "schizophonia" (introduced in 1977) to emphasize "acoustic dislocations" and Gregory Bateson's term "schismogenesis" (introduced in 1936) to discuss "patterns of progressive differentiation through cumulative interaction" (Feld 1994a, 269). The trope "schizophonia to schismogenesis" is used to "describe some dynamics of the mutualistic process by which ever more commercial and noncommercial music is subsumed under the heading of 'global culture'" (258). For Feld, "schizophonia" evokes

"mediated music, commodified grooves, sounds split from sources, consumer products with few if any contextual linkages to the processes, practices, and forms of participation that could give them meaning within local communities" (259). Finnish new folk music, as a composite of various transformed regional musical styles and borrowed elements, seems to exemplify these ideas about sounds split from sources, but as a contributor to both a national and a global culture it does not readily fit into Feld's "resultant state of progressive mutual differentiation." This is principally because the differentiation of which Feld writes is restricted to being played out in terms of the relationships between Western pop musicians' dominance over, and audience spectatorship of, non-Western musicians, with resulting struggles over "authenticity" and "musical ownership." In looking at new folk music in Finland I have been as concerned with relationships between musicians within the nation-state, and in the reimagining of folk music and place through creative responses to various musical resources.

5. Examples include the *mbira* played by Kimmo Pohjonen in "Yxi Kaunis Papillinen Polska" (Kalaniemi 1992), the *tama* played by Badu N'diay in "Paris-Dakar" (Piirpauke 1989), and the *kora* played by Malang Cissokho (1990).

6. I am grateful to Britto Vincent for this communication.

Bibliography

Abrahams, Roger D. 1992. "The Past in the Presence: An Overview of Folkloristics in the Late Twentieth Century." In *Folklore Processed: In Honour of Lauri Honko on his 60th Birthday, 6th March 1992*, edited by Reimund Kvideland, Gun Herranen, Pekka Laaksonen, Ann-Leena Siikala, and Nils Storå, 32–51. Helsinki: Suomalaisen Kirjallisuuden Seura.

Aho, Kalevi. 1985. *Suomalainen Musiikki ja Kalevala* [Finnish music and the *Kalevala*]. Helsinki: Suomalaisen Kirjallisuuden Seura.

Alakotila, Timo, and Arto Järvelä. 1988. *Nuottivihko 1* [Notebook 1]. Kaustinen: JPP.

———. 1990. *Nuottivihko 2* [Notebook 2]. Kaustinen: JPP.

Arnberg, Matts, and Christina Mattsson. 1995. Liner notes to *Folk Music in Sweden: Låtar från Orsa och Älvdalen*, 1–15. CD. Caprice Records CAP 21476.

Asplund, Anneli. 1978. "Ballads: A Part of the Medieval Finnish Folk Song Tradition." In *The European Medieval Ballad: A Symposium*, edited by Otto Holzapfel, Julia McGrew, and Iorn Pio, 51–60. Odense: Odense University Press.

———. 1981a. "Kansanmusiikki nyky-Suomessa" [Folk music in contemporary Finland]. In *Kansanmusiikki* [Folk music], edited by Anneli Asplund and Matti Hako, 234–39. Helsinki: Suomalaisen Kirjallisuuden Seura.

———. 1981b. "Riimilliset kansanlaulut" [Rhyming folk songs]. In *Kansanmusiikki* [Folk music], edited by Anneli Asplund and Matti Hako, 64–124. Helsinki: Suomalaisen Kirjallisuuden Seura.

———. 1981c. "Pelimannimusiikki ja Uudet Soittimet" [Pelimanni music and new instruments]. In *Kansanmusiikki* [Folk music], edited by Anneli Asplund and Matti Hako, 125–63. Helsinki: Suomalaisen Kirjallisuuden Seura.

———, ed. 1981d. *Balladeja: Suomalaisesta Balladiperinteestä Sävelmät ja Tekstit* [Ballads: The tunes and texts of Finnish ballad traditions]. Helsinki: Suomalaisen Kirjallisuuden Seura.

Asplund, Anneli, and Matti Hako, eds. 1981. *Kansanmusiikki* [Folk music]. Helsinki: Suomalaisen Kirjallisuuden Seura.

Asplund, Anneli, Juha Kangas, and Vesa Tapio Valo, eds. 1990. *Kulkurista Kuninkaaksi: Matti Haudanmaan Musiikki ja Elämä* [From wanderer to king: Matti Haudanmaa's music and life]. Helsinki: Suomalaisen Kirjallisuuden Seura.

Asplund, Anneli, and Heikki Laitinen, eds. 1979. *Kalevalaisia Lauluja* [*Kalevala* songs]. Helsinki: Offset Oy.

Asplund, Anneli, and Ulla Lipponen, eds. 1985. *Kalevala, 1835–1985.* Helsinki: Suomalaisen Kirjallisuuden Seura.

Austerlitz, Paul. 2000. "Birch-Bark Horns and Jazz in the National Imagination: The Finnish Folk Music Vogue in Historical Perspective." *Ethnomusicology* 44, no. 2: 183–213.

Bakhtin, Mikhail. 1973. *Problems of Dostoevsky's Poetics.* Translated by R. W. Rotsel. Ann Arbor, Mich.: Ardis.

Bartók, Béla. 1976. *Béla Bartók Essays.* Edited by Benjamin Suchoff. New York Archive Studies in Musicology, no. 8. London: Faber and Faber.

Bauman, Max Peter. 1992. "Safeguarding of Musical Traditions. Towards the 'Rehabilitation of the Alien.'" In *World Music: Musics of the World: Aspects of Documentation, Mass Media and Acculturation,* edited by Max Peter Bauman. Wilhelmshaven: Florian Noetzel Verlag.

———. 1996. "Folk Music Revival: Concepts between Regression and Emancipation." *World of Music* 38, no. 3:71–86.

Bhabha, Homi K. 1994. *The Location of Culture.* London: Routledge.

Blum, Stephen. 1993. "Prologue: Ethnomusicologists and Modern Music History." In *Ethnomusicology and Modern Music History,* edited by Stephen Blum, Philip V. Bohlman, and Daniel M. Neuman, 1–20. Chicago: University of Illinois Press.

Blum, Stephen, Philip V. Bohlman, and Daniel M. Neuman, eds. 1993. *Ethnomusicology and Modern Music History.* Chicago: University of Illinois Press.

Bohlman, Philip V. 1988. *The Study of Folk Music in the Modern World.* Bloomington: Indiana University Press.

———. 1992. "The Musical Culture of Europe." In *Excursions in World Music,* edited by Bruno Nettl et al., 191–222. Englewood Cliffs, N.J.: Prentice Hall.

Bourdieu, Pierre. 1984. *Distinction: A Social Critique of the Judgement of Taste.* Translated by R. Nice. London: Routledge and Kegan Paul.

Boyes, Georgina. 1993. *The Imagined Village: Culture, Ideology and the English Folk Revival.* Manchester: Manchester University Press.

Brăiloiu, Constantin. 1984. *Problems of Ethnomusicology.* Edited and translated by A. L. Lloyd. Cambridge: Cambridge University Press.

Branch, Michael. 1985. "Introduction." In *Kalevala,* translated by William Forsell Kirby, xi–xxxiv. London: Athlone Press.

Burke, Peter. 1978. *Popular Culture in Early Modern Europe.* London: Temple Smith.

Clifford, James. 1988. *The Predicament of Culture: Twentieth Century Ethnography, Literature, and Art.* Cambridge, Mass.: Harvard University Press.

Cooke, Peter. 1986. *The Fiddle Traditions of the Shetland Isles.* Cambridge: Cambridge University Press.

Coplan, David B. 1993. "Ethnomusicology and the Meaning of Tradition." In *Ethnomusicology and Modern Music History,* edited by Stephen Blum, Philip V. Bohlman, and Daniel M. Neuman, 35–48. Chicago: University of Illinois Press.

Czekanowska, Anna. 1990. *Polish Folk Music: Slavonic Heritage, Polish Tradition, Contemporary Trends.* Cambridge: Cambridge University Press.

Dahlhaus, Carl. [1970] 1983. *Analysis and Value Judgement.* Translated by Siegmund Levarie. New York: Pendragon Press.

De Chiara, Marina. 1996. "A Tribe Called Europe." In *The Post-Colonial Question: Common Skies, Divided Horizons,* edited by Iain Chambers and Lidia Curti, 228–33. London: Routledge.

Dyck, Noel. 1985. "Aboriginal Peoples and Nation-States: An Introduction to the Analytical Issues." In *Indigenous Peoples and the Nation State: Fourth World Politics in Canada, Australia and Norway,* edited by Noel Dyck. St. John's: Memorial University of Newfoundland.

Enäjärvi-Haavio, Elsa. 1951. "On the Performance of the Finnish Folk Runes: Two-Part Singing." *Folkliv* 14/15:130–66.

Erlmann, Veit. 1993. "The Politics and Aesthetics of Transnational Musics." *World of Music* 35, no. 2:3–15.

Feld, Steven. 1994a. "From Schizophonia to Schismogenesis: On the Discourses and Commodification Practices of 'World Music' and 'World Beat.'" In *Music Grooves: Essays and Dialogues,* by Charles Keil and Steven Feld, 257–89. Chicago: University of Chicago Press.

———. 1994b. "Notes on 'World Beat.'" In *Music Grooves: Essays and Dialogues,* by Charles Keil and Steven Feld, 238–46. Chicago: University of Chicago Press.

Ferguson, James, and Akhil Gupta. 1992. "Beyond 'Culture': Space, Identity, and the Politics of Difference." *Cultural Anthropology* 7, no. 1:6–23.

Ferris, William, and Mary L Hart, eds. 1982. *Folk Music and Modern Sound.* Jackson: University Press of Mississippi.

Finnegan, Ruth. 1989. *The Hidden Musicians: Music-Making in an English Town.* Cambridge: Cambridge University Press.

Folk Music Institute. 1985. *Rapapallit ja Lakuttimet: Muinaissuomalaisia Soittimia* [Rapapallit and lakuttimet: Ancient Finnish instruments]. Folk Music Institute Publication 18. Kaustinen: Folk Music Institute.

Frigyesi, Judit. 1996. "The Aesthetic of the Hungarian Revival Movement." In *Retuning Culture: Musical Changes in Central and Eastern Europe,* edited by Mark Slobin, 54–75. Durham: Duke University Press.

Frith, Simon, ed. 1989. *World Music, Politics and Social Change.* Manchester: Manchester University Press.

Garofalo, Reebee. 1993. "Whose World, What Beat: The Transnational Music Industry, Identity, and Cultural Imperialism." *World of Music* 35, no. 2:16–31.

Gaskill, Howard. 1996. "Herder, Ossian and the Celtic." In *Celticism,* edited by Terence Brown, 257–71. Amsterdam: Rodopi.

Gilroy, Paul. 1987. *There Ain't No Black in the Union Jack: The Cultural Politics of Race and Nation.* London: Routledge.

Glassie, Herbert. 1995. "Tradition." *Journal of American Folklore* 108, no. 430:395–412.

Goehr, Lydia. 1992. *The Imaginary Museum of Musical Works: An Essay in the Philosophy of Music.* Oxford: Oxford University Press.

Goertzen, Chris. 1997. *Fiddling for Norway: Revival and Identity.* Chicago: University of Chicago Press.

Goldstein, Kenneth S. 1982. "The Impact of Recording Technology on the British Folksong Revival." In *Folk Music and Modern Sound,* edited by William Ferris and Mary L Hart, 3–13. Jackson: University Press of Mississippi.

Gronow, Pekka. 1987. "The Last Refuge of the Tango." *Finnish Music Quarterly,* no. 4:26–31.

Guilbault, Jocelyne. 1993. *Zouk: World Music in the West Indies.* Chicago: University of Chicago Press.

Gupta, Akhil. 1992. "The Song of the Nonaligned World: Transnational Identities and the Reinscription of Space in Late Capitalism." *Cultural Anthropology* 7, no. 1:63–79.

Häikiö, Martti. 1992. *A Brief History of Modern Finland.* Helsinki: Helsinki University Press.

Häikiö, Martti, and Pertti Pesonen. 1992. *President Koivisto on the Finnish Political Scene.* Helsinki: Ministry of Foreign Affairs.

Hakasalo, Ilpo. 1992. *Sininen ja Valkoinen: Suomalaisten Rakkaimmat Sävelmät, 1917–1992* [Blue and white: Most loved Finnish songs, 1917–1992]. Espoo: Fazer Musiikki Oy.

Hall, Stuart, ed. 1997. *Representation: Cultural Representations and Signifying Practices.* London: Sage Publications.

Hannerz, Ulf. 1987 "The World in Creolisation." *Africa* 57, no. 4:546–59.

———. 1989. "Culture between Center and Periphery: Toward a Macroanthropology." *Ethnos* 54:200–216.

———. 1996. "Amsterdam: Windows on the World." In *Transnational Connections: Culture, People, Places,* 140–49. London: Routledge.

Harker, Dave. 1985. *Fakesong: The Manufacture of British Folksong, 1700 to the Present Day.* Milton Keynes: Open University Press.

Hautala, Jouko. 1969. *Finnish Folklore Research, 1828–1918.* Helsinki: Finnish Society of Sciences.

Heikinheimo, Seppo. 1992. "'Suomi saa vielä Karjalan takaisin': Mestarisellisti Rostro-povitsh lausui Lappeenrannassa profeetallisia sanoja" ["Finland will get Karelia back yet": Prophetic words from the master cellist Rostropovich in Lapeenranta]. *Helsingin Sanomat*, September 5, 1992..

Heikkilä, Johannes, and Olli Penttilä. 1989. "Kokoelma Suomalaisia 'Etnisen' Musiikin Yhtyeitä Keväällä 1989" [Finnish "ethnic" bands in the spring of 1989]. *Musiikin Suunta* 11, no. 2:57–62.

Heiniö, Mikko. 1990. "Aatteen Vallassa: Näkökohtia Musiikki-Instituution Käsitteeseen" [In the power of ideas: Viewpoints of the concept of music institution]. In *Etnomusikologian Vuosikirja 1989–90* [Ethnomusicology yearbook 1989–90], edited by Vesa Kurkela and Erkki Pekkilä, 7–37. Jyväskylä: Suomen Etnomusikologinen Seura.

———. 1992. "What Is 'Finnish' in Finnish Music?" *Finnish Music Quarterly*, no. 1: 2–11.

Helistö, Paavo. 1989. "The Clarinet in Finnish Folk Music." *Finnish Music Quarterly*, no. 1:30–33.

———. 1991. "Konsta Jylhä." *Uusi Kansanmusiikki*, no. 6:24–25.

———. 1992. "Otto Hotakainen." *Uusi Kansanmusiikki*, no. 1:20–21.

Herzfeld, Michael. 1982. *Ours Once More*. Texas: Texas University Press.

Hobsbawm, Eric, and Terence Ranger, eds. 1983. *The Invention of Tradition*. Cambridge: Cambridge University Press.

Honko, Lauri. 1979. "A Hundred Years of Finnish Folklore Research: A Reappraisal." *Folklore* 90, no. 2:141–52.

———, ed. 1988. *Tradition and Cultural Identity*. Turku: Nordic Institute of Folklore.

Huxley, Steven D. 1990. *Constitutionalist Insurgency in Finland: Finnish "Passive Resistance" against Russification as a Case of Nonmilitary Struggle in the European Resistance Tradition*. Helsinki: Finnish Historical Society.

Ilomäki, Henni. 1998. "The Image of Women in Ingrian Wedding Poetry." In *Gender and Folklore: Perspectives on Finnish and Karelian Culture*, edited by Satu Apo, Aili Nenola, and Laura Stark-Arola, 143–74. Helsinki: Suomalaisen Kirjallisuuden Seura.

Iltanen, Kimmo. 1989. "Digelius Music Oy: Maailmanmusiikkiputiikki" [Digelius Music Company: A world music boutique]. *Musiikin Suunta* 11, no. 2:28–40.

Jalkanen, Pekka. 1992. "Finnish Popular Music: What Makes It Specifically Finnish?" *Finnish Music Quarterly*, no. 4:24–29.

James, Burnett. 1983. *The Music of Jean Sibelius*. London: Associated University Presses.

———. 1989. *The Illustrated Lives of the Great Composers: Sibelius*. London: Omnibus Press.

Jarvenpa, Robert. 1989. "Unfamiliar Compatriots: Role Ambiguity in Finnish Field Research." *Ethnos* 54:31–44.

Järviluoma, Helmi. 1997. *Musiikki, Identiteeti, ja Ruohonjuuritaso: Amatöörimuusikkoryhmän Kategoriatyöskentelyn Analyysi* [Music, identity and grass roots: Analysis

of the categorizations of amateur musicians' groups]. Ph.D. thesis, University of
Tampere.

———. 2000. "Local Constructions of Gender in a Finnish Pelimanni Musicians
Group." In *Music and Gender,* edited by Pirkko Moisala and Beverley Diamond, 51–
79. Urbana: University of Illinois Press.

JIFMC [Journal of the International Folk Music Council]. 1955. "Resolutions: Definition of Folk Music." *Journal of the International Folk Music Council* 1955, no. 7:23.

Karinen, Ville. 2001. *Folk Music Revival in Finland: Changing Notions of Authenticity.*
B.A. diss., Queen's University Belfast.

Koivisto, Mauno, and Pertti Paasio. 1990. *Finland in the Changing Europe: Major
Speeches by Dr. Mauno Koivisto, President of Finland and Mr. Pertti Paasio, Minister
for Foreign Affairs.* Helsinki: Ministry for Foreign Affairs.

Korhonen, Mikko. [1987] 1994. "The Early History of the Kalevala Metre." In *Songs
beyond the Kalevala: Transformations of Oral Poetry,* edited by Anna-Leena Siikala
and Sinikka Vakimo, 75–87. Helsinki: Suomalaisen Kirjallisuuden Seura.

Kotirinta, Pirkko. 1992. "Kultuuri" [Culture]. *Helsingin Sanomat,* July 24, 1992.

Krohn, Ilmari, ed. 1975. *Vanhoja Pelimannisävelmiä* [Old folk tunes]. Hämeenlinna:
Suomalaisen Kirjallisuuden Seura.

Kun, Josh. 1997. "Against Easy Listening: Audiotopic Readings and Transnational
Soundings." In *Everynight Life: Culture and Dance in Latin/o America,* edited by
Celeste Fraser Delgado and José Esteban Muñoz, 288–309. Durham: Duke Univer-
sity Press.

Kurkela, Vesa. 1989a. "Mambo: Maailmanmusiikin Valoa Kansalle" [Mambo: Educat-
ing the public about world music]. *Musiikin Suunta* 11, no. 2:41–46.

———. 1989b. *Musiikkifolklorismi ja Järjestökulttuuri: Kansanmusiikin Ideologinen ja
Taiteellinen Hyödyntäminen Suomalaisissa Musiikki ja Nuorisojärjestöissä* [Music
folklorism and organization culture: The ideological and artistic utilization of folk
music in Finnish musical and youth organizations]. Suomen Etnomusikologisen
Seura publication 3. Jyväskylä: Suomen Etnomusikologisen Seura.

Kurkela, Vesa, and Anu Laakkonen. 1989a. "Mistä Oikeastaan On Kysymys?" [What
really is the question?] *Musiikin Suunta* 11, no. 2:3–7.

———. 1989b. "Värilliset Pipot Päässä Soitellaan" [Musicians with colored caps].
Musiikin Suunta 11, no. 2:47–56.

Kuusi, Matti. [1978] 1994. "Questions of Kalevala Metre." In *Songs beyond the Kalevala:
Transformations of Oral Poetry,* edited by Anna-Leena Siikala and Sinikka Vakimo,
41–55. Helsinki: Suomalaisen Kirjallisuuden Seura.

Lahtinen, Matti. 1991. *Evaluating Music Policy: Applying an Ethnomusicological Frame
of Reference to the Study of a "Political System Directing the Production of Music."*
Työpapereita [Working papers]. Helsinki: Arts Council of Finland.

Laitinen, Heikki, and Hannu Saha. 1988. *A Guide to Five String Kantele Playing.* Kaustinen: Kansanmusiikki Instituutti.

Lander, Patricia S. 1991. "Finnish Identity in a Changing Europe." *Ethnos* 56:242–55.

Layton, Robert. 1965. *The Master Musicians: Sibelius.* London: Dent.

Lehtinen, A. 1991. *Northern Natures: A Study of the Forest Question Emerging within the Timber-Line Conflict in Finland.* Helsinki: Geographical Society of Finland.

Lehtiranta, Erkki, and Kristiina Saalonen. 1993. *Musiikkijournalismi: Musiikin ja Median Kohtaamisia* [Music journalism: The relation between music and the media]. Helsinki: Sibelius Academy.

Leino, Pentti. [1985] 1994. "The Kalevala Metre and Its Development." In *Songs beyond the Kalevala: Transformations of Oral Poetry,* edited by Anna-Leena Siikala and Sinikka Vakimo, 56–74. Helsinki: Suomalaisen Kirjallisuuden Seura.

Leisiö, Timo. 1983. *Suomen ja Karjalan Vanhakantaiset Torvi ja Pillisoittimet* [Early Finnish and Karelian horn and woodwind instruments]. Kaustinen: Kansanmusiikki Instituutti.

———. 1986. "Joiku: Songs in Samiland." *Finnish Music Quarterly,* no. 4:36–53.

Levanto, Marjatta. 1991. *Ateneum Guide: From Isak Wacklin to Wäinö Aaltonen.* Translated by Harald Arnkil. Keuruu: Otava Publishing Company.

Levin, Theodore. 1996. "Dmitri Pokrovsky and the Russian Folk Music Revival." In *Retuning Culture: Musical Changes in Central and Eastern Europe,* edited by Mark Slobin, 14–36. Durham: Duke University Press.

Lewis, Bernard. 1976. *History: Remembered, Recovered, Invented.* Princeton, N.J.: Princeton University Press.

Ling, Jan. 1997. *A History of European Folk Music.* Rochester, N.Y.: University of Rochester Press.

Linke, Uli. 1995. "Power Matters: The Politics of Culture in German Folklore Scholarship." *History and Anthropology* 9, no. 1:1–26.

Livingston, Tamara E. 1999. "Music Revivals: Towards a General Theory." *Ethnomusicology* 43, no. 1:66–85.

Llobera, Josep R. 1994. *The God of Modernity: The Development of Nationalism in Western Europe.* Oxford: Berg.

Lloyd, Albert L. 1982. "Electric Folk Music in Britain." In *Folk Music and Modern Sound,* edited by William Ferris and Mary L. Hart, 14–18. Jackson: University Press of Mississippi.

Lönnrot, Elias. 1984. *Kalevala.* 25th ed. Mikkeli: Länsi-Savo.

———. [1907] 1985. *Kalevala, the Land of Heroes.* Translated by William Forsell Kirby. London: Athlone Press.

Louhivouri, Jukka. 1992. "The Symbiosis of Church and Folk Music." *Finnish Music Quarterly,* no. 2:27–30.

Louhivouri, Jukka, and Rauno Nieminen. 1987. *Paimen Säveliä: Teppo Revon Paimen-soittusävelmiä* [A shepherd's tunes: Teppo Repo's shepherd compositions]. Helsinki: Suomalaisen Kirjallisuuden Seura.

Mac Craith, Mícheàl. 1996. "The 'Forging' of Ossian." In *Celticism,* edited by Terence Brown, 125–41. Amsterdam: Rodopi.

Manuel, Peter. 1993. *Cassette Culture: Popular Music and Technology in North India.* Chicago: University of Chicago Press.

Meintjes, Louise. 1990. "Paul Simon's *Graceland,* South Africa, and the Mediation of Musical Meaning." *Ethnomusicology* 34, no. 1:37–73.

Melucci, Alberto. 1982. *L'invenzione del presente: Movimenti, identità, bisogni indi-viduali.* Bologna: Il Mulino.

Meyer, Leonard B. 1989. *Style and Music: Theory, History and Ideology.* Philadelphia: University of Pennsylvania Press.

Mitchell, Ritva. 1989. *The New Measures for Financing Arts and Culture: A Survey of European Experiences and Innovatory Initiatives Adopted in the 1980s.* Helsinki: Arts Council of Finland and Council for Cultural Co-operation, Council of Europe.

———. 1991. *Patterns of Cultural Participation and Consumption in Finland in the 1980s.* Työpapereita [Working papers]. Helsinki: Arts Council of Finland, Research and Publications Unit.

Mitchell, Ritva, and Rod Fisher. 1992. *Professional Managers for the Arts and Culture? Training of Cultural Administrators and Arts Managers in Europe.* Helsinki: Arts Council of Finland and Cultural Information and Research Centres Liaison in Europe.

Mitchell, Ritva, and Sari Karttunen. 1991. *Why and How to Define an Artist? Types of Definitions and Their Implications for Empirical Research Results.* Työpapereita [Working papers]. Helsinki: Arts Council of Finland.

Mitchell, Ritva, and Eija Ristimäki. 1992. *Survey on the Economic Situation and Social Status of the Artist in Finland.* Työpapereita [Working papers]. Helsinki: Arts Council of Finland, Research and Publications Unit.

Mitchell, Tony. 1996. *Popular Music and Local Identity.* London: Leicester University Press.

Modood, Tariq, and Pnina Werbner, eds. 1997. *The Politics of Multiculturalism in the New Europe: Racism, Identity and Community.* London: Zed Books.

Moisala, Pirkko, ed. 1994. "Ethnomusicology in Finland." *Ethnomusicology* 38, no. 3: 399–422.

Monson, Ingrid. 1999. "Riffs, Repetition, and Theories of Globalization." *Ethnomusi-cology* 43, no. 1:31–65.

Muikku, Jari. 1989. "Traditional Values in a Modern Light." *Finnish Music Quarterly,* no. 1:46–48.

Nettl, Bruno. 1964. *Theory and Method in Ethnomusicology.* New York: Free Press.

———. 1978. *Eight Urban Musical Cultures.* Chicago: University of Illinois Press.

———. 1983. *The Study of Ethnomusicology: Twenty-nine Issues and Concepts.* Chicago: University of Illinois Press.

———. 1991. "Introduction." In *Comparative Musicology and Anthropology of Music: Essays on the History of Ethnomusicology,* edited by Bruno Nettl and Philip V. Bohlman, xi–xvii. Chicago: University of Chicago Press.

Nettl, Bruno, and Philip V. Bohlman, eds. 1991. *Comparative Musicology and Anthropology of Music: Essays on the History of Ethnomusicology.* Chicago: University of Chicago Press.

Neuman, Daniel. 1993. "Epilogue: Paradigms and Stories." In *Ethnomusicology and Modern Music History,* edited by Stephen Blum, Philip V. Bohlman, and Daniel. Neuman, 268–77. Chicago: University of Illinois Press.

Olwig, Karen Fog, and Kirsten Hastrup, eds. 1997. *Siting Culture: The Shifting Anthropological Object.* London: Routledge.

Paasivirta, Juhani. 1981. *Finland and Europe: The Period of Autonomy and the International Crises, 1808–1914.* Translated by Anthony F Upton and Sirkka R. Upton. London: Hurst and Company.

Pekkilä, Erkki. 1990. "C. A. Gottlund ja Kansanmusiikki" [C. A. Gottlund and folk music]. In *Etnomusikologian Vuosikirja 1989–90* [Ethnomusicology yearbook 1989–90], edited by Vesa Kurkela and Erkki Pekkilä, 192–204. Jyväskylä: Suomen Etnomusikologinen Seura.

———. 1990, ed. *Hiljainen Haltioituminen: A. O. Väisäsen Tutkielmia Kansanmusiikista* [Silent inspiration: A. O. Väisänen's treatise on folk music]. Helsinki: Suomalaisen Kirjallisuuden Seura.

Phillips, Caryl. 1987. *The European Tribe.* London: Faber and Faber.

Pietilä, Riitta. 1992. "Singing High and Loud: In Search of the Karelian Sound." *Finnish Music Quarterly,* no. 2:46–48.

Porthan, Henrik Gabriel. [1778] 1983. *Suomalaisesta Runoudesta* [On Finnish poems]. Translated by Iiro Kajanto. Vaasa: Suomalaisen Kirjallisuuden Seura.

Rahkonen, Carl. 1983. "The Concept of Ultrastability as Applied to a Study of the Finnish Kantele." *Suomen Antropologi,* special issue on ethnomusicology, 239–41.

Ramnarine, Tina K. 1996. "Folk Music Education: Initiatives in Finland." *Folk Music Journal* 7, no. 2:136–54.

———. 1998. "An Encounter with the Other: Sibelius, Folk Music and Nationalism." In *Proceedings from the Second International Jean Sibelius Conference, 1995,* edited by Veijo Murtomäki, Kari Kilpeläinen, and Risto Väisänen, 166–73. Helsinki: Sibelius Academy.

Raskinen, Minna. 1991. "Kanteleet Maailmalla" [Kanteles in the world]. *Uusi Kansanmusiikki,* no. 5:47.

Rasmussen, Ljerka Vidíc. 1996. "The Southern Wind of Change: Style and the Politics of Identity in Prewar Yugoslavia." In *Retuning Culture: Musical Changes in Central and Eastern Europe,* edited by Mark Slobin, 99–116. Durham: Duke University Press.

Reily, Suzel. 1998. "The Ethnographic Enterprise: The Venda Girls' Initiation Schools Revisited." *British Journal of Ethnomusicology* 7:45–68.

Reunala, Aarne. 1989. "The Forest and the Finns." In *Finland: People, Nation, State,* edited by Max Engman and David Kirby, 38–56. London: Hurst and Company.

Rice, Timothy. 1994. *May It Fill Your Soul: Experiencing Bulgarian Music.* Chicago: University of Chicago Press.

Robertson, Roland. 1990. "Mapping the Global Condition: Globalization as the Central Concept." In *Global Culture: Nationalism, Globalization and Modernity,* edited by Mike Featherstone, 15–30. London: Sage Publications.

———. 1991. "Social Theory, Cultural Relativity and the Problem of Globality." In *Culture, Globalization and the World-System,* edited by Anthony D. King, 69–90. Basingstoke: Macmillan Press.

———. 1995. "Glocalization: Time-Space and Homogeneity-Heterogeneity." In *Global Modernities,* edited by Mike Featherstone, Scott Lash, and Roland Robertson, 25–44. London: Sage Publications.

Rosenberg, Neil V., ed. 1993. *Transforming Tradition: Folk Music Revivals Examined.* Urbana: University of Illinois Press.

Russell, Ian, ed. 1986. *Singer, Song and Scholar.* Sheffield: Sheffield Academic Press.

Sachs, Curt. 1962. *The Wellsprings of Music.* Edited by Jaap Kunst. New York: Da Capo Press.

Saha, Hannu. 1984. *Finnish Features: Folk Music in Finland.* Helsinki: Ministry for Foreign Affairs.

———. 1988. "*Kantele:* New Life for Finland's National Instrument." *Finnish Music Quarterly,* no. 1:20–29.

Schade-Poulsen, Marc. 1997. "Which World? On the Diffusion of Algerian Raï to the West." In *Siting Culture: The Shifting Anthropological Object,* edited by Karen Fog Olwig and Kirsten Hastrup, 59–85. London: Routledge.

Schlesinger, Philip. 1987. "On National Identity: Some Conceptions and Misconceptions Criticized." *Social Science Information* 26, no. 2:219–64.

Shepherd, John. 1991. *Music as Social Text.* Cambridge: Polity Press.

———. 1993. "Difference and Power in Music." In *Musicology and Difference: Gender and Sexuality in Music Scholarship,* edited by Ruth A. Solie, 46–65. Berkeley: University of California Press.

Sibelius, Jean. [1896] 1980. "Joitakin Näkökohtia Kansanmusiikista ja sen Vaikutuksesta Säveltaiteeseen" [Some reflections on folk music and its influence on the development of art music]. *Musiikki* 10, no. 2:86–105.

Slawek, Stephen M. 1993. "Ravi Shankar as Mediator between a Traditional Music and Modernity." In *Ethnomusicology and Modern Music History,* edited by Stephen Blum, Philip V. Bohlman, and Daniel M. Neuman, 161–80. Chicago: University of Illinois Press.

Slobin, Mark. 1982. "How the Fiddler Got on the Roof." In *Folk Music and Modern Sound,* edited by William Ferris and Mary L. Hart, 21–31. Jackson: University Press of Mississippi.

———. 1993. *Subcultural Sounds: Micromusics of the West.* Hanover, N.H.: Wesleyan University Press.

———, ed. 1996. *Retuning Culture: Musical Changes in Central and Eastern Europe.* Durham, N.C.: Duke University Press.

Small, Christopher. 1987. *Music of the Common Tongue.* London: Calder.

Smith, Anthony D. 1990. "Towards a Global Culture?" In *Global Culture: Nationalism, Globalization and Modernity,* edited by Mike Featherstone, 171–91. London: Sage Publications.

———. 1994. "The Politics of Culture: Ethnicity and Nationalism." In *Companion Encyclopaedia of Anthropology: Humanity, Culture and Social Life,* edited by Tim Ingold, 706–33. London: Routledge.

Solie, Ruth A., ed. 1993. *Musicology and Difference: Gender and Sexuality in Music Scholarship.* Berkeley: University of California Press.

Spencer, Jonathan. 1990. "Writing Within: Anthropology, Nationalism, and Culture in Sri Lanka." *Current Anthropology* 31, no. 3:283–300.

Stokes, Martin, ed. 1994. *Ethnicity, Identity and Music: The Musical Construction of Place.* Oxford: Berg.

Strathern, Marilyn. 1988. *The Gender of the Gift: Problems with Women and Problems with Society in Melanesia.* Berkeley: University of California Press.

Sykes, Richard. 1993. "The Evolution of 'Englishness' in the English Folksong Revival, 1890–1914." *Folk Music Journal* 6, no. 4:446–90.

Talve, Ilmar. 1997. *Finnish Folk Culture.* Helsinki: Suomalaisen Kirjallisuuden Seura.

Tarkka, Lotte. 1998. "Sense of the Forest: Nature and Gender in Karelian Oral Poetry." In *Gender and Folklore: Perspectives on Finnish and Karelian Culture,* edited by Satu Apo, Aili Nenola and Laura Stark-Arola, 92–142. Helsinki: Suomalaisen Kirjallisuuden Seura.

Tarkkanen, Jussi, ed. 1985. *Leikarit Nuottivihko 1* [Leikarit notebook 1]. Espoo: Leikarit Ry.

Tawaststjerna, Erik. 1976. *Sibelius.* Vol. 1, *1865–1905.* Translated by Robert Layton. London: Faber and Faber.

Taylor, Julie. 1987. "Tango." *Cultural Anthropology* 2, no. 4:481–93.

Timonen, Senni. 1985. "Lönnrot and His Singers." In *Kalevala 1835–1985: The National Epic of Finland 1985,* 24–29. Helsinki: Helsinki University Library.

———. 1998. "Every Tree Bites Me: North Karelian Lyric Poetry." In *Gender and Folklore: Perspectives on Finnish and Karelian Culture,* edited by Satu Apo, Aili Nenola, and Laura Stark-Arola, 201–35. Helsinki: Suomalaisen Kirjallisuuden Seura.

Toivonen, Tapani, and Mauno Järvelä. 1991. *Kyläsoitto* [Village playing]. Kokkola: KP-Paino.

Tolvanen, Hannu. 1989. "Foreword." *Musiikin Suunta* 11, no. 4:1.

———. 1991. "The New Wave of Finnish Folk Music." *Finnish Music Quarterly,* no. 2: 37–39.

Tuomioja, Erkki. 1991. *Europe and the Nordic Fringe.* Vaasa: Finnish Committee for Europe.

Turino, Thomas. 1993. *Moving Away from Silence: Music of the Peruvian Altiplano and the Experience of Urban Migration.* Chicago: University of Chicago Press.

Väisänen, Armas Otto. 1928 *Kantele ja Jouhikko Sävelmiä* [Kantele and jouhikko tunes]. Helsinki: Valtioneuvoston Kirjapaino.

———. 1936. Sibelius ja Kansanmusiikki [Sibelius and folk music]. In *Kalevalaseuran 16 Vuosikirja* [Yearbook 16 of the Kalevala Society], 276–88. Porvoo: Werner Söderström Osakeyhtiön Kirjapainossa.

———. [1970] 1990. *Hiljainen Haltioituminen: A. O. Väisäsen Tutkielmia Kansanmusiikista* [Silent inspiration: A. O. Väisänen's treatise on folk music], edited by Erkki Pekkilä. Helsinki: Suomalaisen Kirjallisuuden Seura.

Vakimo, Sinikka. 1998. "Elderly Women on the Dance Floor: Pensioners' Dances as a Cultural Scene. In *Gender and Folklore: Perspectives on Finnish and Karelian Culture,* edited by Satu Apo, Aili Nenola, and Laura Stark-Arola, 376–402. Helsinki: Suomalaisen Kirjallisuuden Seura.

Van Elderin, Louis P. 1993. "Värttinä between Tradition and Modernity: In Search of the Meaning of Finnish Folk Music." In *On the Borders of Semiosis: Acta Semiotica II,* edited by Eero Tarasti. Publications of the International Semiotics Institute at Imatra, no. 4. Imatra: International Semiotics Institute at Imatra

Vaughan Williams, Ralph. 1934. *National Music.* London: Oxford University Press.

Wallis, Roger, and Krister Malm. 1984. *Big Sounds from Small People: The Music Industry in Small Countries.* New York: Pendragon Press.

Waterman, Christopher A. 1990. " 'Our Tradition Is a Very Modern Tradition': Popular Music and the Construction of Pan-Yoruba Identity." *Ethnomusicology* 34, no. 3: 367–79.

Werbner, Pnina. 1997. "Afterword: Writing Multiculturalism and Politics in the New Europe." In *The Politics of Multiculturalism in the New Europe: Racism, Identity and Community,* edited by Tariq Modood, and Pnina Werbner, 261–67. London: Zed Books.

Westerholm, Simo. 1991a. "Hiski Salomaa: 100 Vuotta" [Hiski Salomaa: 100 years].
Uusi Kansanmusiikki, no. 2:21–23.

———. 1992. "A Living Tradition: The Story of Finnish-American Music." *Finnish Music Quarterly,* no. 4:30–36.

———, ed. 1991b. *Otto Hotakaisen Nuottikirja* [Otto Hotakainen's notebook]. Kaustinen: Kansanmusiikki-instituutti.

Wilson, William A. 1976. *Folklore and Nationalism in Modern Finland.* Bloomington: Indiana University Press.

Yung, Bell. 1987. "Historical Interdependency of Music: A Case Study of the Chinese Seven-String Zither." *Journal of the American Musicological Society* 40:82–91.

Ziff, Bruce, and Pratima V. Rao. 1997. *Borrowed Power: Essays on Cultural Appropriation.* New Brunswick, N.J.: Rutgers University Press.

Discography

This discography lists commercial recordings (audio and video) of the Finnish music referred to in the main text.

Cissokho, Malang (with Hannu Saha). 1990. *Lotus.* CD. Eino EICD 1.

Folk Music Institute. 1988. *Vanhat Kansansoittimet* [Old folk instruments]. Videocassette. Folk Music Institute KIV-2.

Hedningarnar. 1992. *Hedningarnar Kaksi!* CD. Silence Records SRSCD 4717.

Hotakainen, Otto. 1989. *Mestaripelimanni The Master Musician, Otto Hotakainen.* LP. Olarin Musiikki OMLP 17.

JPP. 1983. *Järvelän Pikkupelimannit.* EP.

JPP. 1986. *Laitisen Mankeliska.* LP. Olarin Musiikki OMLP 9.

JPP. 1988. *JPP: New Finnish Folk Fiddling.* LP and CD. Olarin Musiikki OMLP/ OMCD 15.

JPP. 1990. *I've Found a New Tango.* CD. Olarin Musiikki OMCD 32.

JPP. 1992. *Pirun Polska* [Devil's polska]. CD. Olarin Musiikki OMCD 37.

JPP. 1994. *Kaustinen Rhapsody.* CD. Olarin Musiikki OMCD 53.

Kalaniemi, Maria. 1992. *Maria Kalaniemi.* CD. Olarin Musiikki OMCD 40.

Karhu, Santtu, and Talvisovat. 1990. *Airotoi veneh/Syvysharmavus* [Oarless boat/ Autumn greyness]. Single. Eino EIS 2.

Karhu, Santtu, and Talvisovat. 1991. *Omien aigoin legendat/Aunuksen Anja* [Legends of our time/Anja of Aunus]. Single. Eino EIS 3.

Koinurit. 1990. *Yllätyspaartit* [Surprise parties]. CD. Olarin Musiikki OMCD 34.

Local Off. 1992. Local Off Featuring Värttinä. CD. Sonet SPIRCDS 013.

Musica Sveciae. 1995. *Folk Music in Sweden: Låtar från Orsa och Älvdalen.* CD. Caprice Records CAP 21476.

Nelipolviset. 1979. *Kalevalaisia Lauluja* [Kalevala songs]. Audiocassette. Suomalaisen Kirjallisuuden Seura SKSK 2.

Paakkunainen, Seppo. 1992. *Symphony no.1, "Juoigansinfoniija."* Performed by a studio orchestra from Tallin, conductor Paul Mägi, soloists Karelia group and Nils-Aslak Välkeäpää and Johan Anders Baer. CD. DATCD 11.

Peltoniemi, Eric. 1992. *Kävelin kerran / Velisurmaaja* [I once walked / The brother slayer]. Single. Eino EIS-6.

Piirpauke. 1989. *Zerenade.* CD. Rockadillo Zen CD 2017.

Primo. 1984. *Haltian Opissa* [The sprite's apprentice]. LP. Olarin Musiikki OMLP 8.

Salamakannel. 1989. *Salamakannel* [Lightning kantele]. CD. Olarin Musiikki OMCD 25.

Salamakannel. 1992. *Koivunrunkorakkautta* [Love of the birch tree trunk]. CD. Amigo AMFCD 2005-2.

Värttinä. 1989. *Musta Lindu* [Black bird]. CD. Olarin Musiikki OMCD 22.

Värttinä. 1991. *Oi Dai.* LP. Spirit LP 4.

Värttinä. 1992. *Seleniko.* CD. Spirit 517.467-2.

Värttinä. 1994. *Aitara.* CD. Mipu. MIPUCD 302.

Värttinä. 1996. *Kokko* [Bonfire]. CD. Nonesuch 79429-2.

Index

accompaniment, instrumental, 91–92, 42, 184, 211

accordion, 61, 151–52, 168, 177, 184; Magdeburg, 152

activists, 47–48

aerophone instruments, 57, 76, 151, 221n. 3; birchbark, 184

aesthetic criteria: demands, 15; judgments, 108–9; sensibilities, 149, 197

aesthetics: of the exotic, 86; folk, 113, 218; global musical, xv; popular, 201; revival, 48, 76; of synthesis and change, 215

Agricola, Mikael, 28

agriculture, 97

Aino, 34

Ala-Könni music courses, 126–33

Ala-Könni, Erkki, 51, 53, 162

Alakotila, Timo, 160, 162, 168

American folk-rock, xvii, 50, 59, 62, 149

American revival movement, 14

Angelin Tytöt, 182, 184

anthropologists, 17

appropriation, 180, 192, 196

arrangements, musical, xii, 15, 79, 169, 219

art, national, 6, 8, 32, 63

art music, 4, 6, 14, 20, 59, 63, 82, 204, 208

Arts Council of Finland, 202–3

Asamaan, 126, 184, 187, 192–93. *See also* Walli, Hasse

Asplund, Anneli, 53–55, 60, 74

Ataneum Art Gallery, 26

audiences: competing for, 69, 198, 200; for Finnish folk revival, 62; global, 210; for new folk music, xii, xv–xvi, 107, 113, 177–78, 205; portraits of, 27; responses, 181, 191, 193, 210; urban, 79, 83–84, 87, 182

auditions, 133

"Aunuksen Anja," 178–80, 207

aural skills, 71

authenticity: historical, 36; musical, 158, 160, 200, 214; notions of, xviii, 108; questioning, 48, 113, 191, 234n. 1; tropes of, 66

Baer, Johan Anders, 183

ballad, xviii, 11, 39, 134–39, 141, 149, 151, 174, 207

banjo, 148, 153, 184

Bartók, Béla, 4–6, 14, 20, 75, 222n. 1

bass, double, 151, 153, 158–59, 167–69, 211

Becker, Reinhold von, 30

bell, 184

belonging: national, 81, 88; sense of, 23

biographies, musical, 20, 58, 63, 150, 168

Bohlman, Philip, 14, 134, 234n. 3

Boolabus, 190–91

borders, 34, 38, 91; areas, 11, 31, 36, 89; geopolitical, 12; politics of, 182; struggles over, 8. *See also* boundaries

Borenius, 36, 74

borrowing, 174; musical, xvii, 22–23, 168, 174–75, 195, 197, 202, 208, 210–11, 216–

borrowing (*continued*)
18; from "others," 22–23, 135, 173, 200; of
tradition, 30, 36, 196, 215
boundaries: musical, xviii, 3, 23, 58, 136,
149, 180, 210, 218; national, xiii, 22, 196,
215, 217–18; political, 8
bouzouki, 184
bowing: style, 128–29; articulation, 130
Brăiloiu, Constantin, 4, 20
brass bands, 11
British folk-rock, xvii, 50, 59, 62
British revival movement, 14

canon: folk music, 139, 142; Norwegian
folk, 48; recorded folk music, xiii, 93,
143, 159, 184, 204, 206
celebration, national, 135
change, xiii, xvi, 13, 15–18, 22, 66, 87, 214;
in instrument construction, 149; musical, xi, xvi, xvii, 12, 76, 147, 154, 157, 175,
193, 197, 211, 214–15, 219; political, 12, 18;
rapid, 4
character, national, 167
choices: creative, 213; musical, xviii, 90,
108, 175, 196–97, 202, 210–11, 217–18
choirs, 11, 59, 61
chorales, folk, 51
Cissokho, Malang, 184–85, 198, 216
clarinet, 59, 151–52, 154
classification: issues, 5; systems, 40, 74
Cold War, 8
collaborations, musical, xviii, 174, 192, 198,
216–18
collective cultural consciousness, 7
collectivity, 17, 19, 37
collectors, xv, 4, 32–33
commodification, musical, 197, 204
commodity, music as global, xix, 200
communication, global, 197
comparative research, 29, 37
competition: dance, 85, pl. 6; folk music,
81–82, 154, 157, 198; "world" and "folk"
labels as aspect of, 198
composers, 6–7, 21; art music, 5, 21; folk, 160

composition: art music, 6; concerns of,
167; folk, 50, 161–62, 167–69, 173–74; issues of, 20, 196; new folk music, 79, 93,
149, 160–61, 169, 187, 214; old pelimanni,
11; oral, 161; original, 15, 70, 139, 142, 192;
processes of, 21, 160–61
concepts: of change, 14; of folk music, 5, 16,
50, 204, 213; of gender, 101; of identity,
19; of world music, 210; temporal, 17
conceptualizations, musical, 186–87, 214
conflict, 15, 178, 181
contemporary folk music. *See* new folk
music
continuity, 3, 4, 13–18, 22, 58, 66; musical,
xvii–xviii, 125, 147, 150, 157–58, 160, 211,
214
copyright, 204, 207–10
creation myth, 1, 43
creativity, 7, 16, 20, 139, 210; impulse toward, 16; process of, 20–21, 70, 197,
208–10, 215–16, 219
Cuban drumming, xvii, 76–78
culture: global, 175, 202, 215; national, xix,
6, 195, 204, 214, 217; views of, 9, 19, 203,
205, 216

dance, 139, 193, 205; music, 59, 61, 107, 161.
See also folk dance
Department of Folk Music (Sibelius Academy), 57, 67–84, 176–78, 218
difference: assertions of, 18, 216; construction of, 21; experiences of, 194; fictions
of, 217; layers of, 142; musical, xviii, 19,
79, 133, 180, 182, 192, 198, 201–2, 217; national, 9; discourse of (nationalist), 21,
31. *See also* ideology
diversity, musical, 19, 79
drums, 59, 61, 168, 182, 184–86, 195
dynamic range, 113

education, 9, 54–55, 64–65, 69; folk music,
xii, 52, 132, 211; programs, 214; systems,
xi, 68, 70
Education, Ministry of, 192, 210

Ekman, Robert, Wilhelm, 26–27, 53
elements: borrowed, 198; musical, 15, 18, 58, 78, 81, 89, 93, 186, 197–98, 215
"Ellun Sottiisi," 163
emotion, 9, 114, 188
encounters, musical, xviii, 176, 185, 217–18
ensemble, 128–29
epic, national, xvii, 6, 10, 47. See also *Kalevala*
Estonian songs, 72–74, 85
ethnography, 14, 202
ethnomusicology, 14, 215; focus of, xvi, 12, 216; at home, 221n. 2; challenge to basic paradigms in, 226n. 5
Etnosoi Festival, 83, 85
Europaeus, D. E. D, 32
examinations, 81–82
exchanges: asymmetric, 201; global, 85; musical, xvii–xviii, 4, 113, 173, 175–76, 181, 184, 192–93, 215, 217
experience, 13, 17, 19, 23, 89, 114, 177, 194; musical, 58, 89, 218
expression, 188; localized, 200; musical, xvii–xviii, 5, 20, 33, 43, 212, 217; national, xiv, 37–38, 211, 215, 217

Fairport Convention, 59–60
fiddle: as instrument, 11, 147, 151–54, 158–60, 169, 184; performance, 150; repertoires, xviii, 48, 150–53. See also violin
fiddlers, xiv, 11, 150, 152–57, 191, 196, 228n. 3 (chap. 7)
fiddlers' societies, 12
fiddling, 160–61; of Ostrobothnia, xvii, 160, 174; of the Shetland Islands, 14; around the world, 211
Finnish-American communities, 141
Finnish Democratic Youth League, xii
Finnish Literature Society, 11, 13, 31, 39, 53–54, 60, 65, 74, 92, 162
Finnish nation, 3, 6–7, 11, 43. See also nations
Finnish Performing Music Promotion Center, 192, 198, 207–8
Finnish Society for Ethnomusicology, 201

Finno-Ugric: languages, 176; music, 59, 113, 181; peoples, 75, 86, 91, 180–81
flexibility, creative, 16
flow, musical, 16
flute, 59, 61, 177; wooden, xiv
folk dance, 84–85, 142, pl. 5, pl. 6
folklore: material, 28–33, 35, 37; musical, 6; research, 10, 27–28, 30, 32, 34–37, 43, 54, 63, 74
folklorists: debates of, 20; Finnish, 4, 10–11, 13, 34–36; performance involvement of, 50–51, 53–58, 136
Folk Music Institute: archives of, 13; as center for research, 52; directors of, 54, 60; initiatives launched by, 64; publications and recordings of, 161, 206–7; teaching at, 125–28, 132–33, 158; pl. 8
folk music scholars, 13, 49, 51
folk music scholarship, xi, xv, 4, 12, 14, 19–20, 213
folk revival: bands, 207; experiments, 174; musicians, xii, 160, 182–83; period, 13, 161; movements, 13–14, 22, 38, 51, 58; movements, in Finland, 47–53, 75, 124, 150–51, 169; movements, in Hungary and Russia, 48–49
folk-rock, 14, 59, 66, 177
folk singers, 33–34
folk song, 21, 28, 33, 51, 54, 59, 61; electronic treatments of, 14; knowledge of, 7; texts, 3, 6, 20, 28. See also song texts
forest symbolism, 93
foxtrot, 153, 168
frontiers, 20, 109, 175, 180

Gallen-Kallela, Akseli, 32
Geminiani, Francesco, 157
gender, 89, 93, 99, 101–2, 107
genealogy, musical, 16, 175
geographic-historical method, 215
German folklore scholarship, 9
globalization, 216–17; of cultural flow, xv, 174; of industries, 203, 204–5, 208; and transnational spaces for music, 200

guitar, 59, 61–62, 136, 138, 144, 146, 168, 182, 184; acoustic, 177; electric, 177, 210–11; bass, 59, 177

"Häämarssi," 164
Haapasalo, Kreeta, 26–27, 53, 146, 156, 160, 214
"Halikon Markkinat," 129–30
harmonica, 177
harmonium, 151, 157–59, 161, 169, 219; electric, 219
harmonization, 139–40
Haudanmaa, Matti, 162, 221n. 3
Hedningarnar, 92
Hegel, William Frederick, 9
hegemony, creative, 23
Hellström, Martin, 162
Helsinki Day, 84
Helsinki, 51, 87, 182–84, 193–95
Herder, Johann Gottfried von, 4, 9, 29, 34, 43
historic sound documents, 207
histories, musical, xvi, 12–13, 27, 156, 168, 175
homogeneity, musical, xvii, 196, 205
Hot Club de Karelia, 157
Hotakainen, Otto, 128, 154, 161, 167
hybridity, musical, xvi, xviii, 23, 80, 194, 216

identity: affirmation of Finnish, 85–86, 135, 141–42, 211; construction of, 181; marker of, 159, 187, 203–5; minority, 80; musical, xviii, 7, 23, 79, 181, 198; national, 17–19, 22–23, 30, 34, 37–38, 42, 49, 52; regional, xvii–xviii, 8, 52, 79; as relational, 10–11, 37
ideology, 49, 203; communist, 15; nationalist, xvi, 13, 85, 89, 108–9, 202–3; of place and time, xv; political, 11; state, 183, 202
Ilmatar, 1
imagery: landscape, 93–94; textual, 113; traditional, 101
imagination, national, 12, 216
imperial rule, 3

improvisation, 21, 47, 55, 58, 60–62, 64–65, 71–72, 76, 87
independence, creative, 7; political, 7, 9
individual, focus on, 20
industry: music, 148, 203–5; recording, 200
influences: cultural, 217; global, 174; musical, 14, 88, 91, 109, 142, 148, 184, 196, 218
Ingria, 32, 74
innovation, 15–16, 158; creative, 19, 175; individual, 211; musical, 15, 132, 158, 169, 175
inscription, of the national, 12
inspiration, musical, 6–8, 22, 43, 47, 195, 211
institutionalization of folk music, 49, 63–64, 197
instrumental groups: amateur folk music, xii; improvising, 183
instrumentation, 168
interaction, musical, xviii, 186, 192, 197, 215
International Folk Music Council, 4
interpretation: freedom of individual, 92; musical, 58, 132, 141–42, 149, 192, 214, 218
intervals, in part singing, 91
Irish-Finnish musical scene, 190–92
Ismael Lo Pro, 184

Järvelä, Arto, 71–72, 139, 196, 207, 213, pl. 15
Järvelä, Mauno, 155–57, pl. 10
Järvelä family, 156
Järvi, Ernst, 162
jazz musicians, 47, 58–59, 61
jenkka, 59, 152
"Johanneksen Polkka," 131
joik, xviii, 59, 80, 182–84, 195, 199, 217, 219. See also Saami
jouhikko, 57, 67, 75, 142, 151, 177, 210
journalists, xi, 133, 201
JPP: membership of, 71, 129, 156; performances, 83, 130, 156–57, 173; as proponents of Ostrobothnian traditions, 150, 158–60, 162; stylistic features of, 153, 167–69, 196–97, 211, pl. 11, pl. 16

Juoigansinfoniija, 183
Jurva, Matti, 178
Juslenius, Daniel, 28
Jylhä, Konsta: as composer, 160–61; as icon, 50–54, 63, 107–8, 158, 204; as Ostrobothnian fiddler, 66, 132, 150–51; in relation to Järvelä family, 156

Kaasinen, Sari: interview with, 89–93; as promoter, 184; responding to technomix, 197; on Värttinä, 210, 219
"Käin Minä Kaunista Kangasta Myöten," 56–57
Kalaniemi, Maria, 83, 154, 157, 161, 174, 190
Kalevala: as epic, 1, 6–7, 10, 21, 24–27, 29–38, 43, 54–55, 69, 74, 181, 212–13, 219–20; material, 53–55; melody, 40, 56, 59; meter, 38–40, 51, 54–55, 65, 151, 176, 181, 217; as song tradition, xiii, 28, 39, 41, 51, 54–57, 64–65, 73, 151
Kalevala Society, 54, 75
Kantavaras, 157
kantele, 11; concept, 146–49; electric, 147–49, 174; features of, 40; in historical perspective, 151, 156; in the *Kalevala,* 25–27, 212–13; repertoires of, 41, 62, 75–78, 174, 184–85, 210–11; as symbol, 43, 53, 142, 202–3; in teaching and performance, 57, 64, 67–69, 82, 85, 90, 126–27, 132, 161, 214–15, 218–19
Kanteletar, 137
Karelia: region of, 8, 31, 36, 67, 75, 88, 91, 109, 152, 174, 177, 195; Russian, 11, 33, 176; Soviet, 178, 180–81
Karelia (revival band), xiii, 58–59–60, 62, 183
Karelianism, 11, 81, 176, 181
Karhu, Santtu, 176–78, 180–82, 192, 207
Kärki, Toivo, 140
katrilli, 152
Kaustinen, 51–55, 124–27, 135, 150, 152, 155–57

Kaustinen International Festival of Folk Music, 51–53, 134–35, 138, 168–69
Kaustinen Purppuripelimannit, 53
Kaustinen Rhapsody, 196
Kaustinen wedding choir, 156
keyboards, 184
"Kiiriminna," 197
"Klockar Samuell Dikström," 155
Kodály, Zoltán, 4, 6,
Koinurit, xii, 71, 83–84, 87, 143–44, 157, 219, pl. 4
"Kolan Oskan Polska," 128–29
"Konevitsan Kirkonkellot," 41, 62
kora, 184–85, 198, 216
Korkkijalka, xiv, 84, 190–91
"Korppi," 109–12
Krannin Laki, 157
Krohn, Ilmari, 4, 11, 154, 162
Krohn, Julius Leopold, 32, 35–38, 210
Krohn, Kaarle, 36–37
kruunuhäät, 152
"Kruunupyyn Katrilli," 165
Kukko, Sakari, 58, 60–62, 109, 186
Kullervo Symphony, 7, 21, 32, 222n. 5
Kuula, Toivo, 162
"Kylä Vuotti Uutta Kuuta," 184

labels, 198, 200
Laitinen, Heikki, 51–52, 54, 57–58, 69, 207
landscape, 8, 89, 93–94, 97, 149; national, 42–43, 223n. 8; urban, 199
"Lännen Lokari," 143
League of Finnish Youth, xii
learning, xiv, xvii, 82, 127, 142; processes, 15, 67, 70, 214
lectures, 74–75
Leikarit, 162
Lemminkäinen poems, 37
Lencqvist, Eric, 29–30
Liivi, 176–78, 180, 181
local-global: debate, 201; frameworks, 174; questions, 202
Local Off, 197

Lönnrot, Elias, 6, 20, 27, 29–38, 40, 43, 53–54, 60, 74, 89, 173
lullabies, 151
Lutheran Church, 36
Lutheranism, 28
lyric songs, 55, 114

"Maalarin Franssin Sottiisi," 130
Malinen, Ontrei, 33
mandolin, 144, 147, 153, 174
manuscript analysis, 162
marches, 152, 162, 167
markets: commercial, 55, 191; global, xii–xiii, xvi, 23, 63, 68, 113, 200, 202–5, 208, 214, 216; music, xii–xiii, xv, 197, 200; national, xvi; world music, 14, 18, 113, 205
mass movements, 11
mazurka, 11, 152, 167
mbalax, xviii, 126, 185, 192–93, 195, 198–99
mbira, 216
meaning, 195, 197, 216; musical, 174, 197–98
media, 8, 13, 16, 107, 133, 209; agencies, 50, 213; mass, 148, 200, 204
melisma, 40
melody, 40–41, 62, 90–93, 140, 182; folk, 6; line of, 29, 73, 167, 169; pattern of, 20
memory, 13; collective, 4; musical, 21
micromusics, xvi
midsummer celebrations, 84–86
"Mie Tahon Tanssia," 99–100, 102, 105–7
migration of tradition, 29–30. See also geographic-historical method
"Miinan Laulu," 197
minimalism, 185
minuet, 11, 152, 167
modernity, 15, 86
modernization, 4, 14, 51
mouth harp, 151
Mozart, Leopold, 157
multiculturalism, 194; politics of, 193
multiplicity: of identities, xviii; of voices, 34; musical, 19, 23, 174, 196

music, as product, 33, 195, 200, 203–4, 208–10
music making, professional, 91, 127, 133, 156, 191, 214, 218

Näppäripelimannit, 157
nationalism, 9, 17, 86, 216, 225n. 2; in construction of folk music, 3, 8, 23; enterprise of, 4, 11, 17, 43; movement supporting, 5, 7, 9; period of, 181; projects promoting, 20, 23; sensibilities of, 6, 11
nationalists, 3–4, 17, 36,
nation building, 7, 10, 31, 34
nations, 9, 17–19, 21, 29, 33–34, 42, 169, 173–74, 202, 215, 217
nation-state, 8, 10, 34, 47, 52, 80, 175, 181–83, 217
N'diay, Badu, 193, 195, pl. 18
N'Dour, Youssou, 184, 186, 198
Nelipolviset, xiii, 54–55, 57–58, 66, 89, 114
network: institutional, 64–65; global musical, 173, 219
New Europe, 194
new folk music: borrowings, 5, 22–23, 173–76, 196; composing, 58, 75, 79; education, 78–79; as focus of study, xi–xviii; as folk revival, 13, 47–50; groups, xii, 9, 55, 83, 88, 143, 150–51, 157; as marker of identity, 19, 202, 215, 217; as musical category, 18, 38, 198; recorded canon of, 205–7; in relation to continuity and change, 13–17, 147–49, 214, 219; repertoires of, 55, 182–83; representations of, 88, 168, 205; in rural contexts, 124–25, 134–35
new folk musicians: discourses of, 15–16, 27, 66, 80, 87, 141, 148, 173–74, 202; as followers of tradition, 113, 160–62; as performers, 133, 139; practices of, 13, 40–42, 58, 89, 169, 175, 196–98, 200, 210–11, 214–18; as representatives of Finnish folk music, 205
new musical developments, 7

new musics, xi, 58, 217, 225n. 2
Niekku, xii, 58, 69, 83, 157
Nikulanpelimannit, 157
notation, musical, 72, 76–78, 129, 130, 132–33, 162
notebooks, 161–62
nyckelharpa, 71, 225n. 3

"Oi Dai," 93–96
"Olin Sairas Kun Luokseni Saavuit," 190
onomatopoetic lines, 91
organizational culture, 11
organological research, 75
originality, 6, 16, 211
ornaments, xiv, 128, 132
ostinato, 144
Ostrobothnia, 47, 52, 85, 128, 138, 150, 152, 154, 158
otherness, 199, 201
Ottopasuuna, 151

Paakkunainen, Seppo, 42, 58–62, 65, 213, 225n. 9, pl. 2
Papp Sarr, 192–93
Paraske, Larin, 7, 214
particularism, 202–3
Pavolini's tune, 21–22
Peace of Hamina, 9
pelimanni: amateur groups, 150; history, 151–55, 157; *mestaripelimanni*, 85, 128, 132; musicianship, 154, 160; repertoires, 174; research interest in, 11–12, 162; societies, 11; traditions in the Finnish folk revival, 47, 50–53, 59
Pellervoinen, 25
Peltoniemi, Eric, 125, 135–36, 138–39, 141–42, 146, 149, 207, 216
pentachord, 40
percussion, 184, 211
performance: contemporary folk music, 114, 150, 169, 181–83, 191–92, 196, 200, 203–4; contexts, xvii, 14, 72, 81–82, 86,

134, 198, 205, 208, 213–14; elements, 15; organizing, 86–87; practice, 17, 41–42, 75; projects, 57; traditional, 3, 16; variation in, 20–21. *See also* style
performer-composer, 160–61
Perttunen, Arhippa, 31, 33
philosophy, political, 9
phonograph, 204
piano, 61, 140, 168
Piirpauke, xiii, 58, 60–62, 193
Pinnin Pojat, xii, 71, 157
Pirnales, xii, 69, pl. 3
pitch, 73, 184
Poems of Ossian, 29, 223n. 2
Pohjantahti, xiii, 83, 182
Pohjonen, Kimmo, 139, 173, pl. 15
policy: Finnish foreign, 108; formulation, 203, 224n. 8; makers, 65, 202; making, 13, 64, 204
politics, xi, 8, 21; cultural, xii, 49; nationalist, 6
polkka, 59, 161
polska, 71, 152, 154, 162, 167, 173, 210
polyphonic monologue, 32
popular music, 4, 13–14, 18, 63, 153, 168, 179, 200–201, 203
Porthan, Henrik Gabriel, 28–30, 41
postcoloniality, 194
power, 88, 102; national, 10; political, 9–10; relations of, 209; state, 10
Primo, xiii, 57, 66, 89, 185
"Progelaulu," 143–46
promotion: music, 177, 192, 205, 207, 210; of the region, 52
propaganda, 179
proverbs, 28
public imagination, 47
public sector systems, 203

racism, 193–95
radio, 63–64, 141, 179, 209
"Rahapolska," 129

Raskinen, Minna, 191, 202–3, 214–15, 217–19
Rautavaara, Tapio, 138, 140–41
record companies, 16, 203, 205–7
recordings: archive, 54, 58, 60, 92; commercial, 66, 205–7, 214; for learning, 62, 72, 91; as object, 208; in world music markets, 200, 202–3, 205
records, of folk music, 53–55, 206
refugees, 86, 113, 193–94
rehearsal, 81, 93, 129, 139, 187, pl. 9, pl. 15
rekilaulut, 143
repertoires: church hymn, xii; creative treatments of, 15, 82; folk, 4, 57; instrumental dance, 11; JPP's, 150, 211; *Kalevala,* 55; recorded, 178, 197; song, 34, 39; Värttinä's, 88
Repo, Teppo, 21, 63, 214
representation: of collective action, 38; of folk music and musicians, xiii, 10, 16, 49–50, 52, 65, 75, 108, 168, 200, 204, 210; of identity, xvi, 13, 85, 135, 146, 198, 200; musical, xii; of musical unity, 18–20, 21, 22, 38, 49–50, 52, 65, 75, 85, 102, 108, 135, 168, 174, 198, 200, 204–5, 210, 213; of the nation and national culture, 15, 19, 205; sonic, xix, 204–5; visual, 158–59
revival movements. *See* folk revival
revivalists, in Finland, xvii, 47, 50. *See also* folk revival
rhyming songs, 11, 39, 151
rhythm: consistency of, 128; patterns of, 78, 187, 193; structure of, 186–88; variety of, 39
riff, 187
Rinta-Nikkola, Samuel, 154, 162, 173
"Rissakka," 77
rock musicians, 47, 58, 61
Roma, 76, 80–81, 85–86; music, 76, 80, 217; song, 190
romantic nationalism, 10, 13, 27, 30
Rome Convention, 208–10
"Roots in Finland," 125, 135–36, 138, 149, 169, pl. 14

"Ruotsalaispolska," 166
"Ruskoi Reggae," 174
Russia, 8–11, 27, 109, 152
Russian Orthodox Church, 36

Saami, xviii, 76, 81, 86, 141, 182–84; music, 76, 80, 175, 181–83, pl. 17; musicians, 219; political status, 182; shamanic beliefs, 182
Saastamoinen, Ilpo, 58, 61–62, 182
sabar, 83, 186, 192, 217
Saha, Hannu: as performer, 57, 60, 135–36, 146–49, 185, 198; as researcher, 132, 138, 141–42, 207, 221n. 4
Salamakannel, xii, 55–56, 71, 130, 147–48, 157
Salomaa, Hiski, 143, 228n. 3
"Satumaa," 188–90
saxophone, 59, 61, 151, 153, 183, 210
school curriculum, 64–65
"Schottis från Övermark," 131
schottische. *See* sottiisi
score, musical, 20, 128; notated, 153, 160–61, 167, 214
selection, musical, 196
selectivity, 175
self-determination, national, xiii, 3, 9
shaman, 24, 40. *See also* Saami
Sharp, Cecil, 4
shifting spaces, 200, 219
Shindig, 190
Sibelius, Jean, 6–8, 14, 32, 42–43, 68–69
Sibelius Academy, 65, 68–69, 133. *See also* Department of Folk Music
similarity, 190
"Sinimani Seele," 73
Širgo, Ivana, 67
SKS. *See* Finnish Literature Society
Slobo Horo, 83
Snellman, Johan Wilhelm, 9–10, 31, 84, 203
social determination, 196
society, national, 202–3
solidarity, political, 21
songbooks, 137–40, 160

song texts: of gendered experience, 89, 97–99, 101–2; joik, 183; Liivi, 178; tango, 188–90; Värttinä's, 91–96, 98–107, 109–12
sorrow, as folk theme, 109
sottiisi, 152, 167
sources, notated, 13, 214
space, musical, xvi, 108, 214; global, 19, 72, 176, 197–98, 208, 210–11, 215, 217; national, xii–xiii, 5, 212–15
specialization, of folk musicians, 204, 214
spirit, national, 34, 210
standardization, 197
structure, musical, 4, 167, 187
style: joik singing, 184; musical, 58, 78–79, 93, 133, 158, 177, 213; pedagogic, 72; performance, 132, 153–54, 184, 196–97; regional, 88; researching, 29
Suana-aho, Antti, 162
suspended minor sevenths, 187
Sweden, 11, 28, 152; kingdom of, 9
Swedish language, 35
symbols: of ancient heritage, 147, 149; of cultural cohesion, xviii; of identity, 18–19, 22, 43, 52, 142, 146, 204–5; key, 101; of the nation, xvi, 27, 54, 202; programmatic, 7; of unity, 19
symphonic discourse, 7
symphony orchestra, xiii, 59, 183
syncopation, 144, 186

talkoot, 153
Tallari, xii, 128, 130, 157, 161, 228n. 1, pl. 9
Talvisovat (folk-rock band), 177, 180
tama, 83, 193, 195, 216–17
tangos, 61, 159, 167–69, 174, 186, 188, 190, 195, 198–99, 217; dance venue, 159, 191; instrumental, 168
Tapiola, 43
teaching: methods, 7–78, 126–30, 132; practice, 217
technique: classical violin playing, 156; fiddle playing, 153–54; violin bowing, 129; vocal production, 113

techno-mix, 197
ternary form, 144
"Texas Blues," 173–74, 210
texture, instrumental, 184, 211; musical, 173
theatrical performances, 11
timbre, 151, 159–60, 169, 182, 195, 211; vocal, 88
tin whistle, xiv
Tolvanen, Hannu, 83, 200
tonality, 161
total system, 202
tradition: as concept, 19, 47, 50, 107, 162, 197; dynamic of, 22; preservation of, 139, 149, 210; reinterpreting, 70, 87; transmission of, 71, 89
tradition bearer, 14
transcription, 78, 92, 167, 189
transformation: creative, 196, 217; elements of, 48; of musical material, 2, 11, 210, 217; of the person, 97; of society, 51
transmission: changes in, 14, 148, 168; models of, 16, 71, 89, 108; processes, 17, 72, 114, 125, 160, 206, 213–14
trends, 54, 197; aesthetic, 12; artistic, 7; dance, 153; general, 13, 50; global, 168, 198, 200; musical, 7, 60, 125, 201; stylistic, 150
"Tumala," 98–99, 101–5
tuohihattu, 67
Turku romanticism, 29–30, 223n. 3
Tuulenkantajat, xiii, 83, 207

universalism, 202–3
urbanization, 4, 12, 51

Väinämöinen: as embodiment of Finnish nation, 43; as mythical hero, 1, 24–25, 27, 212; research writings on, 30–31, 37; songs about, 55–56
Väisänen, Armas Otto, 4, 21, 40, 63, 67, 74–75, 78, 162
"Vaka Vanha Väinämöinen," 55–56

Valkeapää, Nils-Aslak, 183, 192
"Vanha Sodessi," 76
variation: in instrument construction, 147–48; musical, 20–21, 40, 55, 64, 72–73, 185
Värttinä, 88–94, 97–102, 107–10, 113–14; as new folk group, 9, 53; in performance, 83; in the context of Finno-Ugric tradition, 181; recorded interpretations of, 184, 197; pl. 7. *See also* song texts
Vaughan Williams, Ralph, 14
"Velisurmaaja," 136–38, 207
Vepsa Kirja, 162
Vesala, Edward, 59
violin, 59, 91, 129, 156–57, 167–68, 177. *See also* fiddle
Virta, Olavi, 188
visual motif, 159
vocal styles: experimentation, 113; lines, 197; traditions from the eastern regions of Finland, xiii, xvii, 11, 47; two-part texture, 92

"Vot I Kaalina," 93

Walli, Hasse, 58, 61–62, 184–88, 192–93, 195, 199, 213
waltz, 11, 59, 61, 85, 152, 161–62
wedding songs, 55, 74, 97–99
Wimme, 219
wind ensembles, xii
Winter War, 8, 109, 177
women's social roles, 97
woodwinds, 168
world music: definitions of, xv, 197, 208; Finnish new folk music in relation to, 5–6, 23, 135, 169, 174, 200, 211; rise in, xiii; stage, 13, 168, 173, 181, 200, 213; views of, 22, 84, 198, 201, 216
world musician, 61, 198, 202

Yamar, 192–93
"Ylikuun Polkka," 161
"Yxi Kaunis Papillinen Polska," 154–55, 173